MESSENGERS
OF THE
GODS

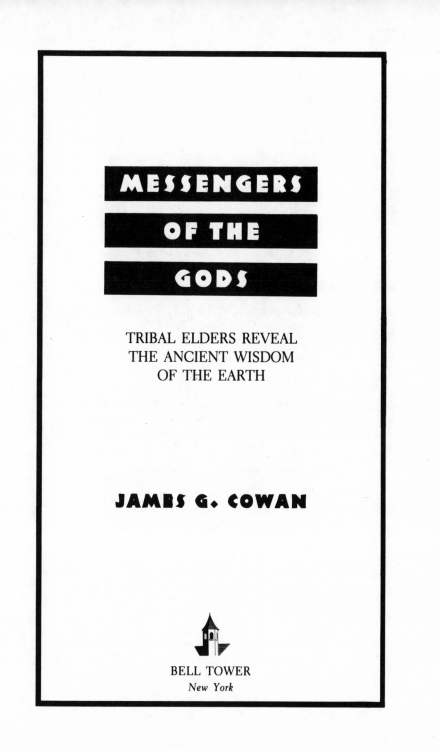

MESSENGERS
OF THE
GODS

TRIBAL ELDERS REVEAL
THE ANCIENT WISDOM
OF THE EARTH

JAMES G. COWAN

BELL TOWER
New York

Published by Bell Tower, an imprint of Harmony Books,
a division of Crown Publishers, Inc.,
201 East 50th Street, New York, New York 10022.
Member of the Crown Publishing Group.
Random House, Inc. New York, Toronto, London, Sydney, Auckland

Bell Tower and colophon are registered trademarks of Crown Publishers, Inc.

Manufactured in the United States of America

Library of Congress Cataloging-in-Publication Data
Cowan, James, 1942–
Messengers of the gods : tribal elders reveal the ancient wisdom of the earth
/ James G. Cowan. — 1st ed.
p.   cm.
1. Australian aborigines—Rites and ceremonies. 2. Mythology,
Australian aboriginal. 3. Ibans (Bornean people)—Rites and
ceremonies. 4. Torres Strait Islanders—Rites and ceremonies.
I. Title.
BL2610.C68   1993
299'.92—dc20   92-30329
                                                           CIP

ISBN: 0-517-88078-4 (pbk.)

10 9 8 7 6 5 4 3 2 1

First Edition

For Howard Sandum, *literatus*

Two people were instrumental in making this book possible.
Toinette Lippe of Bell Tower, whose faith in the project
was unfaltering, and Jill Ker Conway,
who brought us together in the hope
that among us all we might provide
a forum for the indigenous peoples of the world.
To them both I offer my heartfelt thanks—
on behalf of the voiceless throughout the world.

CONTENTS

Nomad peoples, shepherds, hunters, farmers and even cannibals, may all, by virtue of energy and personal dignity, be the superiors of the West.

—Charles Baudelaire

Civilization is not a solitary achievement but the unending converse we hold with one another over the centuries and over the world.

—Kathleen Raine

This earth has all the exoticism washed out of it.

—Henry Michaux

INTRODUCTION

The realm of traditional peoples holds a strange fascination for many of us who live outside its frontiers. On those few occasions when we do manage to cross over into its territory, we often find ourselves affronted by its wild and untrammeled spirit. It seems to us that such peoples have no cares, nor do they look to the future with anything like the same concern as we do. They appear to exist in a timeless vacuum whereby their immediate concerns are confined to survival and the ritual practice of their beliefs. In no way do they embrace the broad spirit of our age, with its emphasis upon achievement, success, and the acquisition of goods. Instead, they allow themselves to inhabit a region dominated by what the early Christians once called "principalities and powers."

Nonetheless, at a time when we in the modern world are increasingly finding ourselves at a loss for answers to the problems confronting us in the areas of economics, social justice, the environment, agriculture, disease, overpopulation, and pollution (to name a few), some are looking to these peoples in an attempt to discover whether they have solutions other than those based upon rational thought or scientific endeavor. After all, traditional peoples have lived in, and to a large extent preserved, a balanced relationship with the world for countless millennia. The forests and animals in their care, the Arctic wastelands with their slender population of fish and seals, the steppes and deserts whose pastures are often so meager—all these regions have supported their ageless presence with a certain benign grace. It seems that whatever they have taken from their respective environments, traditional peoples have learned how to compensate by engaging in an unremitting dialogue with nature itself. In other words, humankind and nature have learned how to discuss what is good for both, and then act in accordance with decrees that each respect.

This is an interesting supposition: that we have a responsibility to consult with nature before we act in our own self-interest. In the past, I think we have always assumed that nature was in some way passive, that it had no feelings, that it was there principally to acquiesce to our needs. We called nature "she" and demanded from her an invincible love without fear of betrayal. She possessed all the generous qualities of a mother whose only desire was to see us satisfy our own needs. Yet at the same time we did not wish to see nature as anything more than an abstraction, something whose built-in regenerative qualities would overcome all obstacles caused by excessive exploitation. She was, after all, always regarded as a kind of cornucopia, a boundless receptacle of abundance. Nature was seen as a willing workhorse, a machine almost, which could be made more efficient by genetic interference, manipulation (how battery hens must long to sleep through a night of darkness at least once in their lives!), or what is euphemistically termed *environmental management*. Yet while in Borneo researching this book I saw at firsthand how such a science-based system of management has brought the trees of the forest to their knees, causing irreparable damage to the cultural landscape existing beneath the forest canopy.

The truth is we have dismissed the notion of natural knowledge as being in any way a reliable guide because we consider it to be a nonempirical science. Seduced by the sirens of the laboratory, we have tied ourselves to the mast of scientific discovery in the hope of negotiating every shoal that threatens to destroy us. In a very short time we have managed to develop such a vast array of knowledge that no one library building can contain it. We are awash with information—information that at once enthralls us while at the same time causes us, without knowing why, to experience feelings of impotence. We do not know how to deal with what we know, because we are made aware that all knowledge is entirely conditional. It is liable to be superseded by new intellectual imperatives and discoveries at any given moment. Icons of permanence no longer grace the walls of our minds—or, indeed, our hearts. Instead, we are drawn in by the flickering image, the shifting scenery of transience that in turn generates a kind of knowledge that resounds for a short while, then falls back into the realm of silence and is lost to us. Nor can we conceive of a canon of belief that stands outside of the current opus of science-based information. Yet it is to this canon of belief—this earth-wisdom possessed by traditional people throughout the world—to which we must now turn if we are to treat what is clearly nature's ailing condition. That is, if we ourselves want to survive.

Of course, understanding how traditional peoples think about their environment demands a unique gesture on our part. For a start, we have to learn how to respect nature as no longer being there simply to serve our needs. We have to learn how to see it as a separate entity possessed of an arcane integrity of its own. It is this capacity to see nature both as a separate entity and as a friend that characterizes the philosophic stance of such peoples. They recognize nature as a living entity, not just as an organic component but as a force dominated by spiritual and earthly imperatives particular to itself, to its own interior life. This force is defined in a variety of ways, depending on which people we are dealing with. But underlying all such definitions is a sense of reverence for nature as being the incarnation of a reality that is able to transcend all representation and analysis. Traditional peoples, therefore, express their relationship with nature in an entirely different way, one not governed solely by a consideration of their own well-being.

It is this "different way" that is the subject of this book. For many years I have wanted to explore what it is that makes the worldview of traditional peoples so remarkable. Why do they see life so differently from us? What is it that binds them to their forest, their island, their piece of earth in a way that any severance of this relationship brings on a cultural crisis of one form or another? What special property resides in such traditional environments that cannot be approached or understood except under the guidance of certain men of knowledge? This, then, was the object of my search. I had to seek out these men of knowledge—these "messengers of the gods" so to speak—wherever they might happen to be, and ask them to teach me how to go about approaching nature in the true spirit of complicity.

In the course of my travels I was to learn important truths from these men. All those I met possessed detailed knowledge of the sea, the forest, and the earth, and their knowledge changed my life. I learned, first, that their wisdom was not contained in libraries, encyclopedias, or even data bases. These men looked to an entirely different method of retention and storage. It was through the art of myth and story that they understood the mysterious "interworld" of nature. Scientific concepts, for all their elegance and clarity, do not have the power to penetrate the veil of mystery that lies between their way of thinking and that of nature itself. Only the myth and its practical expression through ceremony and ritual enables a person to make contact with the timeless truths that exist beyond this veil. In the act of revealing to me what they knew, my "messengers of the gods" influenced me in more ways than I could imagine.

Clearly, I had to learn how to abandon certain precepts and categories. In order to enter into the realm of myth, I had to allow myself to accept its paradoxical nature. To look for, or even expect, a neat ending, even a moral, was to demand much more than it was designed to present. If one of my "teachers" chose to tell me about himself by relating a myth, then he did so with a much more mysterious agenda in mind. Perhaps he was not trying to tell me anything about himself at all. Perhaps, instead, he was attempting to reveal something about his "spiritual conception." Perhaps he wanted me to accompany him on a journey to a place ruled by the imagination, not the senses. It seemed that knowledge of the earth—for him, at least—partook of imaginative encounters with its *invisible* possibilities as much as those designed to make living easier.

The men that I met were simple people. They lived in thatched huts on the beach or in the forest, or as semi-exiles on the edge of towns. They did not own much other than a few necessities— a boat, some farm tools, or a stretch of mythic territory in the bush. Nor did they have any "future" in the way that we might understand it. But what they did possess in abundance was the gift of memory and the humility that inspired them to share it with me. They knew consummately their own history and the history of their mythic heroes. These, I soon discovered, were often intertwined as closely as the carved whorls on a mask found outside a longhouse doorway. More often than not they found it difficult to separate their own history from the heroic endeavors of bird, fish, crocodile, and turtle. Each man of knowledge that I met in my travels confronted me with the same age-old question: How can any of us continue to maintain an exploitative relationship with nature without running the risk of doing permanent damage to its integrity?

I learned, of course, that one must obey the law of nature. Not the so-called survival of the fittest law made popular by Charles Darwin, but a law that was handed down from the gods and mythic heroes. In other words, there is a celestial underpinning of traditional law that brooks neither amendment nor change. In the course of my travels I was introduced to the *Zogo Meer*, or "straight way," of Malu, the divine octopus, among the people of Mer; the law of *Adat* among the Iban of Borneo; and the law of the cloud-faced Wandjina spirits known as *Ungud* among the Aborigines of Australia. Each set of laws governed the conduct of men in their everyday activities as well as in their relationship with the invisible world of nature. As I remarked earlier, these often turned out to be inseparable. Whatever the relative merits of such systems of ethical observance, however, they all had one thing in common: They were designed to help people maintain close contact with the mysterious powers of nature, both as arbitrator and confidant.

I was fortunate. Wherever I went I was able to meet up with

men who recognized the need to communicate this knowledge to a wider world. They were aware of the collapse of the environment caused by excessive exploitation and misuse. They had seen mining sludge cloud the ocean with sulphates, killing their fish; they had watched their forests turned into eroded wastelands by loggers; they had encountered mining companies eager to drill holes or blow up their sacred landscape—and all in the name of material progress. Nor were they immune from the pressures of modernity when it touched them in the form of the cash economy, medicine, and the need to abandon their custom of subsistence living. They had been forced to watch their children drift off to urban centers in the hope of finding work rather than eke out an existence in accordance with the old ways. These men were no longer "noble savages" in the old, romantic sense; they were men afflicted with a profound concern for the collapse of their way of life. They were men of knowledge who knew they had a responsibility to warn the world of an impending catastrophe before it was too late.

More than anything I wanted to assure myself that real nobility could still survive in such a threatened world as ours. The old men I met all managed to present a dignified face at a time when even they knew their days were numbered. I grew to recognize in a man's eyes the depths of his understanding and his wisdom. To me, a true "messenger of the gods" always seemed to embody a detachment in his gaze, even a yearning, that went beyond anything I had encountered before. With a deep-rooted fellowship he was in touch with the spirits of his ancestors, a fellowship that transcended time and space. Death and nature may have absorbed them over the years, but such men lived on as models, providing an extra dimension whenever their stories were told around a campfire or their song sung during a ceremony.

So it was their *gravitas* that first cast its spell over me whenever we met. Sitting under a palm tree by a lagoon, resting in the shade of a longhouse wall, or gazing out over a landscape of rock and gully as we talked, such moments of fraternity inevitably left us feeling as though we had made contact with nature through one another. In a sense, there were always three of us sitting together. The invisible presence of nature having flowed through us in myth and story. Malu, the divine octopus; Sengalang Burong,

the chief omen bird; and Wodjin, the "number one boss" Wandjina—each of these spirit entities joined us in our discussions.
They were the ever-present "third person" in our midst. In the
process, we were able to become every man who ever lived, and
so join that company of invisible spirit heroes who inhabit the
interworld of nature.

Finally, the endless chattering of palms on a windy day or the
cries of omen birds in a Borneo forest managed to impart to me
knowledge of their mysterious language. I learned how to express
myself using the syntax of myth and story. My friends taught me
about Malu's mysterious blue light and about the significance of
the sweet-water turtle's neck bone as symbol of the spirit. In their
company I was able to voyage up the Mandai River along with
other dead souls. At every stage of my journey some old man
managed to make his presence known in order to point me in the
right direction. This is the way of all guides, I decided, whether
they happen to be the legendary Hermes or an old *zogo le* from
the Torres Strait Islands. When you put your trust in those you
meet along the way, it is with the knowledge that each one has
inadvertently adopted the role of a messenger intent on bringing
you news from another world.

Ultimately, I learned that we must all come to terms with the
idea of desecration, both physical and moral, as an unnatural
act generated by ourselves. Nature will not stand for our will-
ful dismissal of its tenets any longer. If the straight way of
Malu, and the law of *Adat* and *Ungud* are to be respected, then
each of us must begin the process of renewal in our own way. My
journeys to the Torres Strait, to Borneo, and to the Kimberley in northwest Australia were the beginning of a process of
renewal for me. I, too, had to learn how to recognize the level
of my collaboration in the business of transforming nature into
a commodity. Furthermore, I had to accept the censure of the
people who told me that it was I who was causing irreparable
damage to the ecosystems of the world. In other words, my inordinate appetite was responsible for the destruction of their
environments.

If I carried away any message from these old men of knowledge,
it came in the form of a greater understanding of the role of the
sea, the forest, and the earth as cultural icons. As well, I will

always cherish the memory of my first encounter with the sweet cacophony of forest noises as I paddled up the Layar River in Borneo. In a bird's trill there was already an echo of a god's voice calling to me from above. The deep-shaded plenitude of the forest bore down, bathing me in the mottled light of a distant sun. It was as though I had been plunged into a limitless space filled with vines, leaves, and flowering orchids. The sheer excrescence of nature overwhelmed me. I knew then that I had begun to make contact with a process that would help me come to terms with my own self-exile from nature's garden.

James G. Cowan
Sydney, 1992

MALU'S

ISLAND

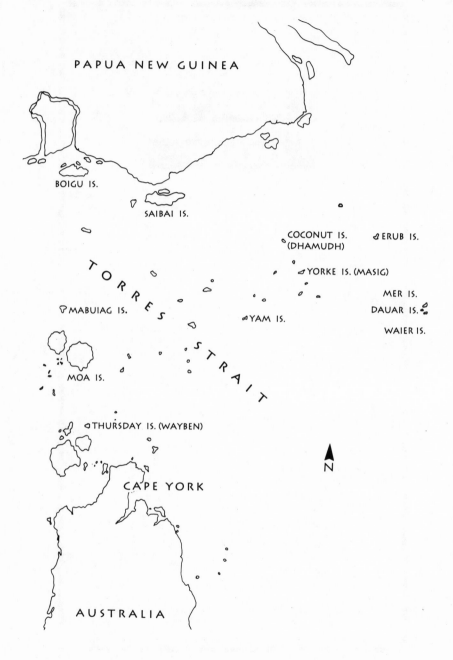

PAPUA NEW GUINEA

BOIGU IS.

SAIBAI IS.

COCONUT IS.
(DHAMUDH)

ERUB IS.

YORKE IS. (MASIG)

MER IS.

DAUAR IS.

WAIER IS.

MABUIAG IS.

YAM IS.

T O R R E S

S T R A I T

MOA IS.

THURSDAY IS. (WAYBEN)

N

CAPE YORK

AUSTRALIA

ONE

Scattered between the northern tip of Australia and the New Guinea coastline, the islands of the Torres Strait drifted into history by way of the charts of the Spanish sailor Luis Vaez de Torres, drawn up after his epic voyage in 1606. Since then, these islands have played host to numerous seafarers—Abel Tasman, James Cook, and William Bligh among them. Cook himself named Tuesday, Wednesday, Thursday, and Friday islands after a midweek encounter with them in August 1770, having already discovered the east coast of Australia on his voyage home from Tahiti. In his log, Cook recorded seeing women on the beach collecting shellfish with "not a single rag of any kind of clothing upon them." Bligh, on the other hand, knew these islands only as the bitter aftermath of a mutiny that forced him to navigate his open boat 4,000 miles across the Pacific to the tiny Indonesian island of Timor in 1789.

Since then, a succession of sailing ships homeward bound to England from the infant Australian colony of Port Jackson has negotiated the dangerous reefs that litter Torres Strait. Some were unlucky, running afoul of the sharp coral on the Great Barrier

Reef, and were wrecked. More often than not, the survivors found themselves victims of headhunters, who saw their skulls as repositories of *zogo*, or sacred power. Torres Strait quickly acquired the reputation among sailors for being an exceedingly dangerous passage populated by "ferocious and mischievous savages" who regarded human heads as the only valid form of currency. Sadly, these early encounters between European seamen and Torres Strait islanders were blighted by fear, suspicion, and mutual distrust. Ritual murder confronted the power of the musket one sunny afternoon, and inevitably Cook's naked nymphs were slaughtered in droves.

Some sort of rapprochement was eventually reached later in the nineteenth century as naval attacks continued to take their toll on the islanders, forcing them to come to terms with the enemy. In the end, those "Pearl Oyster Shell" breastplates that Captain Cook had observed hanging around their necks turned out to be the basis of a lucrative form of commerce for the next one hundred years. Along with Singhalese, Tamils, Japanese, and Koepanger migrants, the islanders were soon drawn into the pearling trade at Thursday Island, where a fleet of luggers was harbored, providing ships' crews and divers for their European owners. For the sum of one pound per month they braved the threat of shark attack, marauding manta rays, and the bends while they combed the seafloor in search of pearl shell.

Using an obsidian knife stuck in a champagne cork, a pearl doctor's task was to transform a blister pearl into a priceless object of beauty. The degree of "shining" in a pearl represented the ultimate quest for any buyer. Seeking out luster and color, using such designations as silver-clouded moon or compass-blue, *rosée rosée*, or the most sought-after *la désirée*, often encouraged a buyer to raise his bid on a pearl as each layer of skin was peeled away. That he might win for himself *la désirée* or merely end up with a piece of worthless baroque was all part of the risk. Pearl skinning was like making a deal with the devil. A man could find himself a prince or a pauper; it all depended on what level of shining the nacre might conceal beneath its surface.

But from the veranda of the Grand Hotel on Thursday Island where I sat one morning, none of this was apparent, even as memory. The sailing ships bearing cannon and trinkets had all departed, the luggers laden with pearl shell and brass helmets no longer lolled at their moorings, and the fateful encounters between Europeans and islanders had faded into history. For the men and women of these islands their entry into history had brought with it other, more fundamental conflicts. As a result of European colonization they had been forced to deal with the loss of something intangible yet intrinsic to their well-being. Like a ritual Bomai-Malu mask hanging on a pole at the entrance to a hut, the memory of their culture gazed down at them, a ghostly apparition, eyeless and empty, yet still retaining that essential power of *zogo* so necessary for its survival.

Devoid of tourists, and populated by a people at odds with themselves, Thursday Island, Torres Strait's provincial capital, today represents a graveyard of conflict and memories. Among its wide streets and leftover houses, its broken-down pubs and shops filled with outdated merchandise, I had already detected a blandness, as if the lives of everyone were being starved of some vital nutriment. Here indeed was a fertile field for investigation. By sharing with these people their desire to come to terms with their identity and heritage, I hoped to resolve some of these same issues for myself.

For while we are being asked to become citizens of the world, many of us find ourselves at odds with the challenge of this new form of internationalism. People still cherish their ethnic diversity in spite of the pressure being brought to bear upon them by others. They linger in forests or on desert plateaus, live in grass huts or in the shade of goat-hair tents, lose themselves among ice-caps or mountainous valleys—and all the while these people, inhabiting countless traditional communities, struggle to preserve their way of life. For many, their customs and beliefs are seen as outmoded, impediments almost to the great task of mobilizing industrial potential. Yet after years of observing traditional peoples in various parts of the world I had begun to ask myself whether we were not urging them on toward extinction for the sake of our own ends. Did we want them to depart this world so that we might take possession of—and exploit—their lands, their resources, and the natural beauty of their environment?

I had become aware of an increasing level of dehumanization going on as a result of the modern world's demand upon people to become more efficient. I had felt for some time that this was against our best interests, that we were being asked to give up certain feelings and sensibilities in the interest of achieving a greater conformity. Economics, not inherent wonders, had become the mainspring of the world. Few of us have experienced the arrival of a god on the beach, or a divinitary act by a bird. Yet these events have been a part of the lore of traditional peoples for much longer than the rules and regulations of modern life have governed us. More important perhaps, they were also a part of my racial memory, and my sympathies were inevitably drawn to their reenactment each time I visited such peoples in their homelands.

I had decided to visit three remote regions of the world where people were still living close to nature, and to their spirit entities. I wanted to make contact with this part of my own inheritance. For many people, the sea, the forest, and the earth constitute an open-air cathedral, the place they visit each day as a simple act of reverence. Wedded to their environment, they have not yet experienced the sense of loss some of us feel when we climb aboard an overcrowded subway and study the faces of our compatriots. They do not see their own vacancy gazing back at them. They do not wonder at the ill-lit tenements in which they live, what debts they have incurred, what illnesses are already at work within their bodies. Instead, they look to their environment to supply them with a sense of beneficence and well-being—that is, if it hasn't already been destroyed by the encroachment of the modern world looking for new sources of raw materials.

I had chosen to talk with the peoples of the Torres Strait, the forests of Borneo, and the rocky landscape of the Kimberley region of Australia in my quest for a greater understanding of this problem. Each of these peoples were in contact with a sacred environment vastly different from mine, and their knowledge, I believed, was vital to the preservation of the world. Encountering their beliefs and the culture heroes that made up their spirit pantheons would be the first step for me. If I were to continue to climb aboard overcrowded subways in the future, I needed to have better reasons for doing so than the ones supplied by the advertisements. Somewhere out there on a lonely beach or under a giant rainforest tree there must be an answer to why traditional peoples have chosen *not* to enter the modern world.

The Torres Strait turned out to be my first port of call. I began my quest by looking up an old friend, Larry Passi, an ex-pearl diver who had retired to Thursday Island, and putting to him a few questions about these matters. We had met at a cultural gathering in Townsville on the Australian mainland some years before. His wife had passed away only a short while earlier. Yet the impression I had that day as we sat on empty gas cans watching the performance of an island dance troupe was of a man struggling to reconcile himself to a loss less tangible perhaps but no less painful than the death of his wife.

Gray-bearded, his large body filling out his open-necked shirt, Larry had talked to me about his past. He had been born on the island of Mer, a volcanic outcrop east of Thursday Island, and the sea had always been a part of his life. Furthermore, his totem was the crocodile, which meant that his relationship with the sea was indwelling. The crocodile in his nature made it clear to me that he rather enjoyed dragging my inquiries below the surface of his mind and digesting them whenever I pressed him for an answer.

Our first meeting upon my arrival on Thursday Island some years later occurred under a fig tree on the grounds of the local Catholic church. I waited for Larry to appear after morning service. He came down the steps amid a bevy of Melanesian mommas, all of them in flower-patterned dresses and wielding parasols. His gray beard appeared bushier than when last we had met. We embraced as old friends before sitting down in the shade of the fig tree. Except for the lingering aroma of coconut oil from those freely perspiring parish women as they departed, we were soon left alone. The death of his wife, however, continued to cast its pall over Larry. I sensed that he was a man with little more than a toehold on life.

He told me that she had been his link with *emeret lu* ("very old things"), the heritage of his people. When she was alive he had wanted to return to the old ways, to the life of the sea. He had wanted to feel the tides wax and wane in his body. But after her death the Church had offered him its hand in lieu of his wife's, and he had reached for it out of loneliness. Regretfully, he felt he was no longer a *zogo le*, a man of power, because of his conversion to the Christian faith.

"It's all gone," he said. "Me, I'm just an island fella washed up on the shore. A piece of flotsam, you might say."

"Is that what you really believe?" I asked.

"Things aren't the same anymore. Not for me, anyway," Larry countered.

"If your wife heard you talking like this, she'd send you packing. I'll bet you never dared say such things in front of her."

Larry stroked his beard. A petal tumbled from its untidy curls. He was recalling their last moments together, walking the reefs of Mer in search of shellfish. The blue world of the sea washed over his thoughts, cleansing them for a moment of the sense of loss that he still felt.

"You know, when she died . . ." he began. "She waved her arms about, flapping them like a turtle. That was her totem, the sea turtle. We call that *lanog*, the last expression of our totem."

"Why was this so unusual to you? You must have seen it many times before."

"Well, no, it wasn't unusual, but it still gave me a shock. She just lay there on the bed like an upturned turtle on the beach. I knew she was going to die then. That's the way it is with our people. We become our totem when we die. If your totem is a stonefish or a stingray, you become that, too. She became a turtle and went back to the sea."

"So now you want to forget all about that? The special relationship your people have with the sea? It doesn't make sense, Larry."

"We're living in a different world today," Larry replied. "I miss those old times, sure. But it's over now, finished. We can't bring them back, the old ways."

"You're talking like someone with nothing left to look forward to. What about your grandchildren? They need to be taught the old ways. You owe it to them."

"I can see that I'm not going to convince you! So why did you fly up here to see me, anyway?" Larry ventured, realizing that he wasn't going to get any sympathy from me.

"I told you," I said. "Your people know things about the sea that people like me have forgotten. It's a special kind of knowledge, not at all like the stuff we learn back home. It seems to me we've got to relearn all this if we're going to survive. That's why I've come to see you. You still have a lot to offer, Larry, even if you think you've lost your *zogo*. Surely the sort of knowledge your people have preserved is what makes the world a better place to live in. You've got to keep it alive for the sake of everyone. If you don't, then we're in for a tough time."

Larry's eyes brightened with interest.

"You really think so?" he said.

"Sure I do."

Heartened by my remarks, Larry finally agreed to act as my guide and interpreter. It was clear that as an old *zogo le* he knew others throughout the islands as knowledgeable as himself. According to him, these old men continue to live secret lives much as hermit crabs do in their shell. Their contact with "very old things," as he called it, kept them alive, vigorous, in spite of their regret at not being able to pass their knowledge on to the young people.

"These fellas come out at night like mud-crabs," he said. "They pick about among the refuse on the beach, looking for bits of the past. That's their way. They like to talk to people who are prepared to listen. Maybe they'll talk to you. Maybe they'll tell you what you want to know."

"So when do we start?" I said.

We agreed to meet the following day so he could take me to visit the first of his friends. I left Larry sitting under the fig tree where he said he wanted to stay for a while. For my part, I wondered whether he would ever allow the sea to surge back into his body. Would he choose again the sea's *zogo*, its life-giving essence, or would he abandon it forever? More than anything he seemed like a man unsure of his next move.

Back at the Grand, I sat on the veranda and gazed at the choppy sea in the bay. Through the salt haze the Australian shoreline was barely visible in the distance. Somewhere out there Larry's wife's totem was swimming. The image of her flapping her arms and legs in imitation of a dying turtle haunted me. Clearly the creature had not abandoned her when her time had come to die. It had emerged from the sea and made its way into her being at the moment of her death. It had embraced her when her spirit had chosen to quit her body. In spite of Larry's insistence that the old ways were all but dead, it appeared that the turtle had not heard the news. Somehow the creature knew that its role in Larry's wife's body was part of the continuing relationship between the sea and Larry's people.

Still, Larry's disillusionment caused me concern. Giving up

the old beliefs meant that he was denying what made him. In our earlier discussions some years ago in Australia, Larry had insisted that he could not divorce his personality from the ocean. According to him, when one of his people died, his spirit journeyed to Boigu, an island off the coast of New Guinea. There it descended a sacred well, and by way of a subterranean stream returned to the sea. Once it encountered the life-giving waters of the ocean the spirit was transformed, becoming *lanog* again, a totem.

"When a child is born," Larry had explained to me that day, "we watch it closely to see what sort of personality it has. If it's a noisy child, we identify it with a bird on a sandbar, screeching. Then we cry out, cry for the bird. 'This is you,' we tell the child. 'The bird is your totem. You have the bird's ways inside you.' Then the child knows who he is. 'I'm a bird on a sandbar,' he cries. He knows why he reacts the way he does, being noisy and talkative all the time. Because he knows his personality comes from the bird. It's the same for me. I fall back on my crocodile ways, especially when the wind blows hard. That way I know I'm safe."

"From what?" I asked.

"Everyday problems, you know. Sometimes you've just got to learn to back off. The crocodile in me tells me when it's time."

"So when the wind dies down, you come up to the surface for a breather."

Larry grinned and continued:

"The sea is our mother. She nurtures us. We can do nothing without her knowing, without her help. She listens to everything we say, even when we dream. She's our medicine, too. When I feel pain in my body, rheumatism say, I go down to the sea in the early morning. I need to smell the ocean, take her into my body. When I smell her, I know that she is breathing new life into me. Then I feel better and the pain goes. Boy, does she make me feel good!"

"The sea sounds like a good doctor, all right. Better than taking pills, anyway."

"Even seashells are close to us," he elaborated. "We walk along the beach and jump into them in our thoughts. We build our folklore on the shell, into its shapes and curves. In this way we always belong to the sea. We can never travel far from her, even in our hearts. Sometimes I ask myself: How can I have a relationship with myself? Well, I know how, that's the truth. I just stare at the coral. All day sometimes I gaze at it."

"You don't get bored?"

"How can I? We island people call it 'watching coral.' We're like seabirds, we only come onto land to dry out. That's why we're always going back to the sea. In the sea we know ourselves. Crocodile, turtle, shark, stingray, dugong—there are a lot of our people out there with different personalities, a different slant on life. The sea makes us feel different."

"I know what you mean. We all like to sit on the beach and watch the ocean sometimes. It's soothing," I said.

"That's not to say the sea doesn't get angry now and then," Larry replied. "The sea has her off days, too, just like us. We got to respect her, though, and not treat her like a child. Aluminium boats and ships don't respect her much. You can see the wounds they cause her with their propellers. The scars on the water go on for miles sometimes. In the old days, our outrigger boats never cut the water the way modern ships do. Because the sea carries us along, not because we tried to plow our way through her. We never hurt the water, never leave wounds. Don't think that the sea ends when she washes up on the beach either. The wind brings her onshore so that she can keep us company at night. We're never far from the sea. She's in our bones."

It was these insights, this homespun wisdom recounted to me that day in Townsville, that had prompted me to want to visit Larry on Thursday Island in the first place. He had intimated to me the existence of a body of knowledge related to the sea that formed the very bedrock of his existence. He had spoken of truths that were linked to the ageless movement of tides, to the screech of birds on a sandbar, to the egg-laying habit of turtles. Above all, he had suggested a way of thinking all but alien to my own. It was clear that Larry did not think of himself as independent from his origins. The sea was his alter ego, his conscience, and all his faculties were tempered by the fluid movement of the tides. Any feeling of separateness he might have felt faded away whenever he was near his beloved sea.

The next morning Larry arrived in a taxi to collect me at my hotel. Together we trundled down the main street and along the coast road to an outlying settlement. On our left, palm trees clung like spiders to the open blue of the sea. Broken fronds lay on the sand like the bones of some archaic sea monster. Residents waved as we passed, and galvanized-iron roofs shone brightly in the sunlight. As the island was no more than two miles long, the journey lasted only a few minutes. Meanwhile, Larry appeared to be more at ease with himself. Our talk the previous day seemed to have relieved him of a considerable burden.

"I want you to meet Mr. Issau," he said. "He's a Saibai man, from near the coast of New Guinea. He's the honorary police inspector here on Thursday Island, but don't let that bother you. He knows a lot of things about the old ways. Watch out, though: He can talk until the tide comes in and drowns you!"

"It sounds to me like there's plenty of *zogo* still left in Mr. Issau," I said.

"There sure is," Larry responded.

Mr. Issau lived alone in a rambling house in the shade by an almond tree. He had converted the rear of his property into a village lean-to: an endless galvanized-iron roof supported by poles. In this way the sea breeze could drift through, cooling those who sat underneath. Abandoned washing machines, broken electrical goods, kitchen bric-a-brac, a model outrigger canoe with its rigging smashed, and ceremonial masks used at dance festivals competed for our attention. The place was reminiscent of a folk museum. Pleased by our visit, Mr. Issau offered us the choice between two equally dilapidated kitchen chairs that threatened to collapse under our weight.

Bald, thick-necked, and with prominent pectoral muscles, Mr. Issau filled the lean-to with his infectious energy. His eyes protruded from his skull as if they were being pressed from behind by the force of his thoughts. When he spoke, his singsong voice threw out sentences in agitated bursts. It seemed as if Mr. Issau had been confined to a policeman's uniform for too long, and now he was relishing the freedom of his recent retirement.

When I broached the subject of the old ways, his manner quickly changed. The easy confidence that came from being an authority figure all his life slipped away, and he adopted a more conciliatory attitude. When he told me that he was a "shallow water" man from the coastal island of Saibai, in contrast to a "deep water" Mer man like Larry, I recognized why his mannerisms were so quick and fluctuating. He was at the mercy of the rapid tidal movements and shifting currents that were a feature of his island birthplace.

"Understanding is like a candle in your body. It lights up all the time, so you know," he announced.

"Mr. Issau's totem is the crocodile," Larry informed me. "That's why we're brothers."

I looked at both men. To be in the presence of not one but two crocodiles left me nonplussed. How was I to deal with their rather formidable presence?

"Luckily neither of you is a shark," I observed. "Otherwise what chance would I have if I swam into one of you out there in the water?"

"You'd be all right," Mr. Issau replied with a laugh. "You see, the shark is the law. He's neutral, that's why we say he's the law. He offers no favors, and eats anything that comes his way. You can't ask any favors from a shark, so don't expect them. That makes him rock-solid, a little distant from all of us. We don't want to get in his way, otherwise he might attack. He doesn't show affection either, but then he doesn't need to. He's the law."

Mr. Issau disappeared into the house at this point and returned with a stuffed crocodile under his arm. This he placed on the table. For the first time I was able to gaze closely at Mr. Issau and Larry's totem. The ridged spine and tail, the half-open jaw lined with teeth, all these suggested some monstrous antiquity. It was as if the three of us were a part of prehistory ourselves.

"For us the crocodile is *augud*," Mr. Issau explained in a whisper.

"What does *augud* mean?" I asked.

"It's part of spirit. *Augud* is the spirit," he replied. "It's what you call sacred. *Augud* is in everything. Nothing can exist without *augud*. It's important for you to know that," he said.

"Maybe you should tell the story about how our families come from the crocodile totem," Larry suggested.

"About Gaizu and Aka, you mean?"

"Yeah. They're important, because they help us to know who we are," Larry responded.

Mr. Issau leaned on the table with both arms. Already he was beginning to sink into that state of reverie from which all good stories eventually emerge.

"Before time," he began, "a boy named Gaizu found a crocodile's egg in a nest. To find one egg like this means good luck. We say, 'The crocodile's egg must be carefully watched.' Gaizu built a pen for the egg on a river bank and kept watch over it until it hatched. He and his ten sisters loved the little crocodile and played with it every day. They called the crocodile Aka."

"Which means 'grandmother,' " Larry said.

"The kids used to climb on her back and go out to sea," Mr. Issau continued. "They always sat on the crocodile's back in the same order—Gaizu in front of Aka's nostrils, four girls on Aka's head, two on her back, and four on her tail."

Mr. Issau ran a finger along the crocodile's spine as he spoke.

"In those days, Aka was a gentle creature," he went on. "At sea, she used to eat seaweed before taking the children home. One day, Gaizu tore the weed from Aka's mouth and threw it in her face. 'Why do you eat such useless stuff?' he demanded. Every time they returned home Gaizu would do the same thing to Aka. He would drag the weed from her mouth and throw it in her face. Aka grew resentful. The next time she took the children out to sea she sank below the surface, leaving them floundering. 'Aka! Aka!' the children cried. But Aka ignored them. She was busy swimming all over the ocean, telling the sharks and other crocodiles of her treatment. Then she came back, and let them climb on her back again, before heading off to a secret place.

"Meanwhile Gaizu saw waves smashing against a reef. It was a dangerous place and he feared they might be thrown against the reef by the surf. He called out to Aka, pleading with her to turn back. But instead Aka rolled over, dumping the children in the sea again. Only this time all of Aka's friends were on hand to eat them up.

"Today we remember Aka in our family names, our totem names, which we identify with different parts of the crocodile's body," Mr. Issau said. "It's our way of remembering who our ancestors were and what they did to Aka, so we don't make the same mistake ourselves."

"Aka is *augud*," Larry emphasized. "She is the single egg, the egg that must be watched over and cared for. When Gaizu and his sisters treated Aka so badly, it was no wonder she reacted like she did. She was tired of being pushed around."

"Before time," Mr. Issau elaborated, "Aka was a gentle creature, happy to feed on seaweed. That was all she wanted. But Gaizu made her angry by not treating her with respect. Gaizu is us. Now Aka's a savage crocodile. That's the way it is with nature. We must always treat it with respect. *Augud* is in everything," he added.

"When someone tells you a story," Larry said. "You got to listen. Everywhere you go in Torres Strait, people have a story to tell you. In these stories you will hear where they came from. It's our way of telling you how we were made."

"We all come from the past," Mr. Issau observed. "You must know the stories if you want to know what made you. They're important."

Mr. Issau stroked the back of the crocodile once more.

"Do you really believe that the crocodile was a friendly creature once?" I asked, my incredulity already stretched by Mr. Issau's story.

"That's what the story says," Larry replied.

"If you don't treat nature rough, it will always be gentle with you. That's what we believe, anyway," Mr. Issau concluded.

I did not see Larry for some days after our meeting with Mr. Issau. The wind had suddenly blown up, so I assumed that he had gone to the bottom of the sea until it finally blew over. This was his way of handling personal dilemmas, I soon learned. Or maybe he was out there somewhere just staring at coral. In any event, I knew that our discussion with Mr. Issau had aroused old memories for him. And these had troubled him more than he was prepared to admit.

A few days later, he finally reappeared. I saw him standing on the grass outside my hotel one morning, his tropical shirt ablaze with color. His stance appeared more upright than when I had last seen him. And he was smiling. It appeared that his time at the bottom of the sea out of the wind had been well spent. I waved to him from the veranda.

"There's one more old fella I want you to meet," he said when I had joined him downstairs. "His name is Lui Bon, and he's a Mer man like me. He can tell you about Gelem."

Gelem. I had not heard this name before. Nor was Larry about to enlighten me. As Lui Bon was an elderly man, a *zogo le* of the old school, Larry felt he must defer to him.

Lui Bon lived with his son in a weatherboard house opposite the local rugby football ground. As we walked up the pathway to his front door the sounds of cheering drifted across the road from the crowd sitting under the trees. Evidently someone had scored. The sea behind the football ground enveloped the ball whenever a player kicked it into the air. And broad-shouldered island boys tackled one another with all the force of waves breaking on the beach.

Mr. Bon received us in the backyard, in the shifting shade of a palm tree. The wind continued to cause a rasping sound among the fronds above our heads. His frail body, quiet voice, and almost birdlike delicacy belied his days as a young man spent at sea as a pearl diver. A gentility characterized his manner so that when he did speak his voice drifted across the space between us with the smoothness of sand.

He spoke of his birth on Mer in 1910. From the Comet tribe, Lui Bon considered himself a "shark person." He spoke of the times when they used to go to sea to catch turtles, using sucker fish tied to a line. The sucker fish attached itself to the shell of the turtle, enabling him and his friends to haul the creature alongside the canoe. Thus, with the aid of one fish, they were able to catch another. Moreover, he told me that his wife, who briefly appeared at the rear door to welcome us when we arrived, was a Torres Strait pigeon person. In Lui Bon's backyard the interplay between man and nature seemed complete.

Lui Bon also told me that his people owned the sea. At first I did not understand what he meant. How could one "own" the sea that shifted about with the currents? The boundaries would have to be as fluid as the sea itself. He then explained how the ocean was apportioned into family allotments, governed by invisible lines drawn between kays, reefs, and sandbars. Whole reefs might belong to one family, and that family then had the exclusive right to the fish and shells within its boundaries. To fish off another man's reef was tantamount to an act of trespass.

Then, without any prompting from either of us, Lui Bon remarked:

"If you want to learn more about our ways, you must make the voyage of Gelem. He is the important one. He made the dugong. My people believe in him."

"He brought the soil to Mer," Larry prompted.

"You must travel to Erub and Mer," Lui Bon urged. "These are the places he visited after he left Moa."

"Who is Gelem?" I asked.

Lui Bon proceeded to tell me the story of a young man who voyaged on the back of a dugong from the western island of Moa to Erub and Mer. A mammal like the whale or porpoise, the dugong feeds on sea grasses in the shallow waters of the strait.

"Gelem used to shoot birds with a bow and arrow made by his mother. Her name was Atwer," he began.

"That means 'criticism' in our language," Larry said.

"He used to give his mother the lean birds he shot and keep the fat ones for himself," Lui Bon went on. "Atwer decided to teach him a lesson. She smeared clay on her face and jumped out of the bush to frighten Gelem. Then she ran off home, washed away the clay, and sat down to wait for him. Gelem told her how he had been attacked by a ghost, but his mother didn't let on what she knew. This happened every time Gelem went out hunting, until one day he noticed traces of clay in his mother's ears. He became suspicious of her, and decided to leave Moa for good.

"Instead of hunting birds, Gelem cut down a number of trees, which he carved in the shape of a dugong. The first tree was too light, and floated too high in the water. This one he told to go to the island of Mabuiag. The next tree he cut down was heavier than the first, but it was still too light for his needs. So he sent this one off to Badu. The third tree was heavier still, but not quite what he wanted either. So he sent this dugong off to the mainland of Australia. Gelem went to sleep that night wondering whether he might ever find the right tree, and so escape his mother.

"His father came to him in a dream and told him to cut down a *baaidem tulu* tree," Larry remarked.

"That's right," Lui Bon added. "He told Gelem to hollow it out in the shape of a dugong. But he would only find the tree when he heard the call of a tiny bird. So Gelem followed his father's advice. He cut down a *baaidem tulu* that a little bird showed him, and made his dugong for the voyage. He filled it with soil, fruit, vegetables, and seed. Then he asked his mother to call him if she should happen to see a large fish swimming near the reef. After that, he climbed aboard his dugong and slipped below the surface. When he drew near his mother, who was fishing on the reef, he surfaced. Atwer cried out for Gelem to come quickly so as to spear a large fish. Instead, Gelem opened the dugong's mouth and laughed and said to his mother, 'You pretended to be a ghost. Well, to teach you a lesson, I'm leaving Moa forever.' He went under the water again and disappeared."

"His mother was brokenhearted. She said, 'Go and lie down at Mer, an island rich in food,' " Larry said.

"This is why Mer has such good soil today, and Moa is so barren. Gelem stole it from Moa," Lui Bon added.

"And how the four different species of dugong were made from four different trees," Larry said with some pride in his voice. "On his voyage east Gelem visited many islands. When he reached Erub and saw Mer in the distance, he knew his voyage was nearly over."

Lui Bon's disclosure of the story of Gelem echoed that of Mr. Issau a few days earlier. Both men had chosen to tell me stories important to their feeling of identity. Their totem and place of origin were embroiled in the exploits of two spirit beings, Aka and the dugong-man Gelem. In telling me of the birth of their world and its people through these myths, they had made me privy to their way of looking at life. I had not expected to be introduced to another way of seeing things so easily. Who would have imagined that four species of dugong found their counterpart in various trees? Or that the crocodile might have been an herbivore until it had been ridiculed by the child in us? Hearing these myths made it clear that both Lui Bon and Mr. Issau felt the necessity to make me a part of their world before I could begin to understand them. By telling me a story, they had handed me an important key.

"You better make Gelem's voyage," Lui Bon repeated his earlier suggestion. "He made the dugong. He made our island. Mer is a place of spirits."

"Maybe I ought to swim there," I said, half in jest.

Lui Bon gave a short sigh, the kind that old men often make when they feel they have made their point.

"That's a good idea," he said. "Because Gelem, he made the world. He's *augud*."

Later, after Larry and I had taken leave of Lui Bon, we paused in the street in front of Mr. Bon's house. The football game was still in progress, but the noise of the crowd hardly disturbed our thoughts. I kept thinking of Lui Bon as he told the story about Gelem and the birth of Mer. His face had been like one of those pearl skinners of the past as he bent over a table, a lamp shining above his head, the sound of an obsidian knife scraping against a soft surface. It seemed that he had finally peeled away the nacre to reveal a pearl of great beauty. This pearl, I realized, was the way the voyage of a god-man had made it possible for his people to discover the truth about their origins. It was the sort of pearl he had wanted me to accept as a gift.

"Larry, I think I'll take Mr. Bon's advice," I said.

A football soared through the goalposts. The crowd cheered.

"Go to Erub and Mer, you mean?" Larry asked, a hint of excitement in his voice.

"Why don't you join me? It would make my task much easier."

But Larry shook his head.

"You will find men living on those islands who know far more about the old ways than I do," he said. "They know a lot of secrets. It's better you see them alone. That way they can talk to you freely. They mightn't like to talk about secret things in front of me. This is the way of my people," Larry said.

"You're not afraid to return, are you?" I challenged him.

"*Bala*, listen," Larry addressed me as "brother" for the first time. "You got to do this thing by yourself. Mer is my past. I know it's always going to be there if I choose to go back. But for you, it is something else. What you can learn. What you can discover about the secrets of the sea. You've got to talk to those old fellas before it's too late. Listen to their stories. They know what it's all about. They know how to make you feel strong again in yourself."

"Build up my *zogo*, you mean?"

"Maybe."

Larry paused and gazed at the sea. Then he said:

"It doesn't mean that what I've lost isn't still out there somewhere, swimming about. The old fellas, they still know all about it. For them the sea is *augud*. It's still a sacred thing. I can't forget that," he added.

"Are you sure you don't want to come with me?" I said.

But Larry had already started down the street. I could see his lips were still trembling a little after his last pronouncement.

"You find Gelem. Then you come back here and maybe we talk about it again," he called out to me.

TWO

The ocean shimmered as our Twin Otter flew into the morning sun. Below us cays, reefs, and pools of anonymous marine life greeted our gaze. Stretches of sand fringed by palms announced the presence of small islands populated by colonies of seabirds and turtles. Fishing trawlers from down south pitched in the swell, their trailing nets supported by countless bobbing buoys. Torres Strait seemed like the rim of the world as we droned on toward Erub and Mer. The trip reminded me of the fear sailors once had about falling over the edge of the world into the abyss. Only the pursuit of knowledge, it seemed, gave them the courage to sail on.

On board the aircraft were islanders returning home. At Yam, Yorke, and Coconut islands we touched down on sandy grass strips where people alighted to the welcoming arms of their families. Flowers garlanded their hair as they embraced. By the time we took off on the final leg to Erub the aircraft was only half full. There were two other Europeans on board, bound for Erub like myself. They were traveling there to attend a memorial service in honor of the arrival of the first missionaries to the region in 1871. For over one hundred years, this day, known as the Coming of the Light, has been celebrated by Torres Strait islanders with the same intense joy as they celebrate Christmas.

I asked myself whether Lui Bon's insistence that I visit the eastern islands might have had something to do with this event. Did he want me to encounter the memory of this confrontation between two cultures on a remote tropical beach? The London Missionary Society's arrival in Treachery Bay aboard the *Surprise* must have seemed like all of that to the young warrior Dabad when he first saw the ship anchor in the bay. In the end I suspected otherwise. Lui Bon's grace in these matters transcended my limited act of hindsight. It was more likely that he wanted me to come to some understanding of his origins rather than engage in any discussion about the role of missionaries. Gelem's arrival on the beach at Erub and later Mer after his epic voyage from Moa represented a far more significant moment for him than the sudden appearance of the *Surprise*. Larry had suggested as much when we were saying goodbye at the airport that morning.

"You'll be all right. Gelem will look after you," he had remarked while we stood on the lawn by the tarmac.

"You seem sure about that," I replied.

"First you got to believe, *bala*. That's important. Gelem, he's the first man. You're traveling in his footsteps. That's what we believe, anyway."

"There's no chance he might lead me astray?"

"You've just got to believe," Larry reaffirmed.

Larry was right, of course. First I had to learn how to accept the reality of myth as part of my life. This was not going to be easy. A man who had abandoned his homeland and transformed himself into a dugong seemed to me like a hard act to follow.

Erub, meanwhile, appeared on the horizon early in the afternoon, a ragged outpost of grassland and palm groves. Fishtraps built of volcanic stones portioned the adjoining reef into watery paddocks. High hills inland made the island seem even more remote than if it had been a coral atoll. Along the coast, huts and houses stood in bamboo compounds. Outboard fishing boats lay on their sides on the beach above the high-water mark. Children ran out onto the sand and waved as the aircraft circled the coastline before making its descent onto a strip carved from the hillside. It pulled up by a pile of shells on the grass and the engines cut out.

An island family offered me a room in their house for a small payment, and I was soon made to feel at home. Of the four tribes scattered around the shores of Erub I found myself a guest of the people of Samsep, whose totem was Nam Kerem, the turtle. The other tribes considered the shark, man-of-war hawk, and the snake as their totems. Though essentially a sea people, the Erubams also relied on their inland gardens. Here yams, cassava, sugarcane, vegetables, bananas, and *wangai* fruit grew on traditional family allotments. For many, the garden was more than just a place where they could grow food; it was also a place where they could enter into a mysterious relationship with the earth.

By profession, an Erubam was either a fisherman or a gardener. He might do both at different times, but he was eventually considered to be one or the other. Gelem, after all, had brought seed and soil with him from Moa, allotting portions to the islands where he landed. The volcanic nature of Erub and Mer came into being as a result of this act of beneficence. Gelem, however, had not stayed very long on Erub. According to legend, when he entered the lagoon near Garsao, he noticed the high hills of Mer in the distance, so he swam there. I was soon to discover why this island, and not Erub, turned out to be his final destination.

The village of Samsep hugged a sandy road skirting the beach. Simple houses made from galvanized iron and plaited palm fronds stood on stilts on either side of the road. There were two shops on the island that relied for their supplies on fortnightly visits by a barge from Thursday Island. Social life, it seemed, revolved around the local church, where everyone gathered to sing hymns on Sunday. Meanwhile, all day and every day the trade winds blew, ladening the air with the smell of salt.

When I broached the question of Gelem's pilgrimage with George Mye, Erub's long-serving council chairman, some days after my arrival, the man was a little reluctant to talk on the subject. He argued that the story of Gelem "belonged to Mer," and that I should explore it with the Meriam people rather than himself. Clearly, certain tales were not common currency to be exchanged with every stranger who happened to ask. In the future I would have to be more circumspect with my inquiries.

If rather reserved at first, George Mye soon revealed himself to be a man of considerable culture. Although he traveled the world on Torres Strait business, he always returned to his house on the beach at Dadamud. Tall and regal in stature, George Mye talked slowly but with emphasis, choosing his words carefully. He was a man who despised gossip of any sort, and yet, as council chairman, it was inevitable that he knew the extent of every political intrigue on the island. He seemed a fitting person to relate the story of the battle between Rebes and Id, the two great protagonists from Erub and Mer. It was the defeat of Rebes by Id that remains to this day an unstaunched wound for many Erubams. Rebes's death is seen as a symbol of cultural loss, of their defeat at the hands of the more powerful Meriams.

"Rebes was a great leader of our people," George related one morning while we sat behind a bamboo windbreak outside his house. "He put the soil in the water at Bramble Kay as a sanctuary for Nam Kerem, the turtle-head god. For that reason alone we see him as important. He helped to provide us with food."

"Why did Id attack him, then?" I asked.

"The Meriams envied my people's abundant stock of turtles because of what Rebes had done," George replied. "So one day Id and his warriors landed at Dadamud in the company of the Masig men, hoping to surprise my people at dawn. Two young men who were fishing off a dugong platform on the edge of the reef saw their war canoes coming and sounded the alarm. When they landed, we were ready for them."

"They fell into a trap."

"More or less," George Mye agreed. "They were forced to retreat to their canoes, leaving many of their companions dead on the beach."

"What happened to Id?"

"He was very angry," George replied. "So angry, in fact, that he decided to come back again a few years later. With some women this time, as he wanted to populate the island with Meriams."

"He wanted to humiliate your people by taking over completely," I reasoned.

George Mye nodded.

"He and his men slipped into Garsao lagoon one night. Although they were noticed by a fisherman from Gazir, the warning came too late. Id's party hid in the scrub and waited for Rebes and his men to reveal themselves."

"Where was Rebes?"

"Up in the hills, sorely troubled by dreams. He knew something was wrong, that's for sure. His rheumatism was causing him a lot of pain, so he ordered his wives to prepare a fire. Meanwhile, down on the beach, one of Id's women noticed a thin trail of smoke emerging from a hillside cave. She told Id about it, and he immediately set off inland with a war party. They soon found Rebes's hideout and prepared to attack."

"Was Rebes ready for him?" I asked.

"Not quite," George replied. "He figured the Meriam warriors must by close at hand, so he ordered his wives to dress him for battle. Even though he was barely able to defend himself, Rebes laid out his weapons on the ground near the fire. If he was going to die then he wanted to do so as a warrior, not as a sick man. He was very proud."

"So Id approached the cave with his men," I said.

"Then he sounded his war drums. Parting the vines hanging over the entrance, he announced his totem: 'Id, shark from the great reef to windward!' Then he hurled his spear at Rebes, killing the old man instantly. In the fight that followed, all of Rebes' wives were killed and beheaded. Very few Erubams were spared that day. Their heads were piled high on the beach near here, before being loaded aboard the war canoes and shipped back to Mer."

"So Id had got what he wanted," I said. "He had conquered Erub, the home of turtles."

"My people were all but destroyed that day. What was worse, the sacred turtle-head of Nam Kerem was carried off to Mer as a war trophy. They were too strong for us. After that, turtles no longer climbed the beach to lay their eggs. Even today we never see them on this island."

George's story of the defeat of Erub was an important revelation for me. I had no idea that Erub's destiny as a place where Christianity would first make its mark in the Torres Strait had been fashioned out of Id's victory over Rebes and the stealing of a turtle god. Or that Erub's future had been determined by the clash of two powerful personalities each eager to abscond with the other's head.

"We lost our birthright when Nam Kerem was stolen," George

Mye said. "That's why we welcomed the missionaries when they came here at the time of the Coming of the Light in 1871."

"The London Missionary Society became a substitute for the loss of your turtle god?"

"Maybe. But we're all Christians now, so Nam Kerem no longer matters."

It was an unusual remark to make—a remark that was more than confirmed by a monument I later discovered by the beach in the neighboring bay of Med. It had been set up as a tribute to the events of July 1, 1871, when the missionaries had first come ashore. It read:

In Loving Memory of Dabad
1871
A Man who Denied his Tribal Law
and Accepted the Good News
of Salvation.

Why had the Erubams wanted to deny their heritage like this? Was it to flaunt their supremacy over Mer in the race toward conversion? It seemed that the loss of Nam Kerem all those years ago had rankled them to the point where they were prepared to do almost anything to avenge their loss to the people of Mer.

Meanwhile, was this the real reason why Gelem had quit Erub's shores and swum on to Mer? Had he encountered a troubled paradise populated by a people stripped of their pride and their god? The story of Rebes lying in his cave, half crippled, awaiting death at the hands of Id, was a disturbing parable. Clearly, Rebes had succumbed to forces beyond his control. He had sacrificed his mind to the mob when his head was torn from his body. The historic trauma of this event was now firmly entrenched in Erubam culture, and it was hard to know whether Erubams themselves pined for Nam Kerem or whether they were content now to sing hymns in the All Saints Church on the beach at Badog.

To find some answers I decided to visit the tiny, shell-encrusted church of All Saints. Inside I noticed the baptismal font surrounded by a frieze of cowrie shells. The altar was built of stone and shells. On the rear wall, behind the altar, the words *Zogo, Zogo, Zogo* had been painted in imitation of the expression of praise, "Holy, Holy, Holy." Multicolored pillars fashioned from crushed coral stood out against the newly painted white walls. Two young island girls of around ten years of age were quietly dusting the pews as I entered.

I soon befriended Ina and Emma, and they invited me home to meet their uncle, Timothy China. When we arrived at the house the old man was sitting on his balcony contemplating the distant sound of the sea. He did not seem at all put out by my desire to ask him questions. He regarded his knowledge as one might a precious ornament that was worthy of occasional display.

Born in 1917, Mr. China had spent his early life diving for trochus shell, then used in the manufacture of pearl buttons. For seven dollars a month he lived aboard a lugger at least eleven months each year, diving on behalf of his Japanese employers. Then he sailed back to Erub for a brief holiday before returning to Thursday Island. It was a hard, often dangerous life, watching friends die of shark wounds or falling victim to the bends. Those were the days when you said a prayer each morning, asking for protection. It was a prayer that Mr. China invariably addressed to Nam Kerem, since his totem was the turtle. When I asked him to recite this prayer for me, Mr. China did not hesitate. Drawing forth a much-folded piece of paper from his wallet, he slowly read his "Song of Mazabkaur" in Erubam, and then he translated it into English:

> Lay thee down there
> In our breast and bosom,
> Call back from the north.
> In beauty, in pride of perfection,
> And style of thy grandeur
> Make thee the sea-ways to the north,
> From the west.
> On thy shell may creep or lie
> Gifts to measure strength of our
> Oars and poles.
> Be laid distantly unspoiled, untrembled
> By the nature of thy makeup and courage,
> O Nam, O turtle god
> Maker of our clan and race totem,
> Spread thy increased treasures
> To wash our shore.

In view of our clans-people in distant lands,
Gather up what thou hast found
Then give it to all.

When Mr. China remarked at the conclusion of this prayer that he found it impossible to be in the same room where turtle meat was being served, I knew how he felt. The creature was himself.

I spent many days on the balcony with Mr. China, listening to his stories. From his vantage point he could gaze at the ocean through the palms and recall how Tagai, the Southern Cross, used to guide his ancestors homeward. By tasting the water, the sailors of old were able to determine whether they were near New Guinea or on course for Erub. Depending on whether Tagai was horizontal or vertical in the sky, they would know whether it was high tide—and so ascertain the strength of the currents. The presence or absence of birds on the wing told them of continuing fine weather or of an approaching storm. Along with the moon, winds, or the movement of currents below the surface, these men were able to sail their outriggers over vast distances in relative safety, knowing that their knowledge of nature would eventually get them home. Such knowledge Mr. China progressively divulged to me on his balcony each day, believing that to withhold it now might mean its end.

"In the old days my people had power," he admitted one afternoon, peering over the top of his battered glasses at Ina and Emma playing on the ground below.

"What your people call *zogo*," I said.

"It's because they had a strong belief in the spirits that gave them their *zogo*," he replied. "I can remember how men used to travel from New Guinea to Erub on no more than a piece of black thread. Nothing stopped them in those days."

"Suspended above the sea, you mean?" I asked.

Mr. China nodded.

"They did it with ease because they had power," he said. "When I was on the luggers years ago I remember how a Solomon Island boy changed into a booby bird and flew back to Erub to ask after our families. It was a still night, and most of us were asleep on deck. Basooki—that was his name—he told us he was going to Erub. Walking to the mast, he suddenly disappeared before our eyes. Next we heard the sound of wings flapping in the night. We sat around asking ourselves what had happened to Basooki. An hour later we looked up to see a booby bird on the masthead. Then we suddenly recognized Basooki on deck carrying a mango blossom. He said he'd picked it in Erub, and that all our families were in good health. I tell you, men were full of power in the old days."

"Did you also listen to the birds?"

"We did. They told us things no one else could," Mr. China recalled. "I remember a family who used to live on Rennel Island some way from here. They always knew when a boat was approaching because the birds told them. Long before the boat sailed into view, the manager used to cry out 'Sail O!' Sure enough, within an hour a boat sailed into the lagoon. A bird warned him of its arrival. We call that bird a *ti* bird. It's a sunbird."

Mr. China then revealed to me information about omen birds that he confessed he had never told anyone. It was a significant moment in our relationship, as I realized that he had finally decided to take me into his confidence. In a sense, he had begun to regard me as a budding *zogo le* like himself. He wanted me to know things about his world that few people had ever been privileged to hear before. For some reason he wanted to make me a part of his life.

He told me about *kiau*, the kingfisher, which has the power of seeing ghosts. If a *kiau* calls out "ekwe, ekwe, ekwe," it is a warning to any passerby to beware of an attack by a ghost from which illness or even death might ensue. Another bird, the *birobiro*, a small migratory bird, always arrives on the island when the yams are ready for eating. The *miaii* is also a "spirit bird," and its cry tells islanders when the banana ceremony has been completed, and when their crops are ready to be harvested. Another bird, the *waru*, sings only at night. A small seabird with a long bill and legs, it frequents the beach at the edge of the water. If a man hears it calling "waru, waru" in the evening, he knows that he must prepare his fishing gear for the morning because a school of turtles will invariably swim past the island. According to Mr. China, these birds act as guides and omen-bearers, foretelling births and deaths.

When I asked Mr. China on one occasion whether he would tell me about the secrets of farming, he grew silent for a time. I wondered whether I might have offended him. Perhaps an omen bird had warned him not to reveal knowledge that he felt might be misused. But I need not have worried. He was merely recalling a time when his garden had been more than a providential plot of land; it had been his small acre of paradise.

"In the old days, our garden was very important to us," he began. "Now we have too much money on the island because of government handouts. The young people have become lazy; they do not want to work in the garden anymore. We rely on the supply boat instead. It's a sad thing: We are no more a strong people.

"But for me, the garden is where I belong," Mr. China continued, warming to his subject. "Every day when I was younger, my wife and I would climb the hill and stay there until it grew dark, working our plot. Everyone did the same. We planted vegetables, bananas, yams, sugarcane. So many good things. We were never hungry in those days."

"Did you perform ceremonies in your garden to encourage the crop to grow?" I asked.

"Sure we did. The festival of Tamar, I remember, was the big one. A long fence was built at the back of the gardens. This was to act as a windbreak in the windy season. At Tamar time we would lay out food offerings along the foot of the fence, and then we would dress up to dance. We would attach feathers to our shoulders, just like they used to do when preparing for war. 'We can fly, we are strong!' we used to cry out and then dance. This was our way of thanking Augud for making our gardens grow."

"Did you plant your crops at any special time?"

"Yes, when the tide was low. Never at high tide. At low tide you could see the rocks above the waterline, which meant that we would have a good crop next season. We believe the rocks are like fruit: The more of them you see the more fruit will grow. Also we believe that with the rising tide powerful forces, forces for growth, are being pressed back onto the land. The sea's *zogo* is good for the garden: It helps our plants grow strong and tall. We always harvest our crop when the tide is going out."

"How did you plant your crops?"

"I never dig a hole and plant my seed in direct sunlight," Mr. China replied. "Always early in the morning or in the afternoon. Even then I stand between the sun and the hole, so that my shadow protects the earth. The sun is a good thing, a powerful thing with plenty of *zogo*. But it can also be hard—too hard some-times for young plants. We must protect them, make sure the sun leaves them alone. We have to be gentle with our garden."

"Did you ever say a prayer for your garden?" I asked.

"Always. Always we pray for fish, for food, and for plants. It's our *lawar* prayer, our food prayer. It's the same as the Lord's Prayer. We say, 'Give us food for this day and another day.' That way, we ask Augud to look after us, to feed us."

"What happens in the garden now?"

Mr. China shifted uncomfortably in his chair. Something appeared to be bothering him.

"The gardens are overgrown," he confessed. "Very few people go up there anymore. Some old people, perhaps. I know old Daisy Solomon and her family still work their plot. But the rest, they sit in the village waiting for the government handout each month. Our people are being ruined by too much easy money."

Listening to old Mr. China speak on his balcony, with the sound of palm fronds rustling as he spoke, made me wonder whether we were discussing the same things sometimes. His feelings for the earth and sea about him always reflected an intimacy, a level of communion between himself and nature not available to people like me. It was as if he acknowledged some link, a "black thread" so to speak, that enabled him to bridge the gap between the world as he saw it and its spirit counterpart. Even his manner of speaking, the way he paused before revealing certain information, implied that he was conscious of his *zogo* and how it should be imparted. In contrast, I was left still grappling with the difficulty of how a man might transform himself into a booby bird and travel to a far place. Mr. China seemed aware of my difficulties, and he went to great lengths to make me understand the world from which he came.

I also learned how such knowledge could cause discord when people used it in an untoward way. George Mye spoke to me one day about *maid*, a method of inflicting disease and death upon a person. *Maid* involved sneaking up on a victim, or perhaps lying in wait for him, then knocking him unconscious. A curse was placed on him, together with a loss of memory, so that when he awoke he would have no knowledge of what had happened. It was said that this man would die within a relatively short period of time.

Pouri pouri, another technique derived from New Guinea sorcerers, could be used to kill a man from a distance. It did not require a physical encounter as with *maid*, but the end result was much the same. The man sickened and died. He could only be restored to health if the curse was lifted, or if the perpetrator was unmasked. If either of these events did not happen, the man grew weak to the point where he was little more than a living skeleton.

Thus I was made aware of the darker forces at work on the island, forces that had to be contained by ritual and ceremony if they were not to become too destructive. Both George and Mr. China made it clear to me that all their rituals in the past were designed to maintain a balance between light and shade, between the extreme conditions that nature sometimes unleashed. Cyclones, drought, and severe storms needed to be neutralized. Garden pests had to be eliminated. Illness had to be assuaged. All these things fell into the category of being considered demonic events, and so had to be isolated by some form of cleansing ritual.

Nonetheless, walking the main street of Samsep each day with the thought of Nam Kerem and its link with turtle abundance in my mind, I often asked myself whether Erubams were in possession of a special faculty. Their island represented a multilayered existence for them. It provided them with food, shelter, and a way of life. It offered them a mythic identity in the form of a turtle god and the heroic demise of Rebes. But most of all it saturated their lives with the sensation of belonging elsewhere, in an imaginative realm where everything is possible. Like Gelem, they had, in a sense, become amphibious, able to exist in two dimensions at the same time.

I had learned a good deal from men like Mr. China and George Mye. In spite of believing that their culture was in danger of disappearing, they had introduced me to much that I had not heard before. Not so long ago it appeared that men like them did indeed have the power to transform themselves. They had been capable of living within a spiritual landscape and performing feats that today's generation could no longer emulate. How many men could travel to New Guinea on a black thread or change themselves into a booby bird in order to bring back news from a wider world?

Mr. China and George Mye had taught me that a gap had opened up between what men like themselves knew to be true and what the next generation merely regarded as superstition. These men were the last link with the old ways, with the sacred garden that bestowed the first fruits of prayer, and a law that had been both understood and feared. Unfortunately they had not yet learned how to come to terms with this loss, nor forge new links with what was fast becoming for them a memory only.

It was time to move on. In the wake of Gelem and now Id it seemed that the island of Mer beckoned. Would I discover Nam Kerem's lost head, the decapitated head of an ancient and noble system of belief, or would I find myself once more casting my net among a shoal of questions I had not been able to successfully land in the past? Clearly Mer held secrets that were central to the survival of Torres Strait culture and of the sea as its icon. It was up to me to discover them for myself.

THREE

Paul Gauguin, the French painter who lived on Tahiti for many years, must have felt on occasions as I did as I sat alone of an evening in the parish guesthouse on the beach at Mer. Gauguin had voyaged to the fringe of the world in order to encounter something wild, the untrammeled freedom of nature. His dissatisfaction with nineteenth-century bourgeois values caused him to flee Europe and pursue what he called "solitude and savagery." I was beginning to understand what he meant. Knowing that there were still people left in the world who regarded nature as their comrade-in-arms struck me as important. Already I had been told that there was a Meriam family on the island who owned the constellation of Tagai. If a man believed he could actually possess stars in the sky, then I was sure Gauguin would have regarded him as a worthy study for a portrait.

Sometimes I thought Mer itself might have been part of that constellation. The island certainly manifested a particular luminosity when it came to signaling the strength of its *zogo*. Gelem, the first man, creator of dugongs and arch-deceiver of mothers, had chosen his ultimate point of landfall with an eye to impressing those who came after him. The dugong that was himself had become the central outcrop of the island. Behind the shack where I was living, the massive slope of Gelem bridged the southern tip of Mer, a dugong-shaped hill that dominated the island. When Gelem arrived from Erub he had lain down beside Mer facing east. But when the east wind blew up his nostrils he had sneezed, discharging the smaller islands of Dauar and Waier, lying a few miles offshore. Then he had rolled over to protect himself from the east wind, though not before issuing vegetables, fruit, seed, and soil from under his left arm. These he scattered about the island so that today Mer is a fertile place, rich in natural growth.

My shack was built below Gelem's flipper among a cluster of houses where all eight tribes of Mer now lived. Before the arrival of the missionaries in the 1870s, the tribes used to live around the entire coastline, tending their gardens inland and working their fish traps on the reef and outer kays. Since then, the parish church had become the center of island life, which in turn had encouraged the scattered tribes to come together and reside on the west coast. Now the people lived out their lives, punctuating each phase with a birth, a death, a tombstone-opening ceremony, a dance festival, and the occasional feast when someone was fortunate enough to spear a dugong. Weaving mats or fashioning the elegantly feathered headdresses, known as *daris*, which are used during the dance ceremony, formed a part of daily life. The old days, those days of headhunting expeditions to nearby islands, were over. All that was left to commemorate these events were a few stone clubs tucked away in old men's sea chests.

My first days on Mer were spent getting to know people and trying to formulate in my mind what I wanted to learn from them. Perhaps, like Gauguin, I had come here merely to escape. This thought plagued me since I was as prone as anyone to falling victim to the romance associated with tropical islands. Palm-fringed beaches offer an excuse to lapse into reverie. But I did not want to escape; I wanted to understand more intimately the world that Gelem had created.

Tapim Benny-Father introduced me to his world of holy birds and flowers one morning when I approached him in his house by the beach. Tapim had been born in 1909, and I discovered that his totem was the shark. I recalled what Mr. Issau had said about the shark as a custodian of the law. Already extremely old, his slight figure enveloped in an aura of gentility, Mr. Benny-Father displayed none of the characteristics of his alter ego—at least not in the sense that Mr. Issau had described. His voice was so soft that I had to draw close to him to hear what he was saying. His words seemed to float on air, as redolent as blossoms lying on a bush path. Every time I sat with him I was conscious of being in the presence of a man who had taken nature into himself with all the intensity of a monk. Dressed in a blue *lava lava*, or sarong, he would sit on a stool outside his hut telling stories to anyone who would listen.

At first, Mr. Benny-Father was keen to tell me about Geigi, the great trevally fish, and its link with the island of Waier. According to him, it was a sacred place where Nageg, the triggerfish, gave birth to Geigi. He saw this story as intrinsic to his identity as a Meriam. After all, when he was young, the trevally was one of the islander's principal sources of food.

"Geigi was really a man," Mr. Benny-Father confided in his hushed voice. "He loved to spear fish. Each fish he caught he showed to his mother who named it."

"Presumably this is how these fish were born," I said.

Mr. Benny-Father agreed.

"Anyway, he made himself a set of fish eyes from young coconut leaves so he could swim underwater. Coming up for air one day, he found himself in the center of a shoal of sardines that a man called Iniamuris was trying to scoop up in his net. Geigi kept on returning to the same spot each day to break up the shoal of sardines that Iniamuris was attempting to catch. One day Iniamuris noticed the white soles of Geigi's feet and swept him up into his boat. He cut Geigi into tiny pieces, and cooked him over a fire. Then he ate him, along with his net, the stones from the fireplace, even the hot coals. All that he left was a tuft of Geigi's hair."

"Geigi's mother must have been worried when he didn't come home," I said.

"Of course she was. Nageg waited two days. On the third day she decided to go out looking for him. When she discovered the tuft of hair, she decided that Iniamuris must have killed and eaten Geigi. So she killed him with a club and cut him open. She took out the pieces of Geigi's body and put them together again."

"She tried to bring Geigi back to life?"

Mr. Benny-Father nodded.

"Nageg cut down an ant's nest and placed it on Geigi's head. She hoped the ants' bites might enter his bones. Then she burned the ants off his head, causing him a lot of pain. He soon woke up."

"The ants stung him alive?"

"They sure did," replied Mr. Benny-Father, rather enjoying the effect his story was having.

"To show how grateful he was," he went on, "Geigi placed a horn on his mother's back. 'Go and live in the sea,' he told her, 'and when men try to catch you on a line, lodge your horn in the rock. That way they'll never catch you.' Geigi swam off to live in the deep waters beyond the reef. This is how the triggerfish and great trevally were born."

I was touched by Mr. Benny-Father's explanation of how these fish came into existence. He had revealed to me a belief that had been in his culture for generations. This story had been a part of his secret life, a life not yet overshadowed by his subsequent acceptance of Christianity. He had told me about Geigi not as a gesture of defiance but of complicity. Like Iniamuris, he had allowed me to become caught up in his net of memory in the hope that my thoughts would be chopped into pieces and reconstituted along with Geigi.

The tale of Nageg and Geigi reminded me of the myth of Isis and Osiris. Osiris, the disseminator of civilization and agriculture among the ancient Egyptians, echoed the fish-creating activities of Geigi. He had been imprisoned in a coffin and later cut into pieces by his brother, Set. Just as Nageg had wandered about Waier and Dauar trying to find her son, Isis had wandered the world in search of her brother and husband, Osiris. The Egyptian god's imprisonment reflected Iniamuris's consumption of Geigi. In the end, both gods were cut to pieces by a jealous brother-figure and restored by a loving mother. Osiris's ultimate destination had been the underworld over which he became lord. Geigi retired to "deep water" from which he ruled his domain.

Listening to Mr. Benny-Father relate his story made me aware of how familiar older Meriams were with their mythic origins. Out there in the sea somewhere the triggerfish and the great trevally bore a striking resemblance to Nageg and Geigi. The story contained memories of a time when cannibalism had been a common practice. The idea of rebirth, after three days in limbo is another familiar image. Moreover, the act of placing green ants on Geigi's head in order to fire his spirit suggest a deep understanding of the way life begins. The sting of insight surely has no finer expression than that of green ants rousing Geigi out of his slumber.

When Mr. Benny-Father first whispered the name Malu during one of our conversations, however, I knew I had stumbled upon something important. The tone of his voice intimated that he wanted to tell me a secret, as if to unburden himself in his old age.

"Who is Malu?" I asked him tentatively.

"He's our god. He brought the law to Mer. Malu is *augud*," Mr. Benny-Father said, his voice barely audible.

He would not say anything more about Malu. But the fact that he mentioned *augud* in the same breath confirmed what I had already begun to suspect: A secret mystery cult still existed on Mer. He defended himself by saying that he was no longer a practicing *zogo le*, and so had no authority to reveal any more to me about their god Malu.

"If you want to hear more about Malu, you'd better pay a visit to Kaba Noa. He's the keeper of Wasikor, our sacred drum," he all but whispered.

"Are you afraid to talk to me because of what people might say?"

Mr. Benny-Father remained impassive. His demeanor reminded me of a man who felt he had revealed too much already.

"Talk to Mr. Noa," he replied, beginning to retreat into himself. "I've told you enough. Nageg and Geigi are my stories, that is all I can tell you."

I took his advice and eventually made contact with Mr. Noa. I found him one day seated on a raised platform outside his hut by the beach. In his mid-seventies, Mr. Noa sat as a yogi might, his spindly legs crossed, supporting his aged body. He wore only a ragged *lava lava*. His sunken chest drooped as he bent over a pile of coins laid out on a handkerchief. Together with Daisy, his wife, I had caught him in the act of counting the cost of a new hurricane lamp. Daisy sat on a chair nearby, her frame bent and wizened, barely able to move because of a recent illness. Nonetheless, on those rare occasions when she did speak, her voice retained a certain dignity and strength.

Mr. Noa received me graciously. For a time we spoke of the sea and the garden, two realms dear to his heart. Although he had been a trochus diver in his youth, his later years had been spent working in the garden. According to him, the garden was very important; it was, he suggested, the "Garden of Eden," a place where a man might go to meditate.

"Our young people don't care for the garden anymore," he said. "They have no respect for the old ways. We Meriams are losing our culture. 'When you're born from your mother's belly,' I tell them, we say, 'I kiss you.' That's what we do to the young ones: Kiss them alive with the spirit of *Augud*. But today the young people don't want to listen. They refuse even to speak our Meriam language. How can we survive without our language? These things trouble me deeply."

A tear rolled down Mr. Noa's cheek. From her chair under a tree Daisy looked with sympathy at her husband. Her heart still remained loyal to the old rituals and ceremonies.

"Mr. Noa, I understand that you are the keeper of Wasikor, the sacred drum."

Mr. Noa continued to gaze at his pile of coins.

"May I see Wasikor?" I gently prompted the old man.

Mr. Noa picked up a ten-cent piece and turned it over in his hand. I could see that he was giving my request a good deal of consideration.

"It's inside the hut," he said at last. "Go in if you wish. By the near wall under a blanket you will find Wasikor."

Daisy nodded to me that it was all right to go inside. It was like entering an ancient tomb. Clothing, utensils, old photographs, bows and arrows, harpoons, and ceremonial *daris* hung from nails on the walls. Howard Carter had probably felt as I did when he first entered Tutankhamen's burial chamber. This may have been how Mr. Noa and Daisy lived, but it was also how they *remembered* living. The hut was their gesture to the memory of the old-time thatched beehive hut bearing a ceremonial *bu* shell on its roof, in which they had lived when they were children.

I noticed a boomerang-shaped object under a blanket, standing on a wooden horse. I removed the covering. There before me was Wasikor, the sacred drum of Mer, its lean, black torso and shark-shaped mouth as predatorial as any scavenger from the deep. Wasikor, whose throbbing resonance was a call to perform secret dances in honor of Malu and the cult of Bomai in days past. According to Mr. Benny-Father, who had warned me beforehand, to walk in front of Wasikor was forbidden on pain of death. He had warned me to look for marks cut into the drum's mouth that indicated those who had died by shark-bite in the past.

"Wasikor comes from New Guinea," Mr. Noa announced from the veranda outside. "He was brought here a long time ago. He is all we have now."

"Do you play Wasikor anymore?"

"Not since we lost Nimau."

"Nimau?"

"His wife," Mr. Noa replied. "White people burned her because they did not like my people worshipping Malu. My ancestors managed to hide Wasikor from them. But Wasikor no longer plays. He is pining for the loss of Nimau."

I studied this lonely old bachelor named Wasikor. He lay on his wooden horse, an aged shark whose teeth had been pulled. It did not seem possible that such a chiseled object, so replete in the memory of "very old things," could possibly be silenced in this way. But Mr. Noa had made his pronouncement: Wasikor was mute now that Nimau no longer existed.

"Wasikor used to be played at the secret ceremonies of Malu," Mr. Noa said when I rejoined him outside.

"Mr. Noa, who exactly is Malu?"

Mr. Noa wiped his hand across his face and peered at me for a long moment. He was assessing whether he could share this knowledge with me. In the end, he bent forward and whispered:

"Malu is *augud*. He is the spirit who gave us law."

Then he said:

"I will tell you about Malu. We say Malu smoothes the way. He overcomes treachery on land and sea, at home and away. He came to us one day from the island of Mabuiag, far to the west, in the form of an octopus."

I recalled a piece of sculpture fashioned from concrete that I had seen under a palm tree by the beach in front of the pastor's house; it depicted the geographic relief of Mer in the grip of a giant octopus. The creature's eight tentacles embraced all sides of the island. The image reminded me of Jules Verne's description of a submarine in the grip of a giant squid's tentacles in his celebrated book *Twenty Thousand Leagues Under the Sea*.

"Four brothers—Malu, Sigar, Siu, and Kolka—sailed in their canoe from the west, stopping at different islands on the way," Mr. Noa continued. "At Yam, Sigar decided to stay. Siu decided to stay at Masig. and Kolka decided to live at Aurid. But Malo sailed to Mer, where he was washed up on the reef not far from here— at a place called Begegiz, where his canoe was smashed to pieces."

"Were the people of Begegiz happy when he arrived?"

"Sure they were," Mr. Noa replied. "They cried out, 'You are our god!' That's how happy they felt. They tied him up with vines and told him to wait while they went to fetch food. But Malu broke away and slipped back into the sea. He drifted across to Dauar and Waier where the people called out, 'You are our god, stay here!' They, too, tried to catch him, but he escaped and drifted back to Mer, where he was caught by a woman fishing off the reef: Kabur, her name was. She saw Malu's canoe drifting toward her. Then she saw a log. Next she saw seed pods. But at no time did she see Malu as he really was."

"How did she recognize him, then?"

"We say she saw him as a 'thing.' " Mr. Noa tried to elaborate what was clearly a mystery. "It was Malu who wound his tentacles around Kabur's legs and made love to her while she stood there. She cried out, 'Dog's strength and courage!' We believe that a dog's liver is where strength and courage are made. He impregnated her with these qualities.

"Anyway, Kabur speared the 'thing' that was really Malu and placed it in her basket," Mr. Noa continued. "She climbed the hill to her home at Aud where she showed her husband, Dog, what she had caught. Then she said, 'Dog, here is courage for you. It is a sacred thing.' They couldn't sleep as they watched over the basket.

"Later that night Malu awoke. His eyes lit up, surrounding him in a blue light. This light shone so brightly that Malu disappeared from their hut. All Dog and Kabur heard was the slapping sound— *ibkep!*—that is the sound an octopus makes in the water, as he left. He had gone to visit a tribe over Gelem hill way. He did this on three nights running."

"Couldn't they stop him?"

"How could they? He was a god," Mr. Noa replied emphatically. "But they did follow Malu to see where he went. They set out around the coast. On the way they met some men from Las. Two of them, Sarkep and Dam, followed the couple when they returned to Aud, and soon discovered Malu in his basket. When Dog and Kabur had gone to sleep that night, the two men made a hole in the wall of the hut and stole Malu. Then they hurried back to Las, singing and dancing as they went."

"What happened when Dog and Kabur awoke?"

"Dog knew at once that Malu was gone because all his happiness had left him," Mr. Noa responded. "He was suspicious of Sarkep and Dam so he set out with Kabur for Las. When they reached Las, Dog demanded, 'Who has taken Malu?'

"The men of Las gave Dog and Kabur a pipe of tobacco as a gift," Mr. Noa said. " 'Let Malu stay here with us,' Sarkep said. 'He is *augud*. He is the god for all of us since we are many.' In the end, Dog and Kabur had to accept the loss of Malu."

"He was too big for them, I presume," I said.

"That's right. He was a god, you see, for everyone. The men of Las then invited warriors from all over Mer and nearby islands to celebrate his arrival. They brought presents for Malu, lots of clam and spider shells. Wasikor and Nimau were also presented to the people of Las to be the sacred drums of Malu. This is how the drums came to be on Mer."

"What happened then?"

"The people of Las soon complained because they had to feed too many visitors," Mr. Noa explained. "The men from the other tribes returned to their canoes and proceeded to lay out their sails on the sand. Then they began to dance on them. Each group performed a different dance—the Torres Strait pigeon, the parrot, the dog, and so on. The Zagareb men played the drums. In this way the people of Mer got their dances and the law in exchange for food. When the visitors decided to leave, they took Malu out to the reef and drove a stake through him that broke his back. 'His back is broken!' they cried out. To this day we use only such a stick to break the back of turtles.

"This is our story. This is the way Malu came to Mer," Mr. Noa said, taking a deep breath.

Relating the coming of Malu to Mer had cost Mr. Noa considerable effort. For what seemed like a long time he sat there in silence. Daisy remained hunched on her chair under the tree, her faded cotton dress devoid of movement. Only the cackle of hens in the background interfered with our thoughts.

"Malu brought his law to the people of Mer," Mr. Noa said. "With his tentacles he made the eight tribes of Mer. Each of us is touched by one of his arms. We are fortunate. We say Malu is like the oyster growing on the reef. He can't be moved. He is fixed in his ways. He is inflexible. We also say, You mustn't speak against Malu, or offend him. He is like a thorn in the ground outside a person's home. If an enemy approaches, he will step on that thorn. Malu protects us always."

The Malu story and Mr. Noa's interpretation came as a revelation. What he had related was one of the great myths depicting the transition of a culture from a practical activity to one governed by other values. Malu had voyaged afar just as Gelem had done. But whereas Gelem had arrived bearing natural gifts, Malu had landed on Mer bearing supernatural ones. His many transformations—from canoe to log to seed pods—confirmed his godlike status. Even when Kabur thought she had seen the "thing," already she had presided over an illusion. For Malu transcended all forms. Furthermore, his sexual encounter with Kabur echoed the encounter between the Virgin and the angel. Dog, too, found his sibling in the benign figure of Joseph. I realized that what Mr. Noa had revealed to me was a story that until now only Meriams were familiar with, since they had chosen to keep it a secret from the outside world.

Malu's transforming blue light is the aureole of divinity attached to all manifestations of deity on earth, whether they are the Lord Jesus or the Lord Shiva. Living in a basket in a hut is not that different from the experience of Moses in the bullrushes or Christ in the manger. Kingship thrives in humble origins as Oedipus can testify, being the adopted son of a mountain shepherd. Malu's night journeys to different parts of the island demonstrate his wish to be everywhere at the same time—or, in the Christian context, "about his Father's business." And his final capture by the people of Las effectively announces his spiritual importance for all humankind. He is too big to remain with Kabur and Dog, his earthly parents. His message is for all. No wonder men voyage from afar, each of them one of the Magi, bearing gifts of dance and song. All the world wishes to participate in the birth of a god, whether that god takes the form of an octopus, a divine child, or the sun.

Gelem made the island what it is today. He bestowed natural gifts. He was the forerunner. But it was Malu who initiated the real transformation. Malu's numerous tentacles embraced all the people of Mer. He was the many-armed god, the creature from the deep who was finally lanced to death on the reef much as Christ was on the Cross. In the end his sacrifice became theirs. He taught men how to live. He gave them the law.

All that remained of the cult of Malu was old Wasikor, lying under wraps in Mr. Noa's hut. He was silent, his power to condemn men to death dissipated, his *zogo* gone. I felt sorry for Mr. Noa because he deserved more than to be sitting there counting coins in the expectation of buying a hurricane lamp. This was no match for the blue light of Malu, shining in its basket at Aud. Yet without Nimau, without Wasikor's wife, he was powerless to enforce a revival of Malu worship.

"We say, 'Don't show your teeth to Malu,' " Mr. Noa resumed, his memories floating to the surface of his mind once more. "Otherwise the sharks of the forest—what we call Bomai's men, or the wise men of Las who stole Malu from Dog and Kabur in the first place—they will strike you down. Always you must obey the law of Malu."

"How do you keep in touch with Malu now that Nimau is no longer around?" I asked.

Mr. Noa rubbed his forehead. Determining the sum required to purchase the lamp had become too much for him.

"It is difficult," he said. "We are not strong anymore. But if you wish, tomorrow I will show you how some of us old fellas stay close to Malu. If you come here before dawn I will take you to visit the Tomog *zogo*. We will listen to the *Si* stones. Then maybe you will understand."

"There are stones on this island that talk?" I asked, astounded by what I had heard.

Mr. Noa nodded.

"The *Si* stones are not ordinary stones," he said. "They have a voice. They speak with the voice of Malu."

That night I lay awake in bed listening to the barking of geckos. My encounter with Mr. Noa represented a turning point. So far I had merely been an attentive listener to all the *zogo le* I had met. Nonetheless, Mr. Issau, Larry, Timothy China, George Mye, all these men had intimated the existence of something important concealed in their stories. Yet somehow I had not been able to determine what they were trying to tell me. All I knew was that they were pointing me in a particular direction, toward a deeper understanding of the mysteries that surrounded their world. They had left it to me to come to terms with what they were saying. In a sense, they had left it to Gelem, and now Malu, to reveal their secrets to me. I was their student, awaiting entry into the inner circle of the Bomai-Malu mysteries.

The myths and stories they had related were interesting in themselves, but in no way did I know where they were leading. It was as if I had embarked upon a study into their essential nature without the knowledge to translate their inner meaning. Like a blind man, I was feeling my way while my friends walked on ahead.

Could the myths be the basis of a visionary language, the language of the gods? My new friends, these "sharks of the forest" certainly seemed to think so. They revealed their myths to me in the same way others might engage in a philosophic discussion. They recounted sacred events in order to draw closer to an understanding of them. They felt it important, too, that I should try to learn this language. If I were going to appreciate the world from their perspective, then it was important that I enter into the spirit of mythic interpretation along with them. Malu's appearance as a sacred octopus on Mer taught me that nature has a role to play in expressing its own mystery, just as Geigi's dismemberment taught me how easy it is to become fragmented when one plays around on the surface of life.

The sound of the ship's bell outside the parish church announcing matins woke me the next morning. I dressed and made my way to Mr. Noa's house by the beach. He was already up and waiting for me, wearing his ceremonial sarong, a shark's tooth hanging around his neck. Mr. Benny-Father was also there, sitting on Daisy's chair. Out of courtesy, it seemed, Mr. Noa had invited him along on our excursion to the Tomog *zogo*.

Because of Mr. Benny-Father's inability to walk fast, we very slowly climbed a bush track leading to the center of the island. On the way we traversed a valley skirting Gelem's trail. As time passed I gained a strong feeling that we were journeying to the court of Malu. Furthermore, Mer's forests and grasslands with its high hills seemed a fitting edifice to house his sacred shrine. After about an hour we approached a bamboo thicket. Mr. Noa then led us into a narrow opening on our hands and knees. When we finally crawled through the tunnel, we were in a clearing about forty feet wide.

At first I thought we had stumbled upon a burial ground. Stones were strewn about the clearing, many of them with large shells perched on top. In other places the stones had fallen over and their shells lay on the ground. It was not easy to detect any formal pattern. I decided that Mr. Noa had brought me to a *zogo* place much in need of repair and rearrangement.

Meanwhile, Mr. Noa and Mr. Benny-Father sat down by a field of *Si* stones and shells to catch their breath. Sweat beaded their brows as they contemplated Tomog *zogo*, home of Malu's law.

"This is Tomog. We come here to learn the truth from Malu," Mr. Noa said gravely.

"What do the stones and shells signify?" I asked.

"Our island," Mr. Benny-Father announced softly. "What you see before you is Mer."

"This is a sacred map made from stones. We come here to consult it when we need to know something," Mr. Noa explained. "Each stone and shell is a place on Mer. We read it that way."

"The *Si* stones, they speak to us about sacred things," Mr. Benny-Father added.

Mr. Noa explained to me how Tomog *zogo* worked. In the old days *zogo les* were permitted to visit the shrine at daybreak. They would sit near the rocks and consult them by observing the movement of birds, rats, lizards, even insects. It was important to remain perfectly still before the *Si* stones, almost in a state of trance, and wait for the act of divination to occur. Prior to sitting down to meditate on the shrine, the *zogo le* addressed a prayer to Malu: "Tomog *zogo*, you make me know all things. Tell us the truth." Then the visitors sat cross-legged, their closed fists on their knees.

If a relative or friend were sick it was customary to ask a *zogo le* to consult the *Si* stones to ascertain who had performed sorcery on the invalid. By sitting quietly by the map of Mer, sometimes for many hours, it was possible for the seeker to discover the culprit. A lizard might emerge from a shell, indicating the village or house where the man lived. It was easy then to discover the man's identity, and so accuse him of an act of sorcery. The man would be formally approached and told to cease. Once discovered, the man would take his sorcery-stone and throw it into the sea. As soon as the stone "cooled," the patient would begin to recover from his illness. This was the way Tomog *zogo* worked. It was a powerful agent in the fight against disease and death.

If two lizards were seen fighting and one died, this was a sign of the likely outcome for the man represented by the dead lizard, particularly if he were extremely ill. On the other hand, if a small wild fowl appeared on the sacred ground, this was a sign that a canoe might appear from the quarter indicated when the bird first emerged from the thicket. Should a stream of ants come from the bush to the north of Tomog, the diviners knew they could expect a visit by sailors from New Guinea. If the ants bore sticks in their pincers, this would indicate that the New Guineans were coming with goods to barter.

The permutation of place, stone, insect, or bird offered countless possibilities for augury. Mr. Noa related a story of how a number of men from Sebeg decided to sail to New Guinea. When they did not return in the normal time, people began to fear for their safety. So the *Si* stones were consulted. A line of ants was noticed traveling from north to west until they had reached a stone representing the village of Sebeg. There they disappeared into a crack in the ground. This was interpreted to mean that the men from Sebeg had traveled to the western islands on their way home to Mer. The villagers were informed of the augury. Within days the Sebeg canoes were seen approaching Mer from the west.

Mr. Noa motioned for me to sit down and adopt the same posture as he and Mr. Benny-Father. He had asked the Tomog *zogo* to say something on my behalf. I allowed myself to be carried along by the sound of Mr. Noa's voice as he addressed the *Si* stones. In time, a Torres Strait pigeon landed on a shell on the far side of the Tomog *zogo* and gazed at us. Mr. Noa and Mr. Benny-Father were greatly surprised by this apparition now at roost on the shell. For a while they talked quietly among themselves.

"That's Jack Wailu's house at Las," Mr. Benny-Father observed finally, pointing at the stone in relation to certain others.

"Are you sure about that?" Mr. Noa inquired.

Mr. Benny-Father nodded.

"He moved back there last year, remember? He decided to build his hut where Malu was first taken by Sarkep and Dam."

"What is the pigeon saying?" I asked.

"It's a holy bird," Mr. Noa replied. "He flew in from the west, where you came from. He's telling us how you arrived on Mer by plane. He's also saying that you must visit and talk to Jack Wailu."

"Who is Jack Wailu?"

"He's a strong man, a man of *zogo*," Mr. Benny-Father explained softly. "Jack's gone back to the old ways. He and his wife decided to leave our side of the island because they wanted to live in the old style. I haven't been round to Las myself. It's too far for me to walk these days. But they say they live in a hut they built out of palm leaves and bamboo, just like in early times."

"He leads the dance ceremonies," Mr. Noa added. "You're a lucky man. If the holy bird wants you to visit Jack Wailu, then you'd better go. Normally Jack doesn't talk to strangers. This is a good sign."

"His *zogo* comes from Malu," Mr. Benny-Father insisted. "He's the last descendant of the family that owns Tagai."

"The Southern Cross?" I asked.

"That's right," Mr. Noa said.

I gazed at the pigeon that had taken up residence on the beach at Las in my honor. It appeared the bird had summoned me to a remote part of the island to meet a man who owned stars. The omen bird had spoken. Would Jack Wailu receive me? When I looked up again, the pigeon had flown off.

"You better get going," Mr. Noa said. "Jack's probably got something important to tell you."

"Such as?"

"That's for you to find out," he replied. "He might be planning to tell you more about the secrets of Bomai-Malu. He knows a lot about these things. More than we do, that's the truth! I reckon if we Meriams are going to become strong again, like we were in the old days, we got to listen to Jack."

"That's right," Mr. Benny-Father said. "Jack, he's got it all in his head. His father told him everything before he died."

"Let's hope that pigeon knows where he's taking me," I said.

"Don't you worry," Mr. Noa encouraged me. "Tomog *zogo* never lies. The *Si* stones know more than we do."

"It's Malu talking," Mr. Benny-Father added. "He knows what's good for you, that's for sure. You go to Las and talk to Jack."

The *Si* stones had spoken. I had been directed to a remote beach on the far side of Mer to meet with a man whose emissary was a pigeon. The question on my mind now was: Would this man receive me, or would he turn me away empty-handed?

FOUR

In my shack by the beach I quickly learned how to detect the subtle changes in the tides. As the moon waxed and waned, so, too, did the sea. On Mer it seemed that no two days were the same. Windy days, days of cloud and rain, and days of absolute calm: These were what made everything so remarkably different, so new, so bathed in the glow of dawn each morning. Like a Chinese storekeeper toying with his abacus, I, too, was seduced by each day's incalculable variations.

My shack was equipped with the barest essentials. A small fire for cooking, a kerosene lamp by which to read at night, and a cold shower out back among the banana trees amounted to the sum of my comforts. I had studied each shell on the shelf in the main room, placed them to my ear and listened to the sound of the sea. I had watched geckos pounce on stray insects at night. I had begun to comprehend, if somewhat slowly, that natural knowledge evolves from one's own consciousness. It had been implanted there from the beginning.

What caught my attention most during my stay on Mer were often the more trivial things. A snake cowrie shell glistening on the table; a spear shaft, weighted down by a coconut at one end, hanging from a branch in order to straighten it; a pair of frigate birds, their wings clipped to prevent escape, sitting on a log outside an island house awaiting the pot; an old woman thrashing the sea one windy day with *sim* leaves and calling out "Peace!" to calm the waves; clamshells placed on the ground under eaves to collect rainwater—such things made up the mosaic of life on Mer.

Meeting with the *zogo les* of these islands had already begun to change me. Men like Lui Bon and Mr. China had helped to furnishae0 me with a new way of seeing life. Like the dugong, it was as though I were coming up for air after a long bout of breathlessness. Underwater all I had to guide me were my senses. From these men I learned that legendary figures were often better guides. Swimming deep in metaphor, a man can straddle many different worlds. The nourishment he needs may be better provided by a fish transforming itself into a spirit than a desire to be always in control.

A lot had changed for me since leaving Thursday Island. There, all seemed relatively clear—or clouded, depending upon which way one looked at things. The beliefs held by men like Mr. China or Tapim Benny-Father had not yet been revealed to me. Now I sensed that the men of Mer were prepared to tell me more. They were about to offer me the *sim* leaf of peace in the form of their knowledge of the old ways.

I realized that the sea and the garden constituted a transcendent territory for these men. It was a territory over which they had ranged free in their minds for generations. "Before time" had become a catch-phrase signaling a willingness on their part to cancel out what had been imposed upon them by the idea of history. Gelem and Malu had arrived on Mer before men had conceived of a historical condition to undermine their sense of the sacred. The idea of locating a spirit hero "in time" would have destroyed forever his cultural status. *Augud*, after all, was the invisible principle of creation. It had to find some way of entering the sphere of ordinary life from its haven "outside time" if it was to affect the way men thought.

But the omen bird had spoken. According to Mr. Noa and Mr. Benny-Father, I had now to seek out Jack Wailu, a Torres Strait pigeon man living on the other side of the island. For reasons best known to himself, Jack had chosen to make his home near the reef where Malu had clung to the legs of Kabur and impregnated her with the spirit of *Augud*.

On my way there, I passed through the local cemetery. Headstones, festooned with plastic flowers, graced each side of the track. In the old days, a dead man would have been smoked over a slow fire until mummified. Now, Meriam families saved their money to purchase elaborate tombstones and ship them in from Australia. Because of this the mortuary ceremonies of the past had all but been forgotten.

I soon found myself on a wild stretch of coastline reaching around toward the beach at Las. Fish traps littered the reef at the low-water mark. The sand was strewn with coconut husks, broken shells, and the occasional plastic bottle. High on the island a smoky ridge rose out of the grasslands. Somewhere below that ridge lay Aud, the place where Kabur had taken Malu in her basket. It seemed that every step along the way had its own tale to tell.

After more than an hour I spotted the bamboo palisade that stood outside Jack Wailu's compound. He had built it to protect his huts from offshore winds. Approaching the gateway, I let my shoulder bag slip to the ground. It was heavy, and I was sweating profusely. Then I noticed a middle-aged woman standing between two huts. She was dressed in a sarong, her hair supported on the back of her head by a wooden comb. When she saw me she gave a start, and disappeared inside the far hut.

Presently a man appeared in the courtyard. Slightly built, he wore a tattered shirt and a sarong. His eyes were curiously remote. His nose was beak-shaped, like a hawk. But it was his hair that gave him a forbidding appearance: Gray dreadlocks rose in curls that reminded me of spider's legs. This was Jack Wailu, the *zogo le* of Las, one of the last of the so-called *um le*, or "those who know."

I introduced myself, explaining why I had come to see him. He listened without saying a word. He barely looked at me. When I had finished, I started to think that maybe he was glad I had come after all. Like Robinson Crusoe and Man Friday we were two castaways meeting for the first time. The trouble was we didn't quite know how to begin talking to one another. We had no common vocabulary.

"Sit down. We talk," Jack Wailu said, motioning me toward a palm tree nearby.

His voice was not at all keeping with his appearance. He spoke normally. Twenty years working for the railways in Australia had left him with a relaxed, worldly manner. We sat on the sand under the tree, surrounded by fishing tackle and harpoons.

When I told Jack of my visit to Tomog *zogo* with Mr. Noa and Mr. Benny-Father, he smiled. I realized then that his physical appearance could easily be misinterpreted. Jack had simply become a part of the wild nature of Las. The sea and wind, high tides, and days of loneliness had honed him to a point where nothing about him was extraneous.

"*Gainau*, that's the Torres Strait pigeon. That was me," he replied.

"So it was you who landed at Tomog."

"A part of me did, yeah."

"Why?" I asked.

I probably should not have asked such a question. He appeared reluctant to answer me. Instead he remarked:

"Las is a place of tradition. I came back here from the mainland where I had been working for many years on the railways. You see, I had forgotten about Mer while I was away. With children growing up and mouths to feed—they soon make a man forget. But each spring I always used to remember the smell of *kabir* blossoms. This made me feel unsettled because I knew it was time to go out fishing. The smell of *kabir* blossoms means that something new is in the air. I felt I was missing out on life. The old ways, I had shunted them off on a siding. But the *kabir* blossoms would not let me forget."

"Mr. Noa told me you used to work on the pearl boats," I said.

"I've been a trochus diver, sure. Up and down the Great Barrier Reef in government boats. I've seen men eaten by sharks, others change into crocodiles and swim home to Mer to pick up a plug of tobacco when we ran out. These things were a part of my life when I was a young man. In those days, the bad and the good things were woven together as tight as Malu's basket! We were living in *Augud*, see? The law of Malu, what we call the straight way, we always looked to it for guidance."

"Returning to Las must have been important for you," I remarked.

Jack Wailu's face was expressionless. His gaze had become as still as a Long Tom fish resting in a grotto near a reef.

"My father was born here," he replied. "He was an old *zogo le*, one of the best. He would have nothing to do with the church people on the other side of the island. For him the old ways were better. When I was a boy, he used to take me out on the sand in front of the windbreak and teach me all about Malu. He used to say, 'Do not speak against Malu.' I heard other stories, too. I went to school and heard about Jesus and Mary. We had no choice in those days. White men wanted us to believe what they believed, hoping that we would become like them."

"Which now, of course, you reject."

"They are not of my culture," Jack Wailu explained. "White men made us feel bad because we owned masks, because we danced for Malu, because we had secret ceremonies. This was our way. Your people told us we were wrong. In the old days we cut off people's heads, the heads of our enemies, it's true. But we never tried to take away their culture. We respected our enemies. We didn't try to change their ways. But your people tried to change ours. They took our masks away to museums, they burned our sacred figures and our drums. They told us not to tell our stories. In time our stories lost their *zogo*. When I was a young man I often used to see the old fellas sitting on the beach gazing at the sea with empty eyes. No more could they see Malu. *Augud* had gone away. All they had left were a few hymns and the Bible to satisfy their yearnings."

Jack Wailu's remarks did not come as a surprise. I had been waiting for someone to talk like this for a long time. Islanders could not vent their anger since they had long ago forgotten what it was they disliked most about white people. Generosity and willingness to please had cloaked the sadness they might have felt at losing their culture. In the end, outboard motors and government pensions had partly appeased any feeling of loss. But for Jack Wailu this was no longer acceptable. He wanted to dispense with white man's patronage once and for all.

"When Kabur took Malu up to her husband at Aud," Jack Wailu remarked, "she said to him, 'I show you my secret thing. This is

Augud, the spirit.' She knew, and pretty soon everyone knew, that a god had arrived on our island. We say, 'This is my god to look up to.' In the early days the missionaries did not think we had a good god. Malu, to them, was an octopus, and our belief in him they called superstition. When they came here all the *zogo les* met with them for talks. But the *zogo les* were not satisfied with their answers and returned to Las. Many of my people followed. The *zogo les* said, 'These people do not recognize Malu's law.' Our people tried to resist, but it was impossible. So they became Christians. The accepted the Coming of the Light as the beginning of a new life. They had no choice. Either they learned to pray to Jesus or one day they might be shot as savages.

"When I was growing up, we didn't think about these things," Jack Wailu continued. "I went to church, learned all about Jesus and the Bible. Many of the stories were like ours anyway."

"Your father didn't mind?"

"I told you: He had little choice. If I were to get an education, a white man's education, then I had to be seen as one of them. Church and trochus shell went together. But this didn't mean we had forgotten. On Sunday we may have gone to church, but on Monday we learned about the old ways. My father knew that if we were to remain strong, then we must stay in contact with Malu."

"Is it true that you own Tagai?" I asked.

Jack Wailu laughed. It was the gesture of a man who had long ago reconciled himself to the paradox of owning stars.

"Tagai has been handed down to me through the generations," he explained. "I own the stars, sure. Not as you see them in the sky, but in the form that they came down to earth. You see, Tagai was a man. He owned a canoe, along with his friend, Kareg. One day they were out fishing with a crew made up of the Usiam and Seg people. To you these people are the Seven Sisters and the stars in the belt of Orion. Anyway, while Tagai and Kareg were paddling along, the Usiam and the Seg people decided to eat all the food and drink all the water on board. Kareg saw this happening and called out to Tagai, who was in the bow of the boat. So Tagai strung the Usiam together with a piece of rope and tossed them into the sea. He did the same to the Seg people. Only Kareg, his friend, remained with him on the boat."

"Paddling into the unknown?" I asked.

"Something like that," Jack replied. "Anyway, Tagai and Kareg eventually landed on the island of Dauar. From here they sailed to another place on the far side of Dauar, where Tagai turned into stone. Kareg later sailed the canoe here to Las, where he turned into stone as well."

Jack Wailu stood up and walked to the entrance of the compound. He motioned for me to follow him. Outside he pointed out a crop of stones on the edge of the beach.

"See that long piece of stone?" Jack said. "That's Tagai's canoe. The red stone you see on this side of the canoe—that's Kareg. It's these things I own because they represent the stars in the sky."

"You own the story?"

"The stars are my story. When I am at sea at night, it's always good to know my story is there to guide me. Tagai is a pointer, a guide. We always trust him to stay in the southern sky."

"But," I began, knowing that what I wanted to ask was almost impossible to put into words. "How do you actually own a star or a rock? Who decides such things?"

"Malu does," Jack replied. "He gives us the law that is really the law of *Augud*. Bomai came before Malu. Christians talk about the Old and the New Testaments; well, we talk of Bomai and Malu. They are the same. In the old days, Bomai was the secret name of Malu. No one could mention Bomai's name except the *zogo les*. To do so would have meant death. He was the terrible aspect, before the law came to Mer. It was Malu who gave us the law and so made us caretakers of the world. In making us caretakers he asked us to be responsible for looking after nature. This is why we have totems. Being a part of a totem means that we must respect our animal or our bird. That way we don't make too many demands on nature."

"This is why you care for Tagai?"

"Yeah. The story of the stars belongs to me. I must interpret it for others, to remind them that all of us must take care not to act like the Usiam and Seg people. By drinking too much, by eating too much, we forget to leave some over for others. The food and water on Tagai's boat represents nature. If we use it up without thinking, we run the risk of exhausting our food supplies on the voyage.

"You ask me how it is possible to own Tagai, the stars," Jack continued. "Well, I ask you: How is it possible for you to own a house or a car in your world? You do so because you have exchanged money to buy it. My ancestors offered a story about the Southern Cross so that they might own it. They paid for it with thoughts, with a story. They paid *Augud*."

I now understood what Jack meant by owning Tagai. He was a starholder as we are landholders. His title took the form of two stone outcrops on the edge of the beach that had been given to him by Augud. But more importantly he owned an idea, a concept of concern for his environment embodied in the creation of the Pleiades and the stars of Orion's belt. Whenever he looked up at the night sky, whenever he gazed at the constellation of Tagai, the scene that always greeted him was one of the need for balance and restraint.

Could I own a star? The thought struck me as worth exploring. Does Jack feel Tagai's gravity, or does its splendid radiance merely envelop him? There was a logic to such an act of celestial possession. By bringing Tagai down to earth as a stone on the beach, the infinite and the particular had been brought together. Clearly Jack accepted his role as custodian of heavenly bodies. His job was to care for his inheritance and make sure that everyone understood its message. The stone on the beach had become a tablet inscribed with Malu's law.

Jack asked me to stay with him for a few days. He appeared to welcome the opportunity to speak with me about the old ways. I moved into one of the huts. At night I could hear the sound of the surf breaking against the reef beyond the palisade and the crabs walking on the beach at low tide. Everything about Jack's place spoke of the care he had exercised in re-creating the home of his forebears. An open-air fireplace, rainwater caught in clamshells, sand floors, fish nets, harpoons, elaborate *daris* hanging from the rafters, a few items of clothing—these things made up his world. He had constructed his compound out of bamboo and plaited palm leaves. Above high water lay his outrigger canoe, which he had purchased on an expedition to the Fly River in New Guinea. It appeared that Noretta, his wife, still had more work to do weaving a set of sails for it out of palm leaves.

During my stay with Jack I was made to feel at home. I joined him on the reef when he went fishing. I climbed the slope behind

Las and watched him work in his garden. In the evening we sat on the sand by the fire while Noretta cooked fish caught that day. We drank tea long into the night before retiring to our huts. Sleep came in a gentle movement of the tide washing over the beach outside.

Like friends who had not seen each other for years, we spoke of many things. We were each unburdening ourselves of a lifetime of silence on matters dear to us both. Jack offered me a chance to explore ideas that had been troubling me for a long time. He in turn welcomed the opportunity to talk about his desire to revive the old ways. Sometimes he allowed his true feelings to surface, but normally he kept these to himself. For the most part he seemed reconciled to living the life of a hermit. Residing at Las again had made it possible for him to devote all his thoughts to the task of reviving the law of Malu.

In his garden Jack always listened to the advice of the spirits, Ib and Omai. When the bamboo rustled he knew they were close at hand, eager to converse with him. He was the only man on Mer who had actually seen Gelem. This had occurred when he was a boy on an expedition to Gelem's nostrils high up on the hillside. On his way there he had seen a red-haired man moving naked through the bushland. Jack had followed Gelem to the entrance of a tunnel at the back of the nostrils. Reluctant to proceed farther, however, Jack had returned home to enlist his father's help. But when they climbed up to the nostril together the tunnel had closed over completely. Jack had always regretted not following Gelem into his cavern that day. What he secretly longed for was another chance to follow the spirit of his ancestors deep into the hillside, and so discover more about his origins.

In the meantime Jack Wailu listened to the spirits rustling among the bamboo in the garden. They inspired him to create new songs and dances for the people of Mer. As he remarked, "I get the notes from nature. The words, too. They come from the rustling sound made by bamboo." These he transcribed with his voice and his body. He was constantly at the beck and call of those invisible forces inhabiting the undergrowth, the spirit people, the *nila markrem*. Jack had given himself over to a way of life that served to intensify his powers of concentration. If nothing else Jack taught me how to inhabit different realms. If *puleb* stones could be trusted to watch over a kitchen fire and keep it burning while the householders were at work in the garden, why couldn't a man watch over the fire in his heart while he was engaged in the business of living? Jack felt that a man's heart was similar to the hearth stones that kept the kitchen fires alight in his absence.

As one of the last of the *um le*, or "those who know," all of Meriam culture seemed to reside under his unruly dreadlocks. My good fortune was to have met him when he was ready to share his knowledge. He believed strongly that a bridge must be built so that all men might travel the straight way of Malu. Now that he had traveled so far into Gelem's nostrils in search of the First Man, he felt he was ready to impart some of his knowledge to others.

All of the people I had met on my voyages through the Torres Strait had pointed me in the direction of Las. Like pearl shells, these islands were home to some shining nacre of knowledge. In the process of emulating the skinners of old I had learned to converse in a new language, the language of myth. I had discovered that if I wanted to realize a more intense inner life, then I must be prepared to renounce the security and comfort of so-called given reality. I had to be willing to acknowledge that there was a deeper level that might allow me to transcend ordinary barriers with the ease of a man becoming a crocodile or a booby bird. It entailed risks, of course, but pearl-skinning also involved risks if you wanted to realize *la désirée*, the most lucent pearl of all. Entering the realm of myth involved making an excursion, unburdened by fear, into the nostrils of a spirit.

This was brought home to me one afternoon when Jack and I were sitting on a headland talking. He had been telling me of his attempts to revive the law of Malu, and how he had already fashioned a turtle-shell mask in the god's image. He told me how this was to become the central part of a new dance. All he had to inspire him was a song his father had taught him, a song known as *Zogo Meer*, which he regarded as the Ten Commandments of Malu. He sang it to me that day:

Malu keeps his hands to himself. He refuses to touch
what does not belong to him.

He never allows his feet to trespass on another
man's property. His hands are not grasping.

He never wanders from his path. Walking on tiptoe,
silent and careful, he leaves no sign of his passage.

Never pluck fruit not fit to be eaten. Shun
also fruit that does not belong to you.

Malu is Muiar. *He is holy. People who do not own or belong to*
a place, must behave toward it as Muiar. Regard another man's
fruit on his land as Muiar, just like Malu.

Malu is like bezar, *that lonely, secretive fish.*
Where Malu walks he keeps to a narrow path
invisible to those who do not recognize him.

Let mounds of yams remain undisturbed.
Let vines rot till no trace remains.

Malu says: Allow faded flowers to return to the soil.
You have enough to spare without them.

Stars travel their own paths across the sky.
I must not walk the path of Usiam, or that of Seg.

What Jack had revealed to me that day was central to all men's
activities, whether on land or at sea. And I was grateful for his
trust in me. The law of Malu opened my eyes to the intimate
connection that existed between nature's sustaining role in the
world and the need for right action on the part of men. According
to Jack, Malu gave the people of Las the law when they had stolen
him from Kabur and Dog at Aud. And although the final entreaty
of these commandments appeared to be derived from the Tagai
legend (cautioning men not to be greedy), Jack insisted it was also
a part of Malu's law. The blue light of Malu, a light known as
zeg, shone on the people of Mer, guiding their every action.

"Sometimes you can see the *zeg* light when you're alone at
night," Jack told me one day. "It rises from the sea just as Malu
did before time. When you see that light, you know Malu is looking after you. *Zeg* is the only way Malu shows himself. This is
what we believe."

The blue light of *zeg* seemed to surround Jack as we talked.
"Maybe we should take a trip to Waier," he suggested later.
"What is there to see at Waier?" I asked.
"In the old days they had ceremonies on the island to celebrate
Waiet, the god of fertility. I can show you the place."

Jack then explained to me a bizarre cult that entailed human
sacrifice, orgiastic activity, and the initiation of young men. According to legend, Waiet originally came from the island of Mabuiag in the west. He lived there with his wife and daughter.
Unusually potent, Waiet was inclined to accost young women at
waterholes and seduce them. If he was in a bad mood he often
ordered his followers to cut off their heads. The trouble was that
his followers decided to emulate Waiet one day by seducing his
wife and daughter. This they did, decapitating them after making
love to them, just as Waiet had done to his victims.

In despair, Waiet took his drum and quit Mabuiag for good. He
wandered from island to island much as Malu had done. At last
he arrived on Waier, at a place called Ne, where he came ashore
on the beach and climbed the cliff. There he sat on a ledge and
beat his drum as a gesture of mourning. The sound echoed from
the cliffs and was eventually heard by two women on one of the
headlands. They approached Waiet and sat down on a pile of
coconuts to listen. When he had finished his performance Waiet
immediately seduced the two women.

Waiet's effigy used to sit on the ledge above Ne until the missionaries destroyed it. Even Jack was unsure as to what forms the
rituals took in the old days. There had been talk of castration and
sexual promiscuity, using captives from other islands, but Jack did
not believe that any cruelty was involved. He thought the missionaries had said these things in an attempt to discredit the ceremony.
He admitted, however, that Waiet's effigy was probably phallic.
Jack did recall his father telling him about one rite. It involved
lowering hot coals in a clamshell from a ledge where a fire had
been kindled in front of Waiet's effigy. On the beach below, each
initiate was required to approach the clamshell and transfer a part
of the sacred fire to a cooking fire nearby.

Jack and I decided to sail over to Waier on the next morning's
tide. It was a good opportunity to test the sail Noretta had finished
weaving. When we eased the outrigger into the water and set a
course for the island a light breeze blew up, making our maiden

voyage across the sea a relatively easy one. The bow of the outrigger sliced through the water, and small fish broke the surface in front of the craft. Behind us, Gelem loomed on the horizon, as if watching us from his eyrie high on the hillside of Mer.

Shaped like a horseshoe, Waier rose sheer from the sea, a thorny outcrop of lava and pumice left over from an extinct volcano. The entrance to the lagoon lay between two headlands. It was like entering a canyon whose only vegetation was a fringe of coconut palms growing on the edge of the sand. The cliffs loomed, intensifying the sound of the sea.

Beaching the outrigger, Jack and I walked along the sand. By a large rock known as Korsor we stopped and looked up. Jack pointed out a ledge in the cliff above.

"That's the place where Waiet used to sit and beat his drum," he said.

"From where the sacred fire was lowered in a clamshell to those on the beach below," I recalled.

"Yeah, that's right."

Jack looked about him at the white sand and the fringe of shade under the palms. He seemed to be looking for something—a shell, or perhaps something he'd forgotten from his last visit. It was hard to tell.

"I come here when I need to think," he confided at last. "When I need to ask myself some questions."

"Malu will always be around to help you, Jack. You don't need to worry," I replied.

"It's not so easy. For my people everything lies in the past. We need to make our culture into something we believe in again. It has to grow and be a part of today. This is what I ask Malu about."

"Does he give you any answers?"

"Sometimes. But other times he makes me think I'm wasting my time. The past is dead, a voice keeps telling me. Leave it to die in peace."

"Maybe Malu says this because he knows Wasikor continues to remain silent," I suggested.

"That's true," Jack agreed. "Wasikor no longer comes over here to join Waiet on his ledge. Until he does, I suppose we're all missing out on something."

I looked at the empty ledge above where once the effigy of Waiet sat on his pile of coconuts. I tried to picture a smoking clamshell with its cargo of seminal fire being lowered into our arms. I tried to hear the sound of Wasikor beating out his message around the stony cliffs above where we stood. Seabirds wheeled and eddied. How could we encourage Wasikor to announce Waiet's arrival, to sing of Malu, to celebrate the creation of the hill of Gelem once again? In a way, we were both struggling to bring back a sense of meaning to our everyday lives.

"Jack," I said. "It's only a suggestion, but why don't you bring back Nimau? You know Wasikor will never play again unless his wife returns."

"How can I do that?" he asked.

"Make a new drum. Name it after Nimau. Then create a story explaining Nimau's long absence and her faithfulness to Wasikor. Design *daris* and a new dance to celebrate Nimau's return to Mer. I'm sure Wasikor will break his silence when he sees her again. He will play, I know it."

Jack Wailu's dreadlocks quivered. For a time he did not speak. He gazed at the lagoon as he pondered my suggestion. It was as if his thoughts had already turned toward New Guinea, toward the deep inland forests where the wood for the drums was traditionally harvested. Then he looked at me, his expression one of intense happiness.

"You're right," he said, his voice filled with new resolve. "Wasikor will be overjoyed. So that's what I'll do. Like you say, I'll bring Nimau back to life. It's not impossible. Nothing is. After all, she lives in my heart. Isn't that enough?"

Jack's eyes searched mine, looking for some sign of assurance from me.

"In you, Jack, Nimau never really died," I said, growing excited myself at the implication.

We walked back along the beach in silence. Already Jack Wailu had begun to meditate on the rustling sound of bamboo in his garden. He was listening, hoping to hear the voices of Ib and Omai once more. He was waiting to hear the first notes of a new song these spirits wanted him to learn. Nimau's lament had begun to formulate in his mind. Suddenly he stopped and lightly shifted his feet about on the sand. The imprints he left behind when we resumed walking were the first tentative dance steps of Nimau celebrating her return to Mer.

By the time we reached the canoe the incoming tide had begun

to erase our footprints from the beach. But this did not mean that
they had been erased from Jack's memory. As we readied the outrigger for departure I recalled some of the words from the song he
had recited days earlier: "He never wanders from his path. Walking
on tiptoe, silent and careful, he leaves no sign of his passage."
These words described perfectly Jack Wailu's footprints on the
beach as he struggled to come to terms with his new role. This
man who owned stars, who had become my close friend during
the short time we had spent together, was already beginning the
task of rebuilding the crumbling grass hut that was once Meriam
culture.

As we set sail for Mer I thought of Larry, Lui Bon, and Mr.
Issau on Thursday Island. They had urged me to follow in the
footsteps of Gelem, the First Man. I had fulfilled my promise to
them. In the process I had done more than that, much more. I
had become a part of their vision of a world made complete by
the merging of myth and life. The First Man was none other than
me, voyaging across an ocean of experience looking for a safe
haven. Like Gelem I had lain down, sneezed islands, and brought
with me to Mer new seeds of insight. It was up to others to plant
these and allow them to bear fruit.

The trouble was I hadn't yet learned how to apply these lessons
to myself. Bringing back Nimau sounded like a relatively simple
solution in comparison with what I had to do. At least Jack knew
what Wasikor needed in his life in order to arrest the process of
cultural disintegration among his own people. I, on the other hand,
still had not been able to come to terms with whatever it was that
was missing from mine. Who had absconded with my drum?
Where was the other half of me that was so necessary if I were to
realize a state of personal wholeness? I didn't know. Realizing that
I was capable of providing answers for others but not for myself
did not make it any easier. It seemed that, deep down, I had yet
to come to terms with the importance of making the reality of
myth a part of my own sense of personal growth. I had to bring
to life a Nimau capable of embracing the Wasikor in me, so that
a new song of hope might at last be composed.

"What will you do now, *bala*?" Jack's question broke into my
thoughts. He seemed more at ease with himself than at any time
since I had met him. A broad smile creased his face as he gripped

the rudder and pointed the outrigger in the direction of the beach at Las. As he did so, the wind began to fill the sail, causing it to whisper with pleasure.

"I don't really know, Jack. Move on to some place new, I suppose."

"You've got no Nimau, no sacred drum to take back home?"

"I wish it were that easy," I replied.

"There must be a key to fit your lock out there somewhere. It can't be lost. You've got to find it somehow."

"I can tell you one thing, Jack. If it takes me a lifetime, I'll keep looking," I said.

"Maybe you should stay here for a while and listen to the sea a little longer," he suggested.

"Stare at coral, you mean."

Jack laughed.

"You've been hearing too much island talk," he said.

"Maybe," I said.

"Don't worry, *bala*. Just you look up at the sky at night. Whenever you see Tagai hanging there, know that he's there to guide you back home. It's the story that helps us. The sky is full of stories. We've just got to learn how to tell them to one another, that's all. Then we make everyone a part of the same story."

"Thanks, Jack," I replied, comforted by his remarks. I was already beginning to wonder how I might avoid the fate of Usiam and Seg, those people whose inordinate appetites had caused them to be flung overboard into an infinitely dark void that was the world. Hopefully, like Tagai and his companion, Kareg, I had absorbed enough of Malu's law to act as a *zeg* light while I set out to navigate this unknown ocean myself.

IN THE
FOREST

FIVE

Kuching, Borneo. The city lies on the banks of the Sarawak River surrounded by tropical rainforest. It is a city of motor scooters, deep-shaded greenery, and small shops all crowded together amid the hubbub of commerce. As a trading outpost, Kuching has played host over the years to Chinese and Malay merchants, as well as European adventurers in the mold of the legendary Marco Polo. A colonial whiteness stained by mildew ensures that each building retains its drabness in the face of hot, steamy days. Climate is the city's alter ego, it seems. Pure lethargy and the soporific nature of the tropics governs every action, willed or otherwise. No one remains immune for long from the debilitating effects of lassitude, nor the sensuality of caryatids disguised as shopgirls. Indeed, Kuching represents the completion of a process of urbanization begun when James Brooke, a young Englishman, sailed up the Sarawak River in 1839 in his yacht, the *Royalist*, to found a kingdom of his own.

A Byronic dreamer, James was one of those young men that imperial Britain fashioned with consummate ease during the nineteenth century. Born into a wealthy family from Bath, he attended public school for a short period until he decided to go to sea. His father, returning from India where he had worked for the East India Company until retirement, managed to steer his rebellious son toward a career in the army. Shortly after his sixteenth birthday James, as an ensign in the 6th Madras Native Infantry, set sail for India, where he subsequently went into battle. At Rungpore in Burma, during a horse charge on enemy lines, a bullet in the lung nearly killed him. Hovering between life and death, young James was transported by canoe down the Brahmaputra to Calcutta. There he was ordered back to England in the hope of facilitating a more rapid recovery from his wound.

But James never forgot his river journey away from the battle-field: The deep jungle crowding the banks, the kingfishers flitting bluely overhead, the forest sounds, and sunlight fragmented by branches all seemed to crowd in on him in his opium-induced state. Each day brought with it sensations of traveling farther from his origins among the hedgerows and village lanes of England. He had already entered the mysterious terrain of the Orient where clarities become blurred. Inadvertently James had become a visitor to what Joseph Conrad was later to call the "heart of darkness," wherein a man finds solace by turning his gaze inward upon himself.

Nor did his fascination with the Far East diminish after his four-and-a-half-year furlough in England. Though he recovered and later returned to India briefly as an army officer, he resigned his commission soon after and made his way back home again. His intention was to convince his father to finance him in his bid to establish trading links in the Far East. It was not until James had realized his inheritance on his father's death in 1835 that he was able to purchase the *Royalist* and set sail for Singapore. Unknown lands, the prospect of visiting places "where no white man's foot had been before" lured him toward the East Indies. Borneo in particular interested him. It was there that he hoped to find the descendants of ancient Hindu rajahs believed to be still living in the hinterland.

On behalf of the Sultan of Brunei, he fought the Sea Dyaks (or Iban people) on numerous occasions in an effort to pacify these marauding headhunters who sailed down the rivers to the sea in their war canoes. They threatened the stability of the region, wreaking havoc among offshore shipping and coastal settlements. With his cannon and guns, James carried the battle to the head-hunters, paddling upriver into the interior to attack and burn their longhouses. It was the classic encounter between warrior and European mercenary. The flumed feathers of the chieftains were soon cut to pieces by the withering fire of musket and grapeshot. In a gesture of gratitude following the success of his military exploits, the Sultan of Brunei ceded the western part of Borneo to James, who now became the Rajah of Sarawak with his seat at Kuching. His boyhood dream had been realized.

The Brooke family ruled Sarawak until shortly after World War II, when it was finally ceded to the British. James lived to a ripe old age, eventually dying in England in 1867. He was succeeded by his nephew, Charles Brooke (James never married), who in turn was succeeded in 1917 by Vyner Brooke, the last Rajah of Sarawak. Between the three of them, these men pacified the interior of Borneo and brought a measure of modernity to an otherwise remote world. James, however, unlike many of his contemporaries, was able to identify with his subjects. He was one of the few men of his age capable of seeing in traditional tribespeople a level of civility and culture. At no time did he regard his subjects as inferior beings whom he might exploit for his own ends. He was one of a select band of adventurers who had chosen to quit Europe in search of the purely exotic in foreign lands. For such men there was something infinitely appealing about Oriental customs, which suggested an imaginative escape from the constrictions already beginning to appear as a result of the early industrialization of Europe.

The Hotel Aurora, where I stayed in Kuching, was a far cry from James's colonial residence overlooking the Sarawak River. Kuching's back streets were populated with merchants of all kinds—gold dealers, herbalists, and fortune tellers—most of them relatively late arrivals in this world of the deep forests. The mixture of Malay, Chinese, and indigenous people around me made it difficult to know whether the city was dedicated to trade, government bureaucracy, or industry. Veiled Muslim women bore smiles as easily as their pagan counterparts. Temple, mosque, and church rendered all architecture eclectic in their drive to establish the primacy of one religion over another. The great creeds had come here with the intention of penetrating the mysterious reserve of the pagan

mind and facilitating conversion. In contrast, I had come not to
proselytize but to allow myself to be influenced by the rich myth
life of the Iban people, those old adversaries of James Brooke who
still lived along the inland rivers of Borneo.

I had already begun to ask myself whether conventional systems
of belief truly addressed the deeper concerns of humanity. Like
many of my generation, monotheism had left me scarred inwardly,
and I longed to experience the heterogeneity of traditional thought,
unaffected as it was by strict doctrine or dogma. Since my encounter with the Torres Strait Islanders I had asked myself whether such
systems of belief denied people the joy of creating myths of their
own. It was clear to me that a sense of divine play had existed
among the more thoughtful of my islander friends, an ideal that
I knew they were struggling to retain against considerable odds.
Something told me also that among the Iban of Borneo, these
same people who had once collected human heads as we collect
butterflies, I might learn more about this art of divine play, and
so become a participant rather than an observer in their cosmic
game.

The challenge was real enough, notwithstanding the threat to
our natural environment as a result of increasing economic and
industrial exploitation throughout the world. Here in Borneo I was
about to come face-to-face with the great forests, nature's lungs,
and the extravagant flora that had fueled my imagination since the
day I observed my first orchid. My early memories of the jungle
were filled with its luxuriance, its super-abundance, its sense of
prodigious renewal. The jungle represented an absolute contrast to
all that made up my own experience. There all is available, and
nature's gifts are bountiful. Forest dwellers know that to seek out
more than what is immediately required leads only to waste.

The plumed and tattooed men of the inland rivers and forests
lived a deep imaginal life governed by a host of mythic heroes and
gods. Of course, like my islander friends, they had been headhunters
in the past. Since Brooke's arrival, however, Christian missionaries
had slowly weaned them away from their addiction to human
heads. The last known headhunting raid took place in the 1920s.
Now the Iban people, poets and orators all, have adopted a more
peaceful life-style, cultivating their gardens, hunting wild game in
the forest, performing their ceremonies, and living out a rich dream

life overseen by augurers, shamans, and song-men. Could these people begin to answer those questions that had posed such difficulties for my islander friends? For example, could a genuine myth life survive in the face of an invasion by a cash economy and various heroes of popular culture? Was there any room left for traditional healing practices when confronted by the power of modern medicines? Where did the world-creating activities of the mythic heroes stand now in relation to those theories of evolution, geology, paleontology, or similar modern disciplines? These were some of the questions I hoped to explore with the people I met in Borneo.

The Iban people had originally migrated from the region of Kalimantan in central Borneo. Known as the "wanderers" by the indigenous people, the Iban entered Sarawak by way of the Lupar, Skrang, and Ai rivers descending from the Kapuas Hula Mountains. Fairer skinned and taller than the local inhabitants they conquered, the Iban boasted a genealogy that reached back to the legendary Sengalang Burong, a spirit hero whose character was made up of both divine and human qualities. The divine family over which he presided included his daughter, Tinchin Mas, and his grandson, Serong Gunting. Sengalang Burong means "lion-kite-bird" and his appearance in the world takes the form of the Brahminy kite, a nocturnal bird of prey. But it is his grandson, Serong Gunting, who stands at the head of the Iban spiritual pedigree since he is the son of Tinchin Mas and a mortal known as Menggin.

According to legend, Menggin was fond of using his blowpipe. One day he noticed a beautiful bird alight on one branch, then on another. Its call so captivated him that he longed to make it his own. On his first two attempts at shooting it with a dart from his blowpipe, he failed. But on his third attempt the bird tumbled to earth. When Menggin attempted to collect his trophy from the path he found instead a woman's sarong lying there. Disappointed, he gathered the sarong in his arms and took it home to his longhouse.

Three days later an unknown girl appeared at the longhouse bathing place. She washed herself with the other women and accompanied them back to the longhouse where her beauty was quickly acknowledged by all. The members of each *bilek*, or family room, invited her to remain with them, but she declined. Not until she reached Menggin's *bilek* did she decide to accept his father's invitation—on condition that Menggin return her sarong. Menggin reluctantly agreed to her request. As soon as she had wrapped the sarong about her waist, Menggin found himself so captivated by her presence that he longed to make her his wife. Her radiance filled the *bilek* like the plumage of a bird.

A night of intimacy followed. The young woman agreed to marry Menggin if he received his parents' consent. This Menggin obtained, whereupon the young woman revealed her true identity. She was none other than Tinchin Mas, the daughter of Sengalang Burong. The son born out of this marriage between a spirit and a mortal was named Serong Gunting, whom the Iban believed taught them the principles of agricultural custom and law. More important, he taught them about the stars and the omen birds used when farming and on headhunting expeditions.

As soon as Serong Gunting was old enough to speak, he decided to visit his grandfather's longhouse. There he sat beside Sengalang Burong, who became angered by his grandson's temerity. Serong Gunting argued that since the elder man was his grandfather no invitation was necessary. Then Sengalang Burong proposed a number of ordeals for his grandson in order that he might prove his ancestry. These included a competition for spinning tops, wrestling, and hunting a wild boar and killing it with a small knife. Serong Gunting accomplished all the tasks set before him and Sengalang Burong finally accepted him as his grandson and became devoted to the boy.

Serong Gunting's career as culture-bearer to the Iban included a journey into the heavens where he met with the seven stars of the Pleiades (Bintang Tujoh). These imparted to him the secrets of farming and their involvement in the cycle of the seasons. Later he encountered the three stars in Orion (Bintang Tiga), who explained to him how they, too, could be used in agriculture. Finally, the moon initiated him into the importance of the lunar phases when farming.

Armed with this information, Serong Gunting returned to his grandfather's longhouse and commenced farming. He cut down the forest and planted his crops on the cleared land. Impressed by his grandson's industry and the subsequent success of his enterprise,

Sengalang Burong revealed to his young protégé the secret of taking heed of omens. He told him that aside from fetching water and defecating, there was no more important activity for a man to engage in than listening to the message of omen birds. He, the supreme lion-bird, regarded his seven birds-in-law as rulers over all the activities of men on earth. If a man listened to the omen birds then his life would follow a course mapped out for him by the "king of spirits," Kree Raja Petara. This was knowledge that Sengalang Burong gave to his grandson. And this was the knowledge that Serong Gunting passed on to men. The omen birds, those celestial guides who took the form of seven sacred birds, were destined to be all men's companions in this life.

My journey to Borneo had been inspired by a wish to learn from these birds the secrets of their age-old wisdom. The pantheon of Iban spirit heroes were known to manifest themselves in the world as birds. Since these birds still lived in the forest, it meant that the spirit heroes were also likely to exist. After all, they shared the same world as the Iban do to this day.

I was further reminded of the importance of birds as divinatory aids by the English word *auspicious* (meaning "ominous" or "of good omen"), a word derived from the Latin *avis specere*, which means "to observe the bird." The language of the birds has always been considered an angelic language, a language that men such as Solomon and Siegfried well understood in their time. The language of the birds is associated with the idea of rhythm, the rhythm of oracular expression, which accounts for why the chanting of Hindu mantras and Koranic sutras are regarded as derivatives of this language.

In the past it was common for men to accept the importance of divination in their lives as a way of acquiring foreknowledge. By entering into a special relationship with birds, animals, and sometimes even insects, it was possible to commune with gods by way of their intercession. The practice of augury presupposed an essentially binding relationship between man and nature, to the extent that each required the other if spiritual directives were to be acted upon. Birds occupied the intermediate ground between men and spirits. Hearing an omen bird was tantamount to saying that a man had been noticed by a god, that he was the beneficiary of celestial guidance.

Desirous of celestial guidance myself, I decided to begin my quest at the Sarawak Museum, a short walk from my hotel. Here, among pieces of Stone Age pottery, Chinese vases, and early Hindu statuary, I wandered the corridors, hoping that some object would stimulate my interest beyond that of normal curiosity. I didn't quite know what I was looking for. Eventually I stopped to look at what appeared to be an item of women's clothing woven from cotton. The caption said its design was that of *lepur api*. For some reason I imagined this to be the pattern of the sarong discovered by Menggin on the path after he had shot the sacred bird.

"*Lepur api* means 'red as flames of fire,' " a woman's voice behind me murmured.

I turned to look at my informant. In her mid-twenties, the young woman looked up at me briefly and smiled. It was the smile of someone at ease with information that she did not mind sharing. I was struck by her boldness, especially since neither of us had met before. She seemed to have appeared out of the throng of museum-goers with the express intention of answering any questions I might have.

"Obviously you speak the language," I replied, seeking to discover the woman's tribal affiliations. I could tell she was neither Malay nor Chinese. Her dark, almond-shaped eyes and equally dark hair were those of the indigenous people of Borneo. Moon-shaped and open, her face reminded me of the impenetrable depths of the forest. Gazing at her was like gazing at a patch of sunlight in a jungle clearing.

"I'm Iban," the woman replied and told me her name: Reminda. Then, without any sense of false pride or modesty, she added, "I'm also a pagan."

Her last remark struck me as unusual. No one had ever identified himself or herself to me as pagan before. The tone of her voice suggested that she did not regard the epithet as being in the least demeaning. When she uttered the word it was filled with a sense of raw affirmation, as if paganism itself had come into existence after a long period of decomposition under layers of humus, and was therefore a product of natural growth, like ferns. Here was a person who implicitly understood the path upon which I was traveling. It seemed that I had been approached not by a woman but by a bird in disguise.

Reminda explained a little more about herself: Her family lived in a remote longhouse on the Layar River, upstream from the town of Betong. She had been born in the deep forest into a *bilek* that boasted a long and distinguished genealogy. Her father, mother, brother, and sisters worked the land, growing pepper, bananas, rice, and various vegetables. However, life was hard for her family now that they had to contend with the cash economy; previously, all their wealth had been associated with the forest. Over the years she had watched her father struggle to gather enough money together to pay for her education in Betong, and later in Kuching. During this time gasoline-driven motors had invaded their longhouse in the form of electric generators and outboard motors. These demanded cash payment, which in turn had drawn people like her father deeper into the web of economics. She had watched him age under the strain of having to live two separate lives.

"It has been difficult for my father," Reminda said. "He still lives close to the gods. But he sees my generation moving away to the cities, and growing distant from Iban tradition."

"Yet he encouraged your education."

"He hopes I will one day return to the longhouse to help our people adjust to the modern world."

"Your father is afraid of what the modern world offers?" I asked.

"Of course. He has lived under the reign of the Brooke family, later the British, then the Japanese during the war, and now the Malays. He has experienced occupation and much change during these years. The days of our forefathers, when a man was considered a great warrior only when he had returned with an enemy head, are gone forever. He has lived through these times, and knows that the old ways will never return. I have been educated so that I can teach others to respect Iban culture. He believes this is the only way our culture might be saved."

"You're a teacher here in Kuching?"

"I accompany tourists on behalf of different travel companies," Reminda replied. "I talk to them about Iban tradition. I show them the way of life in the longhouse. This is why I come to the museum. Like you, I'm interested in learning more about my people."

"Then you know about the omen birds," I said.

Reminda looked up at me, her expression more serious now. She glanced about us, as if to assure herself that no one else was listening.

"Come," she said.

Though she did not take my hand, or indeed touch me in any way, I felt nonetheless that Reminda was physically leading me to another part of the museum. In spite of her education and her modern manners I still detected a fluency, a grace in her movements that reminded me of the forest. It was clear that, in asserting her paganism, Reminda had wanted to affirm her allegiance to her people rather than to a broader nationalism inspired by anthem or flag. Already this young Iban woman insisted on the primacy of her world, the world of forest gods, omen birds, and ritual practice. I felt I was in the hands of a budding *lemambang*, or ritual specialist.

Reminda led me to a glass case at the center of one of the museum rooms. Inside was a neatly trimmed tree trunk with various small birds standing on its branches. None of the birds looked remarkable in themselves. The exhibit captions dutifully informed me that these birds bore names in keeping with the best traditions of modern science. I found myself observing a woodpecker, a scarlet-rumped trogon, a rufous picolet, a banded kingfisher, a Diard's trogon, a crested jay, and a white-rumped shama with their accompanying Latin names. All seven birds were frozen into postures bestowed upon them by a taxidermist. If Reminda had not drawn my attention to the exhibit I probably would have passed it by.

"These are the omen birds you spoke of," she remarked.

"They're hardly inspiring to look at," I said.

"You're seeing them only as birds. We see them as spirits. It's their calls that influence us in our daily life. When we hear an omen bird it means that the gods have taken an interest in us. We Iban are thankful to receive their guidance. It's important to know when good luck has been bestowed upon us. This is normal."

"The calls these birds make are designed to influence how you live?"

"Of course. We are in the hands of the *tuai burong*, the man who speaks with the birds. He listens to their message and tells us what we must do. We can do nothing until the birds have been interpreted."

"How do you become a *tuai burong*?"

"First you must be a good farmer," Reminda explained. "A man who knows how to grow rice, and who shows he is able to receive guidance from the gods, it is he who becomes a *tuai burong*. We turn to him for advice when we hear the call of birds, or when we dream."

"Reminda," I began, trying to formulate my request. "I would like to learn more about the omen birds. If that's possible."

Reminda touched her chin. There was delicacy in her movements. I could see that her dark eyes were gathering in the invisible space surrounding these seven sacred omen birds. The forest in her was whispering its soundless message.

"Most people who come to Sarawak want to know only about headhunting, about the savagery of the past," she admitted. "Often we're seen as the descendants of a cruel and uncivilized race. They don't wish to learn about how we're able to speak with the gods, why we seek their guidance. This is at the heart of Iban culture, not the gathering of heads of our past enemies."

"What must I do to learn more about these birds?"

"If you wish, I will take you to my longhouse. There are men living there with much experience of the old ways. Perhaps they will speak with you."

Reminda's offer to escort me deep into the jungle came as a surprise. Our meeting in the museum had been propitious, a sign perhaps that the forest gods were not averse to my encounter with their sacred lore. Did it not echo the meeting between Tinchin Mas, a goddess, and Menggin, a mere mortal? Certainly the item of apparel in the first exhibit, and my first observation of the omen birds, evoked an almost uncanny parallel with various details in their story. I was left with the sensation that Reminda and I had been fated to meet since individually we were a part of a story much larger than ourselves.

"We have a custom among my people known as *bejalai*," Reminda said. "It means to go on a long journey. A young man is expected to make a trip away from his longhouse before he marries. He may travel many miles—to Singapore or Malaysia, perhaps. In the old days a man performing a *bejalai* might visit the longhouses only in his own region. Nothing has really changed. Everyone is expected to experience new things on his travels, and learn more about the world. That's what *bejalai* is for."

"For me to accompany you to your longhouse will be my form of *bejalai*, I presume," I said.

"This is important. To know the omen birds you must speak with a *tuai burong.* Only he knows how to speak with the birds."

"Tell me, does Tinchin Mas mean anything to you?"

"Of course. She's the daughter of Sengalang Burong, and the mother of Serong Gunting. She's also the wife of Ketupong, the most important of the omen birds. It was Ketupong who led the warriors into battle in the old days."

"Her marriage to Menngin and the birth of Serong Gunting were never revealed to Ketupong, her original husband?" I asked.

"Tinchin Mas is a goddess," Reminda reminded me, a hint of reproach in her voice. "She does as she pleases. Besides, her name means 'Ring of Gold.' She surrounds all with her beauty. Not even Ketupong would deny her that right."

Already I had begun to feel a certain familiarity with Sengalang Burong's celestial family. Important events had occurred during the early part of his reign that to this day color the Iban view of the world. That the beautiful Tinchin Mas, that bright ring of gold, had flouted the marriage law and entered into a relationship with another without her husband's knowledge reminded me of the story of Aphrodite and her dalliance with Ares, the Greek god of war. Aphrodite, who wore a golden girdle as seductive as Tinchin Mas's sarong, although married to the smith-god Hephaestus, made a cuckold of him in the arms of Ares. She later seduced a mortal known as Anchises, who, dazzled by her red robes, accepted her into his herdsman hut on Mt. Ida for a night. When she revealed herself as a goddess, Anchises was extremely fearful. Aphrodite, however, informed the herdsman that she would bear a son by him who would inaugurate a new civilization on earth. This part-man, part-god was none other than Aeneas, the founder of Rome. He, like Serong Gunting, the revealer of culture to the Iban, would become a hero to his people and always be remembered with affection. It is interesting to note that Aphrodite's father was Zeus, the supreme god of Olympus, whose celestial counterpart is Sengalang Burong, the bird-god who resides with his family on the mysterious mountain known as Rabong Raminang, lying across the border in Kalimantan.

In both families a forbidden passion involving a divine goddess, the god of war, and an ordinary mortal was instrumental in creating a new dimension to human activity. Both goddesses inspired men with their beauty, and both seduced their lovers with the aid of a magic piece of clothing. Furthermore, Serong Gunting's visit to his grandfather's longhouse on his maturity finds its echo in Aeneas's visit to the underworld to meet with his father, Anchises. Both men in turn learned of their destiny as culture-bearers from grandfather and father. The idea of divine intervention among the affairs of men in order to broaden the concept of custom and law is also a common theme in other mythologies. After all, were not the Ten Commandments received by Moses as a gift "from Jehovah"? Christ's injunction that "no man cometh to the Father but by me" also implies divine intercession, a role ably fulfilled by Serong Gunting, who received the secret lore of the omen birds as a gift from Sengalang Burong himself.

I told Reminda I was ready to travel with her to her father's longhouse immediately. She suggested I pack my bag and be ready to accompany her to the docks at the mouth of the Sarawak River early the next morning. From there we were to join a fast ocean ferry for a voyage across the South China Sea to the provincial capital of Sibu on the Rajang River. Then a bus would transport us to Betong; from there we would travel upriver by longboat.

"Are there still pirates in the South China Sea?" I asked.

Reminda laughed. "No more than there are outlaws ready to attack your stagecoach where you come from," she countered.

At least I knew we were safe from that threat.

SIX

The voyage across the South China Sea in the narrow, bullet-shaped ferry was at times unsettling. The feeling of total enclosure below deck became even more extreme when a sudden rain squall drifted across our bow, causing water to stream down the portholes. The ferry continued to plow through the waves, a slender capsule filled with travelers bound for the safe haven of the Rajang River some three hours away.

During the course of our voyage Reminda told me a little more about herself. Her childhood in the forest had been marked by hearing many stories about her people from her father and her relatives. Before the coming of radio or TV, poetry and stories had been the common form of expression. Every detail of their lives was carefully rendered into poetry or invocation by the *lemambang*, or longhouse bard. He was the liturgical cantor whose task was to chant the full names, honorifics, and nicknames of the spirits. Often dressed in female clothing to protect him while he journeyed through the realm of the spirits, the *lemembang* boasted an excellent memory. He knew more of the ritual incantations than any man in the longhouse. Reminda told me that her people had always been devotees of the word. Their lives were founded upon the mysterious verdancy of their language, which to them was as fertile as the jungle itself.

It seemed that language and a long memory encouraged most Iban to want to recall where they had come from, and to know intimately their family lineage. To Reminda, being familiar with her origins was extremely important. It was with some pride that she informed me that her family tree reached back eighteen generations.

"Our founder was Jelenggai, a warrior who migrated from Sumatra," Reminda explained. "He was the high priest of the stars you call the Pleiades. It was he who taught the Iban how to look up at the sky and see the stars setting, so that people could plant their seeds at the right time."

I was not surprised by her revelation. After all, I already knew Jack Wailu—himself a custodian of stars.

"Who did Jelenggai marry?" I asked.

"Bintang," Reminda said. "Their son, Selamuda, married Manis Muka, the swine goddess. It was Selamuda who introduced the tradition of foretelling the unknown by reading a pig's liver. Selamuda had a son by Manis Muka, but they were left alone when she decided to turn back into a sow again. Another ancestor, a man named Pintiniggi, paddled up the Saribas and Layar rivers to build a longhouse at a placed called Banggai. While he was still on board his longboat, Patiniggi decided to make a fire by rubbing two stones together. One of these stones accidently fell overboard and was immediately transformed into a huge rock that can still be seen today."

"Let's hope we don't run aground on it," I said.

The sky soon cleared over the Rajang, and our ferry made a fast passage upriver. Distant clouds framed the riverbank. Large timber mills lay tucked away among the corridors of rainforest logs that had already made the journey downriver in rope-laced barges, some as long as half a mile. We passed a number of these log islands drifting on the current under tow. Loggers danced from one log to another along their entire length as they attempted to manage their half-submerged cargoes.

Reminda watched these log barges without speaking. I could tell that she was figuring out how much forest had been lost to her people. The orchids, the animals, the birds, insects and fish, the ferns, flowers and deep-clinging vines—all of these were eliminated at a stroke as each tree came crashing down. She must have known that her world was in the process of being destroyed, but her eyes gave no indication of how she felt.

Sibu turned out to be a thriving river port dominated by a Chinese pagoda, endless river traffic, a clock tower boasting a hornbill as a weathervane, and busy streets crammed with all manner of vehicles. Open-air stalls served fresh fish and prawns. Chinese script climbed the sides of banks and commercial offices like spiders, announcing their wares. In air-conditioned offices clerks spent their days adding up figures and authorizing the sale of thousands of cubic feet of timber to the world's markets, while on the river itself tiny sampans bobbed up and down in the wash of cargo ships heading toward the sea. Even in the Taoist temple, which we visited to fill time until the following morning when the bus was to depart, we were greeted by a priest demanding that we purchase from him sufficient "spiritual money" to offer the gods so as to ensure our safe journey. In Sibu, it seemed, religion and commerce were intertwined.

Early the next morning we breakfasted in an Islamic café opposite the bus terminal. There were photographs on the walls of the Ka'aba in Mecca and the tent city outside Mina in Saudi Arabia. Even here, elderly *hadjis* returning from pilgrimage mingled with young Iban men commencing their first *bejalai*. By the time our bus left town and took the road to Betong we were both glad to put Sibu and its mountain of dead logs behind us.

Soon the forest gathered around the bus. Down a rutted road we sped, along deep-shaded gullies and abrupt hills. Streams beckoned as they flowed under bridges. Rows of pepper trees and bananas in forest clearings, along with secluded fish ponds, intimated the private world of Iban agriculture. We had put behind us the discordant sounds of modern life. Here in the jungle it seemed that the birds were still able to celebrate their gift of greenery.

"We Iban believe that the birds made us," Reminda said as we entered a stretch of forest hugging the roadside.

"In what way?" I asked.

"In the beginning, Kree Raja Petara lived alone," Reminda said. "He was a being who could speak, hear, and see—nothing more.

He had no arms or legs. In his loneliness he dreamed of two birds, one male and the other female. These two birds were born into the world, and from then on Petara never made any further attempt to create life, since the birds were his instruments."

"What did they do?"

"First they created the sky and the earth, and later the rivers. When they realized that there was more earth than sky in the world, the birds collected the earth together with their feet to make mountains and gorges. After that, they tried to make men, but without much success. Then they made trees and tried to turn them into men. When this did not succeed they attempted to make men from rocks. But the figures they created could not speak, so they tried again. This time they took some earth and molded it into the shape of a man with a little water. To give him life they put the red gum of the kumpang tree in his veins. When they called to him, he answered. And when they cut him with a knife, blood flowed from his wound. As the day heated up he began to sweat. You see, he had taken on life."

"In a way, all the ingredients of the forest had helped to bring him into the world," I suggested.

"You understand," Reminda replied, pleased at my response. "The birds were so overjoyed that they gave him the name Tannah Kampok, which means 'molded earth'. "

"Is this why the birds are so important to you?"

Reminda nodded.

"They made us," she said. "They work on behalf of the spirits. We can do nothing the birds do not know about."

"When you see all those logs floating down the Rajang River, I suppose you fear for their survival," I said.

"If we cut down the trees, how will the birds continue to live?"

Reminda's remarks were in stark contrast to the rationale that argued for the exploitation of Borneo's forests. Judging by the air of prosperity around Sibu, the traders there had mounted an impressive campaign to affirm their rights to log the forests despite tribal resistance. Since the land did not belong to the Ibans but to the gods, it followed that all men were entitled to partake of their beneficence. In the end, a chorus of circular saws was no match for the cries of numerous omen birds. Not guns, but auditor reports, contracts, and letters of credit were the weapons used by Rajah

Brooke's heirs as they set about cutting down the trees. Without these the omen birds could not survive. The clash between spiritual and material values was never so evident as here in the Borneo forest.

Early in the afternoon we reached the market town of Betong. A small trading outpost boasting a Christian school, a wooden fort left over from Rajah Brooke's time, and a number of rubber and pepper warehouses, Betong catered to the longhouse communities living upriver, providing them with basic supplies and the opportunity to sell any excess produce. Chinese shop proprietors in soiled singlets watched over us as we purchased a few supplies of our own prior to beginning the last phase of our journey. Tinned food, tea, biscuits, sugar, and brandy were the kind of gifts Reminda said her people would appreciate in return for their hospitality.

Later that afternoon we took our place in a longboat that Reminda had arranged to transport us upriver. No wider than a conventional rowing shell, the longboat was manned by four paddlers. Reminda knew these men, so our river journey was punctuated by talk and laughter as everyone caught up with the gossip. In the meantime I became absorbed by the shadowy world of the forest. Here on the Layar River silence, the splash of paddles, the occasional blossom drifting past, the sight of a monkey retreating before our advance, even the hidden meander of the river itself invested me with a sense of well-being.

On the way we passed perhaps a half dozen longhouses. This was my first encounter with how Iban people lived. Built on wooden piers, the communal longhouses stretched for as much as one hundred yards above a cleared patch in the forest. On an open balcony known as a *tanju*, pepper and farm produce were left to dry in the sun. Regular doorways opened into the covered part of the building, called a *ruai*. It was here that the community would gather of an evening to sit on rattan mats and weave cloth or listen to poetry. Inside, each family owned their private *bilek*, located off the *ruai*, where they cooked their meals and slept. On the ground underneath the building a farmyard of chickens, pigs, and dogs wandered about picking up scraps thrown down from above.

When we arrived at Reminda's longhouse late that afternoon we were greeted by a number of her relatives who were bathing in the river. Men and women chattered excitedly as they wound on their sarongs in readiness for the moment when we berthed at the landing. Along with our provisions and baggage we were soon ushered to high ground where the longhouse was located. Climbing an adze-stepped log to the open veranda, I was formally invited to enter the Genswai longhouse as a guest of Reminda's family. A bottle of rice wine known as *tuak* was opened in my honor while we sat around on rattan mats outside the *bilek*. I immediately felt at home among friends.

Reminda introduced me to her family, beginning with her elderly father, Nyanbong. As he was an old man she asked me to address him as Aki, meaning "uncle." Her mother, Banun, a spritely old woman in her seventies, I was asked to address as Ini, meaning "auntie." Her sister, Lundak, and brother-in-law, Jana, made up the rest of the family present at that time, together with a number of small children. Various people from other *bileks* joined us on the mat—as much to satisfy their curiosity at the presence of a European in their midst as to share in the rice wine that was passed around.

Ini and Lundak soon disappeared into the *bilek* to begin preparing the evening meal. Meanwhile my hosts studied me with interest as they drank. I was introduced to the headman, Patrick Wrynkye, an elderly man with easy wit and twinkling eyes. Although I was officially Aki's guest, it was Patrick who orchestrated conversation and made sure that my glass was filled. Aki appeared more retiring, shy in demeanor. He seemed content to remain in Patrick's shadow.

Reminda then asked me whether I would like to wash. Together we slipped away from the gathering and walked down to the landing by the river. In the fading light I watched Reminda discard her sarong and walk into the water. Her gesture seemed so natural as she swam into midstream that I, too, removed my clothes and dove in. As I swam about I felt the fatigue of our journey slipping from me and drifting downstream.

That night we dined on jungle food by the light of kerosene lamps. Vegetables were placed on the floor along with a bowl of rice for each person. Ranged along the walls stood large Chinese vases, their glazed dragon motifs reflecting our movements as we ate. *Tuak* was again brought out and liberally offered. I sat on the hard floor, answering questions as best I could and asking some of my own.

After the meal Reminda informed me that Patrick Wrynkye expected us to join him on his mat on the veranda outside. As the headman, he was entitled to meet formally with any visitors to the longhouse on his section of the *bilek* and inquire into their motives for coming. Dressed in a sarong lent to me by Ini, I accompanied Reminda along the walkway, passing various families at work weaving mats or cloth on simple looms. They nodded politely to us and resumed their work.

Patrick Wrynkye greeted us with a smile. He sat on his mat, his legs crossed under him. Beside him sat another elderly man who was introduced as Sumbeng, the *lemambang*, or longhouse bard. Sumbeng was in his early seventies, possibly older. His ribs showed, and by the light of the kerosene lamp his skin had the look of parchment. There was a feminine quality in his demeanor that Reminda later told me was not unusual among *lemambangs*. Specialists in invocation and chanting that sometimes lasted for many hours, *lemambangs* were often hermaphroditic by temperament. Living so near to the spirits, they frequently adopted an air of sexual ambivalence so as to maintain a distance from their compatriots.

Patrick poured me a glass of local brandy while he plied me with questions. When I informed him that I was interested in learning about the practice of augury, he listened intently, a wry smile on his face.

"So you wish to study the omen birds," he announced in a quaint, old-world English accent that he must have picked up during the time of the Raj. Everything about Patrick denoted a belief in good government. His longhouse was a model of social harmony, a clear reflection on his ability to bring out the best in people.

"I have met others in the world who understand the language of the birds," I replied, informing him of my encounter with the Meriam people in Torres Strait. Patrick was not surprised that others acknowledged the importance of birds.

"This is because birds are the spirits. When we listen to them we are listening to the voice of what you call God," he said.

"Is their lore open to people such as me?"

"It depends," Patrick began cautiously. "The knowledge of *burong rama* [bird augury] is a difficult science. Not every man is graced with the understanding to interpret omens. Of course, birds may appear to all, but to translate what they are saying is revealed to only a few. These men we call *tuai burong*. They are most favored by the spirits. Ketupong, the chief omen bird, watches over their deliberations and guides them in the correct way. Such men are made known to us in dreams. We do not have the power to choose our *tuai burong*."

"Is there a *tuai burong* in the longhouse I could speak to?"

Patrick shifted his weight and rearranged his sarong. He glanced briefly at Sumbeng who sat to one side smoking a cigarette. The *lemambang* pursed his lips, but otherwise made no attempt to converse, not even in the local dialect.

"Your request is perhaps a little incautious," Patrick replied in his quaintly formal English. "We do not know you. You must understand that our *tuai burong* is a most singular man. He is regarded by this longhouse as our true link with the spirits. We would have to be sure of your sincerity before his identity could be revealed. I do not wish to sound impolite, but we Iban regard the knowledge of birds as a great mystery. Before we reveal it to visitors we expect them to show their colors," Patrick added, resorting to a British military term he must have picked up on a visit to Singapore while performing *bejalai* long ago.

I was impressed by Patrick's speech. He had invested all of his previously unspoken thoughts on the matter with a certain dignity. It was not that he wished to dissuade me from making my inquiries, merely that he wanted me to understand the gravity of the issue. As far as he was concerned the knowledge of bird augury was a privilege bestowed upon the elect few. I was not yet one of these, of course, and would therefore have to await my confirmation with patience.

"Is there anything I should know that might help?" I ventured, hoping to smooth over the impasse.

"To understand my people, it is important that you first know of Iban custom," Patrick told me. "This is the basis of how we live, not only here in the longhouse but also when we are in the forest and in the fields. We call this knowledge the law of *Adat*. Such knowledge was revealed to us by Sengalang Burong himself."

Patrick went on to explain in detail the law of *Adat*. It was a term I had never heard before, though he assured me that the origin of the word probably lay in the Muslim concept of *Hadat*, which was an Arabic word for customary law, a word that would have crept into use among the Iban by way of Malay and Indonesian contact along the coast. But for the Iban, *Adat* meant much more than customary law; it signified divine cosmic order and harmony, coupled with a belief that all life and actions should be in agreement. Nor are men the only ones who were beholden to *Adat*. Every creature, every phenomenon or action occurring within the cosmos was subject to celestial decrees, and was required to live and act according to these harmonies.

Patrick also explained that, though the Iban see themselves as standing at the center of the universe, they know they have no control over it. They are only part of a whole that embraces all people and all levels of existence. The universe is inhabited by various groups made up of human, spiritual, animal, and vegetable entities that have some interests in common. At certain times these interests may diverge, thus setting up the possibility for potential conflict. *Adat* exists to ensure harmony in the universe and to promote the well-being of all its inhabitants, not least among them the Iban themselves. *Adat* is designed to promote a mutually satisfactory relationship between men and all the other inhabitants of the universe.

The *Adat* of plants is to grow and be fruitful, each according to its natural disposition. Animals, too, possess individual *Adat* that affects their way of behaving within the natural scheme of things. For the Iban, their *Adat* involves the observation of rules governing social behavior and the performance of ritual acts. To explain the unusual behavior of foreigners, for example, an Iban would say, "That's their *Adat*." While Iban acknowledge that differences of *Adat* interpretation may exist among rival groups, they know that ultimately following the law of *Adat* is designed to promote good relations, health, harvests, and general prosperity. This they call *chelap*, meaning "cool" or "tranquil." Universal order is therefore considered in these terms, while its opposite, *angat*, is considered to manifest itself as "heated" or "feverish." Since both the physical and the spiritual worlds are regarded as being aspects of the same order, there is a requirement to balance these with the use of complementaries rather than that of opposites. Thus the concept a day and night opposing one another, or sight/blindness being set up in antithesis is something with which the Iban feel uncomfortable. They prefer the idea that all things complement one another.

Men are paired with spirits and the spirits of the dead; the body with the spirit, mortality with immortality; what may be seen with the eyes, with the invisible nature of things; objects with their insubstantial essence; the profane with the sacred; and the earth with the sky. The universe becomes an unlimited gathering of siblings that are designed to reflect wholeness. Numerology plays an important part, whereby certain numbers are said to embody sacred attributes. The number three is associated with the expression "Oha!," which precedes most invocations. This number derives its origin from the belief that Petara, the Creator, cried out three times while attempting to bring man to life. Furthermore, the universe can be divided into three parts: the sky above, the earth, and the region below the earth. Its inhabitants also fall into three distinct categories of existence: that of Petara, the realm of the Spirit; Antu, the realm of the dead; and Mensia, the realm of men.

Seven is an even more propitious number among the Iban. It is said that Sengalang Burong and Pulang Gana have five other brothers. Sengalang Burong has seven daughters, and of course there are seven omen birds. The sky is considered to have seven layers, while most sacrifices are sevenfold in order to appease the seven spirits. At the time of important festivals the drums are beaten seven times. Whether in the garden or in the forest the power of seven pervades Iban reality, helping to preserve *Adat* as much as possible.

It follows that an offense against *Adat* disturbs the universal order, producing a state of disorder and the undesirable "heated" or "feverish" state known as *angat*. Such disorder usually results in the appearance of destabilizing events ranging from minor sickness to epidemics and even crop failure. Serious transgressions invariably affect the well-being of the community to the point where a state of sterility may be realized, resulting in the entire natural order ceasing to function properly. When this happens land often becomes sterile *(kudi)* and is unable to produce any crops. *Kudi* implies disrespect, even ridicule or actual interference with the natural order itself. It is also a serious offense to mock or exploit natural behavior. Laughing at dogs copulating, for example, may result in the perpetrators being turned into stone. There are a number of petrified stones throughout the Layar River region that serve as reminders to people not to offend nature.

What is forbidden, therefore, is acting against the law of *Adat*, which is not so much an absolute ethical standard as a yardstick by which the difference between order and disorder is measured. When the Iban encounter difficulties, or when calamities occur, they believe that *Adat* has not been correctly observed. In the case where an individual Iban is judged for a presumed offense by a court of longhouse members, his punishment is not designed to fit the crime so much as to compensate the offended spirit party. The Iban do not use the word *pay* when speaking of a fine. Instead they say one "meets" or "completes" such a fine. If the offender's identity is unknown, it is not entirely out of the question for the headman to "fine" himself so as to restore order between men and the spirit-world.

When the *Adat* is disturbed, the individual, his family, and the lives of all those living in his longhouse are in danger of becoming "heated," "feverish," or "infected." Furthermore, the *Adat* permeates the conduct of every action in the life of an Iban. Kitchen hygiene is preserved by way of the *Adat*, which insists that all longhouse kitchens must be continually in use. If a family moves away from its *bilek* for a time it must take steps to ensure that food is cooked there at least twice a month, preferably at full moon or on the first day of each lunar month. If this rule is broken for any reason, then the family is liable to a fine of two chickens, a knife, and an adze. This is to prevent the entire longhouse from becoming spiritually cold, thus endangering the well-being of the rest of the community.

The law extends to all farming activity as well. A man cannot plant ordinary rice seed until he has first planted his family's sacred rice around the offering platform in the field where a sacred lily always grows. When the sacred rice is planted, he is ready to plant the ordinary seed before that of white, red, and black glutinous rice in strict order of precedence. Not to do so is an offense that may result in a family death at some time during the year. Nor should a farmer arrange his paddy fields around that of another man's in such a way as to confine the latter's too much. This is said to disturb the *Adat* of the land, and so run the risk of jeopardizing the health of all concerned.

Adat affects hunting, fishing, the collection of fruit in the jungle, even the gathering of honey. If a man discovers a bee tree, he is entitled to make a cross nearby and so claim its produce as his own. He then arranges for a climber to accompany him to the tree on the afternoon of the last day of the lunar month. Other members of the longhouse are invited to join them at the foot of the tree and observe the ritual of driving off the bees at dusk. As he performs his task, the climber sings a sacred song, which protects him from being stung by the bees. As soon as the honeycombs have been lowered to the ground they are pressed by receivers to extract the honey. At daylight the ceremony is concluded with a ritual division of the honey, whereby the climber and his helpers receive shares according to their relative importance. Such apportioning is designed to protect the honey-gatherers from attack by a catlike animal that is the guardian spirit of the hive. In this way the *Adat* relating to the realm of bees is not disturbed. Although somewhat reluctantly, the bees have been asked to give up their honey under cover of darkness, thus concealing from them as much as possible the extent of their loss.

"*Adat* is the way we live," Patrick concluded his dissertation— with a flourish of the brandy bottle. Even he seemed somewhat taken aback by the extent of his knowledge. He gave the impression that he had never been asked to explain in such detail the workings of *Adat* before. Nonetheless, I was still unsure whether I fully understood if *Adat* was the manifestation of cosmic law, or whether it was merely an expression of Iban custom.

"When you understand *Adat*, then you are able to become one of us," Patrick added. "But first you must know that we believe all life is divided into two parts. What we touch and see with our senses we call *tuboh*. Everything in life has *tuboh* and can be seen or touched. The spirit side is its counterpart, which we call *semengat*. The more *semengat* a man possesses the more we say he is good. It is like a shadow and, depending on our health, grows big and small within us."

"Are you born with *semengat*?" I asked.

"Yes. But when you are in your mother's belly, *semengat* enters you only after three months. Before that we say the unborn baby is still made of blood. He has no *semengat*. When a man dreams his *semengat* may leave him for a time. If he is dying or sick, his *semengat* also leaves him. The task of a healer is to make sure the *semengat* returns to a sick man's body before it is too late, otherwise he will surely die."

"Can a dying man's *semengat* be asked to return to his body?" Patrick shook his head.

"A man's *semengat* knows when it is time to leave," he replied. "Therefore a healer is powerless to stop the final departure of a dying man's *semengat*. Some Iban believe that we have seven *semengat* souls that leave us one by one throughout our life. When the last leaves us it turns into dew. In the morning, when we feel the dew of our ancestor's *semengat* underfoot, it makes us feel happy. Then we know we are always close to what we believe. This is *Adat*," Patrick concluded after a pause.

Patrick's explanation left me better informed but no wiser. Sitting there in the partial darkness, with only the glow from various lamps illuminating family groups along the veranda, I sensed that perhaps what the *tuai rumah* had been telling me found its source in the forest itself. I had no way of knowing to what extent the language of the birds, indeed the language of nature itself, conveyed its own level of ethics to a living world. What did impress me, however, was the recognition that the Iban gave to nature as a teacher, as an authority on the invisible forces that governed their lives. Although a man's final destination after death was Sebeyan, the land of the dead, his living reality was the result of a complex spiritual nexus between his *semengat*—that is, his spirit or soul— and the law of *Adat*. The inversion of almost every Iban belief in order to reflect its passive dualism merely serves to heighten the need to maintain a balance between all the disparate forces at work in nature.

What Patrick was saying to me suggested that I should be very careful about accepting things at the level on which they appeared. In the topsy-turvy world of gods and men there was no formal exactitude that could be introduced to account for the way these contrasting entities went about their business. Clearly *Adat* was a cautionary device, a way of treading lightly upon the subsoil of existence. It allowed men and nature the opportunity to reconcile themselves each to their chosen domain of activity, and to one another. Each entity, spiritual and natural, was entitled to inhabit its own district or territory while at the same time recognizing that these territories sometimes overlapped. *Adat* was the region where

men and gods came together to converse. It was a region where a
sacred language came into play, enabling both parties to communicate at the highest level possible.

No wonder Patrick treated my initial request to learn more about
the omen birds with some caution. He knew I had a long way to
go before I could begin to understand their language. I must learn
to listen with a new, more refined sense of hearing to the voice of
nature—and translate what I heard in the context of Iban belief.
Meanwhile Patrick, the wisest of men and a true longhouse leader,
agreed to counsel me whenever I might ask it of him.

"It is the way of our people," he said. "In the old days we
hunted for heads, true. This is not a practice I am proud of.
Perhaps my forefathers believed that in taking heads they were
gathering unto themselves more *semengat*. Who knows? My people
also laid claim to knowing important mysteries, mysteries that one
day other people might wish to know. This is why we pride ourselves on our gift of language. We Iban are poets. We believe it
is the way we speak, in our incantations, that we draw near to the
gods. We know that in preserving our tradition, by making sure
each poem is taught to the next generation, we can maintain contact with the time when Sengalang Burong and his brothers lived
among us. Is this not important?"

"It appears you regard the Iban language as the key to all knowledge," I said.

"It is our richest possession. All our stories, all our ritual songs—
these define who we are. We do not exist except in the way we
talk about ourselves. This is why *Adat* is so important to us. *Adat*
is a sacred language, too."

My good fortune was to have encountered a man like Patrick
who was conscious of his responsibility as a culture-bearer, and
who was as equally prepared to share his knowledge. Already he
had made me aware of the potency of language and its ability to
fuel the imagination. I was excited by this realization: We are not
alive until we have entered into a living myth and allowed its
mystery to weave its magic in the form of words. Its ability to
communicate, however, constituted one of its least important func-
tions. What appeared to be more important was that in the act of
articulating a reality with the aid of poetry, its very meaning could
be transcended. This reality had become essential to the Iban heri-

tage. It was a reality governed by the power of nature as the physical manifestation of all divine action.

In spite of being no closer to discovering more about the language of the omen birds, I felt I had made some progress. Patrick's dissertation on the subject of *Adat* had made me privy to a way of seeing the word as an extension of natural activity. My first night in the longhouse had indeed been productive.

Sumbeng, the local *lemambang* sitting at Patrick's side, suddenly cleared his throat. I thought he was about to say something. Instead, he opened his frail chest and began to recite a few lines of poetry in a voice that was filled with controlled modulation. His words seemed to emanate from a region beyond that of his mouth or throat, as if he were drawing upon the service of another organ altogether. He sang:

> *Gayu guru*
> *Chelap lindap*
> *grai nyamai.*

"What is he saying?" I asked Patrick.

"He is wishing you a full life span lived in contentment, good health, and comfort."

"Please thank Sumbeng," I said. Then, suspecting that other meanings might be hidden in those few lines of poetry, I asked, "What else is Sumbeng saying?"

Patrick's eyes twinkled. I could see he enjoyed the verbal interplay that had arisen between us.

"I will tell you," he said. "The word *gayu* hides another word inside. This word is *ayu*, which is a spirit substance that grows in banana shoots. We believe that when a man's *semengat* leaves him at death, this plant also dies. Now *gayu* means 'long life' in our language. It follows, my friend, that imbedded in 'long life'. is the tiny spirit word *ayu*, which leaves at death, too. So what Sumbeng is saying to you is this: While he wishes you a long life, he also knows your life will achieve its own measure, and will end one day. Sumbeng is wishing you good health, but telling you what to expect as well!"

"What he means is that in a long life, death will always be

present," I said, beginning to understand the sublety of the Iban language.

Patrick chuckled. It was evident that he enjoyed explaining the irony of Sumbeng's invocation.

"My mat is always spread for you," he said finally, when Reminda and I made as if to go.

"Thank you, Patrick," I replied, bowing my head as a sign of respect to the two old men sitting before me. In a way, they reminded me of figurines unearthed from the ruins of an ancient metropolis.

"Come," Reminda whispered as she rose to her feet.

"Sleep well, my friend," Patrick replied, raising his hand.

Again I nodded to Sumbeng, who in turn acknowledged my gesture with a nod of his own.

Reminda led me in silence along the darkened veranda. Already the longhouse community had retired to their *bileks* for the night, leaving us to savor the moonlight patterned at intervals on the floor in veranda doorways.

SEVEN

Patrick's revelation that language was like a double-edged sword left me in a quandary. If the power of words could be undermined by a variety of meanings imbedded within them, then perhaps language had been designed with an entirely different function in mind. Perhaps its strength lay in its ability to enchant rather than to explain; its true purpose that of helping to evolve a dream world made up of dream scenery and dream people. Whether in dream or in waking, however, language offers us the opportunity to explore something expansive and self-delighting in ourselves. Through it, our feelings of who we are grow larger.

Clearly the forest held the key to the way the Iban thought. Their language must have been derived from a reality determined by this green world. The deep shade under old trees, the stillness that pervades the forest floor, the shy anarchy of butterflies as they skip along a pathway—these images and many more must have resulted in a desire on the part of my friends to communicate in a language less given to the process of analysis. Could it be that the Iban refused to separate themselves from their environment, as I so clearly had, in order to deepen their relationship with certain mysteries that lay concealed within the forest itself? I began to suspect that the lore of the omen birds was an essential part of this relationship between man, nature, and language.

My early days at Reminda's longhouse were transformed into a voyage of discovery as each event in the lives of my hosts became an object of inquiry. When she was not helping Ina in the kitchen or washing clothes, sewing Aki's torn shirts, or looking after the children while her sister was in the fields, Reminda somehow found time to answer my questions and act as my interpreter whenever I ventured along the veranda of the longhouse to talk with the older inhabitants. She was a true descendant of a goddess. Her deft hands made everything she did appear so easy. I felt that Reminda's warmth and beauty had been enhanced by this renewed contact with her family. She appeared to have relinquished the memory of Kuching and all that it represented with the same grace as she had her sarong at the river when bathing.

We went on long walks together in the forest, visited paddy fields on secluded hillsides, sat on the riverbank, and exchanged gossip with villagers traveling to their longhouses. It was not hard to find out who was ill, who had given birth to a baby, and who had eloped. Meanwhile, the longboats arrowed upstream, their passengers wedged in among kerosene tins and produce. I soon grew accustomed to this world of twigs and leaves as they drifted past, their passage intimating distant communities enmeshed in the age-old secrecy of the river. It was the true artery of discourse, the one method of dispersing all the abundance of the forest.

"In December, the forest is filled with wild orchids. They flower in the trees above," Reminda said to me one day as we sat on the landing, dangling our feet in the water.

"Much as stars do at night," I suggested.

Reminda smiled.

"You're beginning to speak like a true Iban," she said. "We have expressions like that also. We say, 'he has eyes like a prawn,' or 'the night is as long as a blowpipe.' The world may be 'as small as a frog under a coconut,' or 'a man may act like a lion at home, a turtle in the jungle.' This tells you he is boastful but has little courage.

"Let me tell you a riddle," Reminda added, withdrawing one foot from the water. "What is it that you can cut and it will not break, heat and it will not burn?"

I looked at her nonplussed.

"Why, water, of course. It cannot be destroyed. Not like us."

"What are you afraid of, Reminda?"

"What the modern world is doing to us. It is changing all our old ways. Our people are already beginning to question the value of *Adat*."

"Patrick is a strong man. He will not let it happen," I tried to encourage her.

"He is a wise man, I know. But he is also a Christian. This means that he is only half with us."

"Patrick? A Christian?" I said. This news surprised me.

"He attended St. Augustine College in Betong, where he became a Christian," Reminda told me. "After school, he spent some years in Singapore working in a pharmacy."

"This must have been at the time of his *bejalai*," I remarked.

"Perhaps," Reminda replied. "But he also worked for Europeans at the Sarawak Museum before the war, helping anthropologists write down our history. Then the Japanese came, so he returned to our longhouse to become the *tuai rumah*."

"From what I have seen, it appears that Patrick's Christianity sits lightly upon his shoulders."

"Patrick is an unusual man. He is able to live in both worlds. But most Iban who convert to Christianity are not like him. They soon lose faith in Sengalang Burong and the lore of the omen birds."

"Which you believe spells the end," I said.

"Doesn't it?" Reminda asked. "You can see for yourself how few young people like myself live in the longhouse nowadays. We have already gone to the coastal cities to look for jobs. This is what Christianity has done to us. While it has brought us education, it has also made us doubt the value of the old customs. Now we look elsewhere for happiness."

"But you received such an education, and are grateful, surely," I reminded Reminda.

"Not at a Christian college. Fortunately the government schools still allow us freedom of belief, even though Malaysia is a Muslim state. I'm still pagan, remember."

Reminda's remarks echoed those I had heard Jack Wailu make on Mer. It seemed that wherever I went I found myself embroiled in the arguments of various peoples who resented the colonization they had been forced to undergo at the hands of the Church. The undermining of pagan belief by missionaries had caused a great deal of suffering. People like the Iban had been urged to give up what was intrinsic to their culture—their desire to remain in touch with nature's intricate web of truths masquerading in the guise of the physical world. What the missionaries could not accept was that divine entities such as Sengalang Burong and Pulang Gana found their expression *in* matter. These visible and imaginable forms were signs, or pointers, directing the thoughts of the Iban to what lay hidden in the bosom of nature. There resided something mightier, more comprehensive, and less transitory than anything able to be grasped by the senses or the emotions.

Of course Reminda's fears were immediate. She had no way of knowing at what point the process of destruction became irreversible. But I sensed in her concerns a real dilemma. Her education had been derived from a source that she now wished to reject. Her own beliefs were no match for the relentless inroads made by the modern world on her doorstep. Serong Gunting's appearance as a god-man had been cut down to size the instant he had encountered Rajah Brooke's emissaries, although I suspected Brooke's military incursions had been less destructive than the mission societies that followed. These had finally routed the ragtag army of spirit figures that confronted them with a blend of European education, moral injunction, and the dismissal of nature religion as a relic of primitive thought.

Nonetheless, the great trees along the Layar River seemed to offer a fragile haven for the likes of Patrick, Sumbeng, Aki, Ini, and the invisible company of spirit beings under the command of Sengalang Burong, at least for a while yet. But after that, who would protect them from the army of chainsaws when the time came for these to invade their territory? It was a question constantly on my mind as I walked the forest pathways or stopped to gather in the deep silence of the river at dusk.

I decided to voice my concerns to Patrick. With the sound of pigs foraging underneath the longhouse, we sat together one afternoon on his mat, discussing the prospect of the loggers eventually encroaching on the Layar River.

"We came here twenty-five generations ago under the guidance of Sengalang Burong," he said, his twinkling eyes filled with the joy that survival into old age often brings. "We must listen first to the voice of the forest. The forest will tell us what to do."

"The people along the Rajang River did not choose to listen," I countered, recalling the logs I had seen on the river near Sibu.

"Those people are not Iban," replied Patrick with an air of dismissal in his voice. "They are more interested in bartering their forest in return for what the outside world has to offer. So they allowed the loggers to come in. We Iban are much stronger."

"Are you really any stronger than the Kelabit or the Kenyan when it comes to the lure of royalty payments?" I asked, mentioning the names of two Rajang River peoples who I knew were in league with the logging companies.

"We have Sengalang Burong who protects our forest, and we have our god of rice, Simpang Impang," Patrick answered.

"He gave you rice?"

"Let me tell you a story," the old man began. "There once lived a man who discovered that someone had been stealing his rice. He decided to watch over his rice jars from a secret place. One day he saw a snake descend from the rafters above and lick up his rice; this snake he immediately killed. Then a huge body, without shape or recognizable features, came down from the sky and filled the valley. The man cut up this body and cooked it. While it was cooking, the bamboo containers made strange noises that provoked laughter among the women. We Iban believe it wrong to laugh at nature, as you know. The sky turned black with cloud and it rained for forty days. Only one person managed to survive the flood, and her name was Dayang Racha. She crawled ashore on a mountain where she attempted to make fire with two sticks. An ember flew up and touched her on her private parts, causing her to become pregnant. The child she gave birth to she named Simpang Impang, which means 'someone who has only half his private parts.' "

"A male-female person," I suggested.

"Perhaps," Patrick agreed. "Anyway, Simpang Impang was always sad. He decided to kill himself by putting to sea. But a beautiful woman named Indai Jubua came to his rescue and took him home. He began to notice that she often grew hairy and behaved like a garden pest. When she came home she brought home grains of rice. Indai Jubua then asked Simpang Impang to look after her children while she was away in the fields. The trouble was that her children were very naughty. They turned into pests, making life miserable for Simpang Impang. So he decided to pour boiling water over them.

"When Indai Jubua came home her children told her what had happened. Shocked, she told him to leave the longhouse. But as a parting gift she gave him three enormous rice seeds. Then she revealed to him who she really was. You see, Indai Jubua was the Vermin Spirit."

"What happened then?"

"Well, Simpang Impang wandered about, hoping the seeds might dry out. But a gust of wind broke them into many pieces— about the size of what rice is today. Simpang Impang demanded the Wind Spirit pay for what he had done. When the Wind Spirit refused, Simpang Impang decided to attack him with a band of his followers. As they were about to storm the Wind Spirit's house, the spirit cried out, 'Don't you know who I am? I'm a great friend of your father, the Fire Spirit.' "

"Did the Wind Spirit help Simpang Impang?" I asked.

"He gave him a gong, which he told Simpang Impang to beat whenever the wind blew," Patrick replied. "We Iban still beat the gong whenever a big wind blows. It was then that Simpang Impang did something for us. He named every living creature, all the trees, every bird and insect. He did this in consultation with the spirits. But one day when they were sitting together discussing these names a cock flew over and messed on them. The Earth Spirit, Pulang Gana, decided that the cock should be punished. In future, when a man wished to address the spirits, a cock's comb must be cut and its blood sprinkled over any offering. This is how the *biau* ceremony was given to us by Pulang Gana. And this is how the names of everything in existence were handed down to us."

"It was certainly a great gift," I said.

"A gift no amount of money can buy," Patrick added with an air of finality. "Dayang Racha brought us to life once more after our ancestors had laughed at the sounds of nature. She had made fire for us and given birth to the Spirit of Knowledge in the form of Simpang Impang. His father was fire, you see. Meanwhile Indai Jubua had saved Simpang Impang by offering him the gift of rice, and the Wind Spirit had made the seed practical for our use by breaking it into small pieces. Pulang Gana had helped us by naming things so that we might identify all that we saw. Because he was the Earth Spirit, he also revealed to us how to cultivate rice and to build our longhouses. These are the ways of Pulang Gana. He makes the trees grow. He made the earth fertile. This is why we say that our people cannot own the earth. How can you own a god? We are its overseers, nothing more."

Patrick seemed to have all the answers. In the face of the very real threat posed by loggers, he was prepared to marshal a force of gods in his defense! When was the last time I had read of such an act of faith by someone defending his homeland? Joan of Arc, perhaps? The Knights of St. John in their defense of Rhodes? I had no way of knowing whether Patrick held any doubts as to the efficacy of the Iban gods when he contrasted their past exploits with those of his newfound Christian beliefs. He was as enigmatic as a sage in this respect.

At the same time, I was aware that he had revealed an important myth to me. While this myth included details of a flood, it also explained the origin of rice, the beginnings of agriculture, and the reason for certain rituals. More significantly perhaps, the process of naming things saw the introduction of diversity into the Iban world. Through the actions of Simpang Impang, the Iban people were able to control their lives through the use of language. Words were the source of identification and power, a power that they managed to share with the omen birds. It seemed that Simpang Impang's sexual mutilation had been more than compensated for by his command of the word. He could manifest his potency in the world by the very act of naming things.

By now I had begun to realize that a myth does not have to be comprehensible at all levels of consciousness. A myth is like the word *gayu*; it houses deeper meanings that are not always perceptible to normal understanding. A myth may be regarded as a sort of divine language that can be understood only by those well versed in its meaning. Just as a foreign language is little more than a series of sounds to an untutored ear, so, too, is the imagery and events surrounding a myth to an outsider. They represent its syntax, and provide it with its inherent structure. A myth is designed to "flow over" the intellect as a river does over stones. As these are washed smooth of their uneven texture, so, too, is the mind washed smooth of its rationalizations. In a way, I had finally learned how to "listen" to a myth as I might music. Both provoke a deep emotional chord. Both elevate the mind in a way that may be incomprehensible in one sense, yet no less real for being so.

Sumbeng, the longhouse *lemambang*, joined us on the mat. He had brought with him an armful of storyboards bound together with a piece of string. These boards contained ritual information in a language that only a *lemambang* understood. Used as prompters, they help to remind a *lemambang* of the numerous plot details essential to a story. His frail chest looking more like a withered leaf than ever, Sumbeng finally untied the string. Then he arranged the boards about him and studied them closely.

"He wishes to chant a *sabak* in your honor," Patrick whispered, tucking his toes back under his sarong in anticipation. "We call it a mourning song," he added.

Patrick went on to explain to me the plot of Sumbeng's death dirge while the old man drank a tot of brandy and finished off his cigarette.

"We believe that when we die our spirit begins a long river journey to the otherworld in the company of the spirits of our ancestors. On the way our spirit passes through the villages belonging to the birds, who ask us who we are. Even though our spirit is afraid of the unknown, the birds tell us that in the upper reaches of the Mandai River, the River of Death, a glorious land awaits us."

"Paradise," I suggested.

"Heaven," Patrick corrected me with a knowing grin. "Taking courage, our spirit passes through the Door of the Earth with the help of the Spirit of the Worm who helps open this door. Our spirit reaches the landing stage of the Mandai River where a longboat awaits. On the journey upstream our spirit meets with great men of the past who talk of their exploits. Finally, our spirit reaches its own spirit landing, and here it goes ashore. The death party then washes and puts on fine clothing before beginning a procession to the spirit longhouse. They stop at the *nibong* palm. Here the *lemambang* explains how the fruit of this palm must be gathered as a gift for the spirit longhouse.

"When the party arrives at the longhouse, our spirit is invited to fight the cock of his nearest cousin with a bird given to him. Although his cock wins the contest, our spirit still feels homesick for this world, and longs to return. But the spirits of the dead gather around and ask our spirit to look upon the beauty of the forest of the upper Mandai River, the sweet Land of the Dead. At last our spirit begins to feel at home and the *lemambang* who accompanied us is free to return to the Land of the Living. He is given charms to protect him on his return journey downriver. Prayers are said to the Wind Spirit to hasten his longboat on its homeward voyage back to the land of the living."

"Is it true that Sumbeng has sailed up the Mandai River and returned alive on other occasions?" I asked.

"Many times," Patrick responded. "The spirit of *sabak* always protects him."

I gazed at Sumbeng with new respect. Already the old man appeared to have quit our presence as he set a course upriver in the company of his storyboards. They were his spirit paddles.

"He is ready," Patrick whispered, removing a floorboard by the upright and pouring a draught of brandy onto the ground below.

"An offering for Pulang Gana," he said.

At last Sumbeng launched into a death dirge. His voice came from deep down in his throat before he effortlessly delivered his lines. His delivery was reminiscent of plainsong. During his rendition he stopped singing periodically so that Patrick might translate for me. In those moments he bent low over his boards, as if in a state of trance.

Thus he intoned:

Where are you, beautiful Kumbau, dwelling in the loft
And you, Lulong, seated below the roof ridge?
"Why do you call me, kind friend?" Kumbau demanded.
I am inviting you both to the spirit's send-off
At the landing where the chill Mandai River begins.

Do not curse me or die because I wish to journey
To the upper reaches of the Mandai, to send off
The departed. My head is protected by a sheet
And my toes hardened on the point of a spear
So I may safely reach the sacred hill beyond.

Since it is now dusk I will ask he who is so afraid
To die, "Grandfather, why are you lying on the

Veranda, under a sheet next to a betel nut box?"
He replies, "Perhaps I will die and make the journey
To where the river roars for a year and then abates.

"Though my window will be closed against the night
And my room hard to leave with its brass box treasures
Shaped like onions; my kitchen also where my cat
Curls up to sleep—these will linger in memory
When I die like smoke against a cloudy black sky.

"My door of belian wood, fastened as it is with a gun
swivel, and locked with a blade of the best steel,
This too will be hard for me to leave when I die,
Knowing that it was the place where incense burned
To attract visitors and captives with tattooed arms."

Will I explain to you the dome of the universe,
Its beauty as rounded as a broad-brimmed hat?
The door made of lulai wood opens wide, and
The dead man's feet step onto the open ground
Pitching like a fishing boat after a month at sea.

His fingers hold on to a post, fearful of dying.
This post roots him to the ground of his pigs,
To the perch where his fowls always roost,
Where antlers bearing the swords of old men
Hang amid charms designed to attract traders.

"Oh," he cries. "It is so hard for me to die
When so much is left undone. The sale
Of my rice crop needs attending to, and
I still long to see a collection of coconut shells:
My enemies' heads strung from the roof beams."

He calls out to Kumang, a mere glimpse of a girl
Who smolders like a cinder; and to Sudan
With her filters and love charms—she the spirit
Of lightning who glows with all the abundance
Of molten iron when beaten on an anvil.

For she is that girl at the center of the universe
Who travels about in a whirlwind, and who moves
Backwards with the ease of a prawn. Her real name

Sounds like the noise at the heart of a tree, none
Other than thunder dashing against cloud all day.

"What a pity grandfather is dying," she cries out.
Her beauty spots dimpling as stiffly as calico.
For she is the spirit of lowering clouds, younger
By far than her sister of spattering rain, as she
Floats high over the ridged lowlands and forest.

A blue butterfly enters the room, informing him
That a visitor arrives. Perhaps it comes to announce
A man looking for his fighting cock, or a bird
Flying the full length of the longhouse, singing of
The collapse of hills in a tumult of earth and rain.

The dead arrive at the landing, in company
With the Dark Prince who orders the girls to bathe
In the Mandai River: these girls whose braided
Hair looks like a trail of birds in flight, or the furl
Of a hanging sail as it unravels among flowers.

"My children," he cries. "Since I am to journey
To the land of the giant bamboo, prepare all that
I'll need for my new life." The Dark Prince announced,
"Leave your deer horn charm and wild boar tooth
To protect those who store rice when you've gone.

"In their place I give you a charm to make you wise,
A cinder to use when you dye cotton in a trough
And a charm of frozen cobweb to make you agile
As you leap from the landing into the longboat.
These are as cleansing as water from a pumpkin."

Among the birds they walk, into misty clumps
Of trees, Ketupong's abode, until they reach
A forest where the Flower Goddess lives
Hanging from the shield of the day. She is sister
To the omen bird, Beregai, praise-singer of the Dead.

Leaving this place, they meet up with the goddess
Of birds' eggs whose nickname is Bottle Filled with

Light Cloud Hanging. The spirit of unused honeycomb,
She encourages the topmost branches of trees
To crow like fighting cocks before they do battle.

Whose country is this but the land of mad E'it
Who wears her hat upside down, a love sprite
Nicknamed the Girl of Creaking Wooden Planks?
All bee trees are under her spell, and the rope
Honey collectors climb to reach their prize.

Leaving this place, they reach a junction where seven
Paths meet. Whose path is this so coolly dug to the depth
Of one's ribs? A voice cries, "This is the path used by
The butterfly, inviting Sengalang Burong to a feast
From his faraway home on the rim of the sky."

Leaving this place, they meet with the lovely Lengui
Whose orations are as direct as a bridge of brass.
Along with Siba-Iba, she watches over the frontier
Between the living and the dead, a place
Among ponds beneath the shadow of moonlight.

Leaving this place, they arrive at a clump of trees
Resembling a congregation of Malays praying to Allah.
By a stone as bright as a sharp sword they ask,
"What place is this?" To which a piece of clay
With the voice like a Jew's harp replies, "Maid Kawa

Lives here, guardian of the Earth Door, a sprite
Who watches over the flowers of the areca nut
As they fall. The worm goddess, she bathes
In a pool of root water each day, and walks
Backwards as easily as she does forwards."

At the Mandai River grandfather cries out, "Who
Owns this longboat whose roof is made of the skins
Of my Kayan enemies?" The Dark Prince remarks,
"So carefully made from belian *wood in the Malay*
Fashion, my boat is faster than any white man's.

"Decorated with caterpillar carvings, its bow shaped
In the image of a savage boar, my longboat looks
Like an elephant rampaging on a mountain slope

At dusk. The illusion of legs, hands, mouth, eyes,
And toes means that my boat is not a dying craft."

They paddled hard against the current, drifting
Past a stone ledge that stood like a flock of storks
Resisting waves inside a reef. On this ledge
A dandi tree shelters the Tortoise Wizard, whose
Arms are white from shoulder to fingertip.

Passing this place, they reached a riverbend
Littered with the tracks of visiting crocodiles.
"Whose place is this?" they ask. The reply,
"Where Maid Semambu lives, her breasts so
Slack they can be thrown over her shoulders."

After leaving this place, they arrived at a hilltop
Covered in bushes made yellow by the sun's rays
As they light up the world. Here Maid Lulong
Lives, her nudity concealed behind flowers,
Recalling an early death on her marriage day.

How beautiful is the country of Mandai,
Haven of whirlwinds, palm groves, and snakes
Coiled around trunks consuming themselves.
Interlocked branches resound with the wind
Rushing like water over whetstones.

At last they stood on a longhouse veranda
And gazed at a mountain peak on the upper part
Of the Mandai River. Like a box for a crooked
Steel spur, it stood beside a clump of bamboo
High above waters too chilly to touch.

Afar, they saw five peaks like tufts of hair
Decorating the scabbard of an ilang sword.
Below this a river swirls, its current awash
With palm blossoms and unfathomed depths
Still awaiting measurement with one hand.

Beyond is the sea with a floating landing stage
Where a three-masted ship is safely moored.
Look at the elegant first-class cabins on board

All brightly lit and filled with numbered bunks.
Look at the brass ladder ascending either side.

This ladder is glorious, sloping up to the other
World, each precious rung diamond-studded
And brightly shining as it nears the full moon.
There one can see the Fortresses of Heaven,
Blue with gems, diamonds, and gelima stones.

How wonderful is the Sixth Stronghold of Heaven,
Walls aglitter with diamonds and chembaka stones.
How elegant is the Fifth Stronghold of Heaven
With walls made of the purest pale diamonds
That radiate light with all the power of the sun.

How lovely is the Fourth Stronghold of Heaven
Its walls lined with heaped silver dollars.
How fine is the city built on a small hill, whose
Shape resembles that of a coconut shell.
Flowers and gelima stones decorate the roofs.

How beautiful are its walls, shining like pearls.
From afar the city looks like a red hawk, near like
A horse, and closer still like a camel whose wings
Form a crown of gold. Its stately head wobbles,
Breathing forth lightning and thunder over all.

She is a dragon of a thousand eyes, ranging in
Rows down her breast and back. She is custodian
Of a wide lake filled with gold-flecked gravel.
Her house is decorated with fine carvings, its floor
Made of many steps resembling the folds in a turban.

Among these splendid views of the Mandai River
Grandfather sat by his parents on the veranda
And cried, "I have forgotten my country far below,
The vault of heaven watched over by stars
Twinkling at night. This is my everlasting home."

And I, the singer, must quit this place and return
Alive to where the moon is my door in life. I
Descend the ladder of the Dark Prince's longhouse

And make my way to the boat. I take leave
Of the Spirit of Storms whose abode is the summit.

All the words I have uttered come back to reside
In the enclosure of my ribs, in the dark space
Of my lungs. Every day I visit the country of the
Departed, high on the Mandai River. Let me
Remain healthy, uplifted to Mount Rabong.

Let me live to a great age as wide as the water,
My understanding remain as broad as the earth.
Do not wave cocks of bland colors over me
But one of red and white plumage, or a cock
Of red and green with wings of purest crystal.

At the conclusion of his performance Sumbeng lowered his head while Patrick poured him a brandy. His hand trembled as he raised the glass to his lips. About him his storyboards lay like abandoned platters of words. He was exhausted by his efforts. Voyaging along the Mandai River in the company of dead souls had rendered him speechless.

I felt that I, too, had made this voyage in the Dark Prince's longboat to the Land of the Dead. The omen birds had beckoned me, sweet sirens all of them, dressed as they were in the garb of beautiful young women. At every stage of the journey I had been enthralled. The Elysian fields of the upper Mandai were home to a secret tribe of dreamers. For they were dream people inhabiting a dream landscape. And I had entered a dream region where language and nature were intertwined.

"Sumbeng has spoken," Patrick said.

"I am most grateful," I replied. "I feel as if the Earth Door has opened to receive me as well."

Patrick nodded.

"It is a forest world. This is why we must listen to all that lives there," he said.

"The Mandai River is a spirit world, too," I countered.

"Is not the forest around us a spirit world also?" Patrick asked. "Do we not walk in Sengalang Burong's domain each time we take to the path?"

I sipped my brandy.

"Patrick," I said. "You have mentioned the omen birds. When will I meet with them?"

"You have made the voyage to Mandai and beyond. This is good. I think now is the time," the old man replied.

"Who will introduce me to them?"

"Why, Aki, of course. He is our *tuai burong*."

I was dumbfounded.

"I've been a guest in Aki's *bilek* without knowing that he was an augurer?" I said.

"Aki is different from other men. Such men do not reveal themselves, except through their knowledge. They are interpreters of all that is mysterious about the forest. We know there is much that we do not understand, so we look to men like Aki to help us. Aki alone speaks the language of the birds," Patrick added.

Sumbeng made a remark in Iban that Patrick translated for me.

"Sumbeng says that for most of us the forest is our home. But for men like Aki it is different. The forest finds its home in him."

Sumbeng arranged his storyboards into small bundles and tied them together. The Mandai River had returned to his chest, to the secret region of his heart. Our dream journey to the realm of the dead had concluded and the air about us had become drained of words. We were solitary wayfarers once more. Sumbeng's storyboards, each a scrawl of wooden words, had imparted their enchantment and were now silent.

"In Iban we do not just dream," Patrick explained. "We say that we 'eat' the dream."

I understood what Patrick meant. The Iban had learned the art of nourishing themselves upon language, that winding river of words whose current managed to transport them beyond the ordinary. Their reverence for it enabled them to be drawn up into the folds of Sengalang Burong's wings. There, for a short while at least, they became companions of the gods. My privilege was to have made an excursion along this river in the company of one of nature's oracles. Perhaps soon the prospect of talking to the birds in the company of Aki, the longhouse *tuai burong*, would help complete this process of change going on in me.

EIGHT

I awoke early to the sound of people moving about in the darkness.
Sheets were thrown aside as they made their way to the *ruai*. I
looked across to where Reminda lay. She, too, was putting on her
sarong. When I asked her what was happening, she whispered,
"Jana has shot a deer in the forest."

I climbed to my feet and followed Reminda outside. Lying on
a rattan mat before us was a rusa deer, its antlers propped against
the floor. Most of the inhabitants of the longhouse were already
gathered, all chattering with excitement. Patrick crouched by Jana's
shoulder, his sleepy eyes nonetheless keenly observant as he gave
instructions to the hunters who were preparing to cut up the animal.

"Patrick is telling Jana how to share out the deer," Reminda
explained.

According to custom any animal shot in the forest must be
portioned out to all members of the longhouse. The hunters, in
this case Jana and a friend, received the rump, the head, and one
of its hind legs. Those who carried the deer back to the longhouse
from the forest also received a share. The rest of the carcass was
divided up equally among the *bileks*.

"It's our way of making sure no one goes hungry," Reminda said. "We don't often eat meat, so it's important that everyone receives a share."

"Sumbeng isn't here to receive his share," I said.

"He has been troubled of late. His wife informs me that he saw our longhouse being hit by lightning in a dream. It's a bad omen."

"In the meantime, the man refuses to eat?"

"Before he can feel himself again he will have to conduct a *piring*. This is a ceremony to cleanse the longhouse. But first, invitations must be sent to everyone who owns a *bilek*. They must come from Betong and even Sibu. This is the law of *Adat*. Everyone must be present for a *piring*. Otherwise lightning is liable to strike and cause harm to everyone in the longhouse."

I returned to the *bilek* with the intention of drifting off to sleep again. But I couldn't. Lying under the mosquito net, I found myself recalling my impressions of the men cutting up the deer. The wildness of the jungle seemed most concentrated in those moments. The deer's severed head, lying in a pool of blood, looked like a witness to its own death. I felt myself drawn into a liaison with the deer's head as I struggled to make sense of what was happening. The truth was that my voyage with Sumbeng up the Mandai River earlier that evening had unsettled me.

"You seem troubled," I heard Reminda whisper from her bed nearby.

"You didn't tell me your father was a *tuai burong*," I said.

"It's not for me to tell you of such things," replied Reminda, raising herself onto one elbow. A hint of dawn bathed her features in light.

"Our friendship should have made it possible," I argued.

"The omen birds' message can't be bartered away as we might a Chinese vase. Like you, I don't know much about these birds. Nor has my father chosen to tell me."

"How can I talk to him if he will not talk to you?"

Reminda sat up then and gazed at the emerging shapes in the forest through the opening at the rear of the *bilek*. Dawn bestowed upon her an appearance that I had not thought possible. The sow goddess in her seemed to glow.

"It's for my father to decide," she responded at last.

By lunchtime the next day it was clear that Aki had made his decision. While we sat around eating freshly cooked venison and listening to Jana tell of his exploits in the forest the night before, Aki's normally retiring demeanor seemed less in evidence. He ate more than usual. Perhaps, like my friend Jack Wailu, he had come to realize that his knowledge was in danger of being swept aside by the demands of the modern world. More than once I caught him glancing at me as if he were trying to reconcile himself to something important.

At last, when Ini and her daughter were clearing away the plates, Aki motioned me to sit by him. He asked Reminda to join us.

"This man has proved himself one of us," he said to his daughter.

"He wants to know about the omen birds, Father."

"Patrick has told me of his wishes. There is much to learn, tell him. We depend on the birds for knowledge in the way white men rely on books."

"How?" I asked.

"In the old times," Aki said. "Everyone knew the secret of writing. Then a flood came that forced people to swim for their lives. The white man put the secret of writing in his cap, so it remained dry when he reached high ground. The Malay, because he dressed the way his people do, tucked the secret into the collar of his jacket, so it was damp when he finally reached safety. The Chinese put the secret in his shirt while he was swimming, and when he reached high ground, all the letters had run. That is why it is only the Chinese who can read their writing. But the Iban, because he wore a loincloth, tucked the secret into its folds. When he reached high ground he found that the writing had become unreadable. He put it out in the sun to dry, where a flock of birds flew down and stole the secret. That is why we Iban do not write. Instead we must rely on *beburong*, the knowledge of birds, in order to live."

"I understand you rely on seven birds to help you," I said. "Reminda showed them to me in the Sarawak Museum."

"These seven birds are very like people," Aki replied. "Each bird shows qualities that we identify with ourselves. Ketupong we call *burong tengklak*, which means 'one word bird.' We say he is like a man who speaks only one word. Embuas we know as *burong sinu* or the 'pitying bird,' because he always speaks kindly. He is also known as a 'heavy bird,' because we believe he is loaded with success when it comes to our good fortune. Beragai we call *burong tampak*, meaning 'happy' or 'bright' bird. He is a laughing bird because he laughs like we do.

"Then there is Papau who we call the 'unseen bird.' We sometimes call him the 'bird of deceit' since he often blinds or deceives the enemy. He is a bird that lives in deep forest, so we rarely see him. Bejampong is known as *burong gegar*, the 'excited bird,' because he always speaks quickly. Pangkas we know as the bird 'who shouts out.' And Nendak, the last bird, his other name is *burong chelap*, the 'cool bird.' We say of Nendak that he is like someone who gives comfort and shade.

"All these birds live in Sengalang Burong's longhouse," Aki continued. "Each bird has a *bilek* next to his. Ketupong, because he was a leader of warriors in the old days, lives next to Sengalang Burong. Then comes Beragai, Embuas, Pangkas, Bejampong, Papau, and Nendak. But Nendak is a poor bird, so his *bilek* is very small. Not like the other birds."

"Which means he is less important?" I asked.

"Nendak is a cool bird, so it is unlikely that he will augur bad things," Aki said. "This means he has no depth to his character. If I hear his call before I decide to burn off my field, I will know that the fire will not be very hot. I also know that my crop will not be affected. Nendak does not like to hurt anyone."

"How do these birds become meaningful?"

"There are two types of bird omens, Aki informed me. The birds we see unexpectedly are known as a *burong laba*, or 'stroke of luck' birds. These are not often encountered, and are considered to be lucky. Mostly Nendak is one of these. The birds that we deliberately seek out we call *burong jeritan*, and they include the other six that I have spoken of."

"When do you seek them out?"

"In the morning, before we begin work in the fields. This is the best time. It is important to know what they want us to do. We watch how they fly, and how many birdcalls they make. When a bird flies from right to left, it is known as *mimpin*. This is a strong omen for us. But if a bird flies from left to right, we call this *raup*. This is a weaker sign. If the bird flies in the same direction as ourselves, we consider it to be a good sign. When it flies in the opposite direction we know it is bad."

"And if the bird happens to fly both ways?" I inquired.

Aki revealed one of his rare flashes of humor, a demure glance implying that he was aware of the irony of his next remark.

"We call this *mimpin raup*, which means that the bird lacks confidence in itself. We say that it feels shame, and is not sure of its message. What we look for is a *burong laba nganjong*—an omen bird that entrusts its knowledge to us. If it travels with us along the path, or leaves the field the same way it came, this means that the bird is escorting us. We believe its omen to be good. If Ketupong happens to fly across my path while I am sharpening my knife, I know this to be a good omen as well. I must thank Ketupong for the trust he has shown in me, so I make seven offerings in his honor. The first food offering I bury in the field. The second I toss in the river. The third I place on the boundary of my field. The next three I place in baskets and suspend on bamboo poles. And the final one I place in a bamboo post that has been split at the top to make a petal shape."

"What does an offering consist of?" I asked.

"White rice, black rice, cooked red rice, bananas, eggs, and tobacco mostly," Aki said. "These are considered to be the favorite foods of omen birds. If a bad omen has been noticed—say, Beragai is seen flying backwards along the track—then work must stop for a day or two while we prepare the offerings. Sometimes I am asked by a farmer to come to his field and deal with a bad omen. We call this *makai burong*, which means that I must 'eat the omen.' By placing charms in a bowl of water along with leaves from the farmer's field, I am able to make the omen tasteless. Work can begin again in the field as soon as I say that all is well."

"Do you say any prayers?"

"During the *puda* ritual, which happens at this time, I always talk to the gods," Aki said, breaking into an incantation for my benefit:

> O hoi! O hoi! O hoi!
> What is it I hear, the pounding of a tuba root?
> What is it I hear, the swish of a net cast on water?
> What is it I hear, the call of a pheasant?
> What is it I hear, the squawk of a hornbill?
> What is it that scratches the slopes where
>   the gamebirds rest?

What is it I hear, the rattling of a porcupine?
Who is it that calls like a man?
It is my call.
I call because I have been summoned
To send forth an invitation from the farm owner.

"Does a prayer like this always work?" I asked.

"As you know, we Iban believe in the power of words," replied Aki. "When I sing a song like this one, I am singing as the gods might if they were to speak directly to us."

"How can you be sure the gods are listening?"

"What I sing about, the gods revealed to the Iban at the beginning of time. I do not make up the prayers. This is not possible. Words such as these we call *leki sampi*, which means that they are words handed down to us from the spirit world."

Aki's dissertation on the lore of omen birds was stamped with all the authority of a true *tuai burong*. I could see now why he had appeared so guarded in our initial encounters. All his actions were reminiscent of the birds he interpreted. Shy creatures, their knowledge was unlikely to be revealed merely to satisfy my idle curiosity.

"If you wish," Aki added, "you may join me at dawn tomorrow. I will show you how augury is done."

"Is there anything special I should do to prepare myself?"

"Tonight we must not eat, otherwise the birds may not be hungry in the morning. They must be hungry if they are to sing. Do not wash yourself either, as you may cause the birds to get wet and so fall ill," Aki responded.

That night I lay on my mat in the *bilek* and pondered what the morning might bring. Reminda lay nearby, the sound of her breathing barely perceptible above the rest. Feasting on venison at lunch earlier that day had left us all feeling drowsy. Jana, I know, had drunk one too many glasses of *tuak* in celebration of his hunting prowess.

Aki's explanation of the role of omen birds had clarified one thing for me, though. Their language was the language of signs, the interplay of call and flight. A man needed eyes and ears that were attuned to the way these birds rendered their message, otherwise he would not be able to interpret what they had to say. I liked the idea of birds acting as omen bearers. Their freedom, after all, was derived from the life of the forest. The biology of place had been distilled into their very essence, and they carried within themselves a wisdom as liberating as flight itself. Aki had introduced me to a way of recognizing how an individual species might embody the fulsomeness of character over and above its normal bird traits. If an omen bird was able to entrust its knowledge to men like Aki, then it was incumbent upon me to listen closely when my time came to hear their message.

It seemed that I had traveled a long way from my first contact with these omen birds in the Sarawak Museum. To equate their spiritual qualities with their individual genus I now realized was to miss the point. Aki did not see Ketupong, Embuas, or Bejampong and their companions as a typical piculet, kingfisher, or crested jay; of this I was certain. In the true sense he was a seer capable of divining the inner workings of nature. He regarded them as mediums only.

Before dawn Reminda awakened me. Aki was already dressed in his sarong. Together the three of us slipped from the longhouse and made our way inland toward the paddy fields. Although I had visited them many times before, on this occasion I felt that all was not the same. Normally I might have walked along the pathway surrounded by impressions of no particular importance. But now I was aware that something was indeed "in the air."

Presently we arrived at a stretch of country bordering a stand of old jungle trees. An eerie silence permeated the upper layers, and one could feel their dampness. Spiderwebs glittered on the pathway in the morning light. Meanwhile, Aki stopped in front of us in order to collect a number of small sticks from the undergrowth.

"These are *paung burong* or bird omen-sticks," he explained. "We choose sticks that do not ooze sap or contain rubber."

"How do you use them?" I asked.

"In time you will see. Come."

We continued on our way until we reached a shelter built of thatch set back from the pathway. Aki motioned us to follow him as we made our way inside. When we had found a place to sit Aki continued his explanation.

"Augury depends on four things. First, you must consider where the call comes from. Next, you must recognize the birdcall and consider it in relation to others you might hear. Then, as I said before, care must be taken to see from what direction the bird is flying, and how it crosses your path."

"An omen bird can be interpreted differently, depending on individual circumstances?" I asked.

"This is correct. An elderly farmer never wishes to hear Ketupong at the beginning of the season as he knows this will bring with it difficulties for his family. But a young farmer looks forward to hearing the cry of Ketupong as he knows this means good fortune. If a poor farmer hears Pangkas while he is cutting down trees, this is a good omen. But if a wealthy farmer hears Pangkas while he is doing the same, he sees this as a bad omen."

"The birds work in mysterious ways, it seems. It must make your job very difficult," I said.

"What nature wishes from each of us requires vigilance on our part," Aki admitted. "We must learn to listen with more than our ears and eyes. We must learn to listen with our hearts."

By now the morning light was gathering outside. Reminda and I watched Aki prepare his omen-sticks on the ground. His frail, introspective body, so still and yet so much in accord with the air of seriousness that he always managed to convey, was as implacable as stone.

"We must be patient," he said. "It may be that no omen bird will appear today."

"Is there any special omen you hope to hear?" I asked.

"We have two forms of augury. The first we associate with the clearing of rice fields and the conduct of the planting season. This is known as *burong kena manggol*. The second, which is the one we wait for this morning, is known as *burong rama*. It is associated with everyday events such as hunting or fishing."

"Is every detail of your life linked to the omens?"

"All that a man thinks or does is capable of being interpreted by the omen birds," Aki replied. "We Iban are not so smart that we are able to conceal our motives from their gaze."

"Can they foretell death?"

"Of course. Embuas we often call the mourning bird. If he happens to fly into a *bilek* and then sits on your shoulder, this means that someone close to you will die. If he lands on the perch where your chickens sleep at night, this means that your family will live a good life."

"And if you hear two birds calling at the same time?"

"This sometimes occurs with Embuas birds when they call to one another. We regard their omen as *burong surong api*, which means the 'omen of handing fire to one another.' Such an omen signifies that you will have good fortune in hunting.

"If a young man plans to make his *bejalai*," Aki continued, "it is fortunate when he hears Nendak on the left hand side of the track call twice, and then twice more, followed by three calls on the right, and then by five more. He knows his journey will be a lucky one if he hears Nendak call to him in this way.

"Also, we believe that you must be engaged in work of some kind for the *beburong* to be at its strongest. A man who does nothing finds that the birds will not care for him. Birds only talk to those who wish to listen."

Aki's fluency in these matters struck me as being of a very high order indeed. The lore of the omen birds was as integral to the communication between man and nature than anything I had heard before. Nor was he ever at a loss for the right words to explain what he meant. It was as if the omen birds had imparted to him their "coolness," their singular authority. Aki was less a farmer, husband, father, or brother than someone who seemed to enjoy the freedom of the birds themselves. I doubted whether he had ever considered his destiny as other than the interpreter of omen birds.

Meanwhile Aki rearranged his omen-sticks as he waited patiently for the call of a bird. Reminda and I gazed at the forest before us, not knowing what to expect. Still, Aki's remark about being involved in some activity troubled me.

"Aki," I said. "What are we doing that is so important right now?"

Aki turned and looked at me. It was a question he had anticipated.

"I have recently completed seven days of clearing in my field," he said. "This is the time to seek the advice of birds. As you've heard, Sumbeng has had a bad dream about our longhouse. The birds may wish to remark on this as well."

"Will the birds comment on my situation?"

"It is possible. You have journeyed among us to seek knowledge. This is an important activity that my people accept as a part of *bejalai*. The birds may wish to advise you on the success of your future endeavors."

"Shh. I hear a birdcall," Reminda whispered.

We stopped talking. Aki craned forward. A bird called on three distinct occasions off to our right. Immediately Aki picked up three omen-sticks, broke them to the right, then pressed them into the ground near his knee. Again the bird called, nearer to us, its presence more inclined to our left. Aki broke another omen-stick, this time angled to the left, and inserted it in the ground. Then there was silence.

"It was Papau calling," Aki murmured. "He is the unseen bird."

"The bird of deceit," I recalled.

"He is good for us today. He tells me that he has blinded the eyes of the animals and insects that might otherwise have invaded my paddy fields. He is also warning me not to leave my tools in the field after the time of plowing. Otherwise the harvest will be in danger from a plague of insects."

"Why do you plant the omen-sticks in the ground?"

"Sometimes there may be many calls coming together. Breaking the omen-stick to right or left helps me to remember the different calls, so that later I can interpret their message."

After a short interval we heard another bird call as it flew from right to left.

"That was Bejampong," Aki informed us. "You can tell it was him by the excited tone of his voice."

"What did he say?" Reminda asked her father.

"His omen was good," Aki said. "Provided we go ahead and observe the *piring* festival with due care, then our longhouse will not come to any harm. Sumbeng's dream was a warning to us. Bejampong is telling us that we must pay more attention to the rituals."

"Bejampong is not talking to me, perhaps?" I ventured, wondering how Aki could determine which birdcall was linked to each separate event or person.

"You must await the call of Ketupong," Aki replied.

"And if he chooses not to cry out?"

"You will have to be patient," he insisted.

We continued to sit in the shade of the pavilion listening to the sounds of the forest. Many birds entered into the morning chorus that Aki appeared not to notice. They were not omen birds. He was listening for a call that told him that he was in communication with *beburong*, the ringing pronouncements of omen birds.

Eventually there was silence. The birds of the forest had gone off to gather food, leaving us to our thoughts. Aki got up to go. I could sense that he was disappointed—as I was. No bird had come to pronounce on my destiny as we had hoped.

"This is not your day," Aki said.

"The birds don't want to talk to me," I responded.

"The omen birds belong to all men. They do not withhold their message unless a man does not believe in them."

"Perhaps they were shy this morning," I said as we walked back along the pathway toward the river.

"Or you may be an unbeliever," Aki replied.

I glanced at Aki. He did not seem in the least perturbed by his remark. It was a statement of fact as far as he was concerned. How I dealt with it was my own business, not his. The truth was he had discerned how difficult it might be for the omen birds to pronounce on the destiny of someone who had forsaken nature's comforting embrace.

Just then we heard a single, sharp call up ahead. It was hard to tell whether it came from our right or left. Aki motioned us to stop in the hope that the bird might call again. We stood on the path, surrounded by tall trees and the silence of the rainforest. The call came again, this time moving away from us.

"That was Ketupong calling," Aki said. "He has not forgotten you."

I sighed with relief.

"What does he say?"

"His omen suggests that you must follow the straight path. But because his call comes from neither right nor left, it means that you are still afflicted by uncertainty. Ketupong is the warrior bird. He is telling you to be more courageous in your endeavors."

"What more can I do?"

"Ketupong cannot tell you what to do. He is an omen bird, not a guide. He only echoes Sengalang Burong's concern. This is all he can do. The rest he leaves up to you."

At Aki's instigation Ketupong had spoken. I was relieved. To have ventured into the forest and not been noticed would have made me feel even more estranged than I already was. I had not come all this way not to realize the consequences of such an event if it occurred. Aki, the silent one, the man whose oracular talent had been concealed from me until the very last, in the end it was he who had managed to come to my rescue. He had taught me to listen to the sounds of the forest in a mood of deep and abiding reverence. He had taught me to respect the call of birds as the secret language of the spirits. Sengalang Burong and his longhouse company of omen birds no longer struck me as creatures of the imagination. I now considered them to be far more substantial. They were nature's emissaries, sounding forth with their messages or concern and the need for right action. In future, as Aki suggested, perhaps I would have to be more courageous than I had been so far. And I needed to learn how to believe.

I gazed at Aki with new admiration. Here was a man who maintained contact with the spirits using an ancient and time-honored method of augury. He had made me realize how little I was aware of the way nature chose to communicate its message. Birds were as significant as books, the telephone, or a lecture as a method of transmitting knowledge. The call of an omen bird contained as much information as any how-to guidebook. What I had not known, until Aki had called upon Ketupong to make his statement on my behalf, was that I was relying too much on material forms of communication and forgetting those of gesture, song, or birdcall. I was only thankful that the *tuai burong* of Genswai Longhouse had interceded for me.

When we returned to the longhouse later that morning we found that things had changed rather dramatically in our absence. The inhabitants of the longhouse had decided to act upon Sumbeng's dream. Boats were arriving from downriver with people I had never met before; the *ruai* floor had been swept clean and new mats laid out; flowers and quantities of food had been gathered in preparation for a feast. An air of festivity pervaded the longhouse.

"People are gathering for the *piring*," Reminda observed. "You are fortunate. Such events do not happen often."

Ini informed us that Patrick had decided to call the *piring* for that afternoon. Many people had already arrived from Betong and Sibu. Much work had to be done in a very short time to prepare food. Rice wine was produced. By midafternoon people were beginning to assemble on the *ruai* outside Sumbeng's *bilek*. Inside the circle plates of cooked rice, cake, vegetables, fruit, strips of cane, even flowers had been laid out by the women. Bottles of *tuak* passed from hand to hand as the menfolk drank and chatted.

Then Patrick called for order. In a long speech he detailed the concerns raised by Sumbeng's dream in relation to the well-being of their longhouse. It was not often, he said, that such a wise man as Sumbeng should encounter a bad dream. Therefore it was important that they all regarded the omen with gravity. Patrick then went on to enlarge upon the reasons he believed were behind Sumbeng's dream. He had noted the young people wearing jeans they had purchased in Betong. He had also heard rumors that some members of the longhouse wanted a generator installed so that they might have electric light, perhaps even television. These demands, he believed, threatened their traditional independence. Where would their desires stop, he asked them. Next they would require regular visits from the doctor in Betong, thus making it impossible for their own *manang* to practice his craft. In conclusion, Patrick asked others if they might wish to comment on Sumbeng's dream.

Those who felt Patrick's criticisms were leveled at them hung their heads in silence. Finally, after a number of others had voiced their opinions, Patrick asked Sumbeng to begin chanting. The old man began portioning the food into small offerings that he placed on a plate before him. The rest of the company followed his example. Then he opened his lungs and sang:

> *Oha! Oha! Oha!*
> *I call upon the spirits,*
> *The spirits of my grandparents*
> *And my parents—from the graveyards,*
> *From the deathtraps and coffins.*
> *I celebrate with you these rites today,*
> *I ask for your ritual help and assistance.*
> *This I implore, assist at my altar*
> *Pulang Gana, Serong Gunting,*
> *Raja Petara, Sengalang Burong,*
> *Protect us from the lightning*
> *Which threatens our longhouse.*
>
> *Whoever of you (with ill intent)*
> *Can raise the point of his nose,*
> *Can speak with the tip of his tongue,*
> *Can talk from the side of his mouth,*
> *Can curse below the jaw—*

Of evil heart or evil hand,
Pass this longhouse, its wide river
And gardens—pass the rice
The sweet rice, and be broken
By our tuak *brew, killed*
By the headiness of our rice beer
And crushed by our rice cakes,
Follow the sun setting, the sun
As it sinks below the horizon.
Follow the sun dying, the sun
As it dies each night.
Follow the sun into burial,
The sun into darkness.

This I ask of you in the name
Of the omen birds, who watch
Over this longhouse, this home
Of busy farmers and hunters,
Caring wives and mothers.

Sumbeng's words were filled with a kind of majesty as he called upon the spirits to hear his entreaty on behalf of everyone in the longhouse. His dream was an echo of their dreams; his concerns were theirs also. Around the circle the men carefully dropped offerings onto their plates, while one man walked along the *ruai* sprinkling water on all the *bilek* doors.

Patrick rose to his feet, grasped a cock that was passed to him by someone in the crowd, then held it forth so that its comb might be cut. Blood immediately spurted from the wound. He proceeded to walk around the inner circle, allowing blood to fall on each of the offerings. As he passed I felt newly spilt blood warm on my cheek.

"It is a sign for us to leave," Reminda whispered, taking me by the arm.

"But the *piring* isn't over yet," I said.

"We cannot stay to the end, unless you wish to remain here for some days. The longhouse must be sealed off from the world so that it may be made clean. If we leave now we will not endanger the outcome. This is the way of *piring*," Reminda added.

I looked about me at the faces of the men and women I had come to know and respect. They glanced at me with affection, even though I was a stranger to them. The Mandai River beckoned. The solitude of the rainforest with its green life encircled them. While the call of the omen birds drew them back into their world, far from my own. For they had unlocked the secret to the language of the birds and made it theirs.

Reluctantly I climbed to my feet. Patrick noticed me withdrawing, and nodded. His wry smile informed me that he approved of my departure. It seemed strange not to be saying goodbye. Patrick, Sumbeng, Jana, Lundak, Ini, and Aki—they had all shown me the way to the very heart of Iban life. Ketupong had been right: Perhaps I did not know how to recognize the straight path. Perhaps I had yet to learn fully what it was that made a person believe in birds as omen-bearers, as true spiritual entities, and listen to their advice.

Later, walking with Reminda to our longboat for the trip downriver to Betong, I noticed the deer's antler hanging in the sun to dry. For the first time I realized that this deer represented my fugitive self, the self that Ketupong had killed off with the sound of his voice, with his intimation of celestial guidance. Whether I had the courage to overcome the condition of *mimpin raup*, or lack of confidence, and set my mind to heeding his entreaty was another matter. But one thing I did know: I had finally understood what it was like to commune with nature, if only in the measured strophes of a bird at dawn.

"What will you do now?" Reminda asked when we had set off in the longboat.

"Try to remember what Ketupong said to me today, I suppose." Reminda laughed.

"Be more courageous, you mean? I'm not sure I translated exactly what my father meant," she added.

"The truth can never be translated exactly," I said.

"Your visit has helped me, too. For that I must thank you," Reminda said.

"In what way?"

"I see my father through different eyes. Patrick and Sumbeng as well. They really are men of knowledge. When they tell their stories, it is as though they were revealing the history of us all. You made this possible."

"The mountain of Rabong Raminang in Kalimantan is where it all began for your people," I said. "The forest is your sacred book."

"That's true," Reminda remarked, dangling her fingers in the waters so that new ripples began to spread out from the longboat. "The omen birds are like your saints. They give us hope. They are what we look to when we need guidance."

"All people need guidance at some point in their lives. Your people turn to the omen birds, other people turn to prayer. The important thing is we must learn to acknowledge that we're not alone."

Reminda half-turned to look at me.

"This is exactly what *bejalai* teaches us," she said. "Visiting new places means that we learn to see beyond the treetops. Being with you has helped me to climb above them."

"Maybe even to learn how to fly," I added, knowing that Sengalang Burong had finally decided to roost in me.

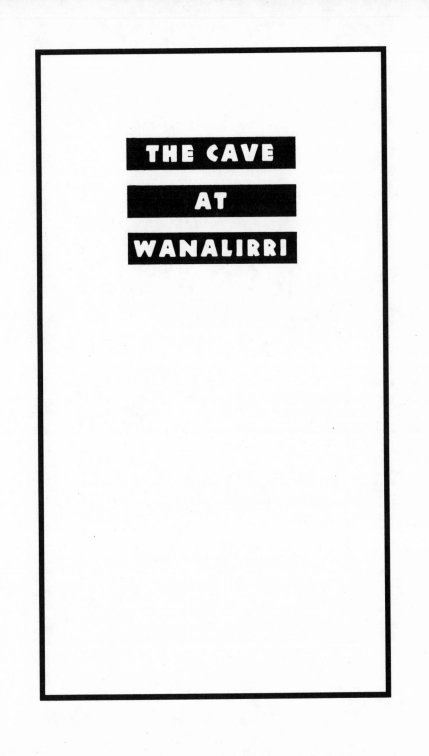

THE CAVE AT WANALIRRI

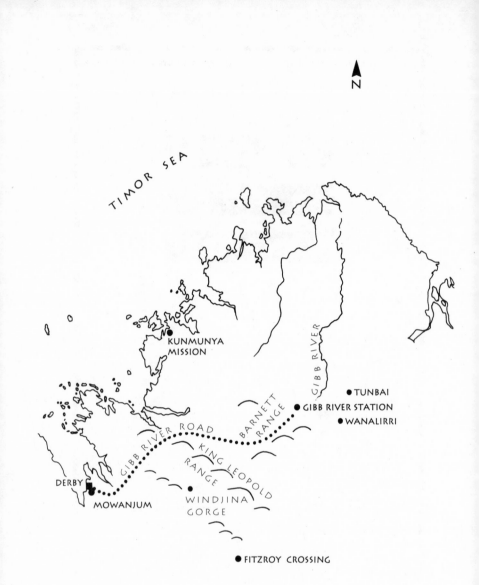

N

TIMOR SEA

KUNMUNYA
MISSION

GIBB RIVER

TUNBAI

GIBB RIVER STATION

WANALIRRI

GIBB RIVER ROAD

BARNETT RANGE

KING LEOPOLD RANGE

DERBY

MOWANJUM

WINDJINA
GORGE

FITZROY CROSSING

WESTERN AUSTRALIA

NINE

It is almost impossible to look at landscape in the context of myth. To see a hill or a rock pool as the incarnation of the Rainbow Snake, it is necessary to identify with nature in a way that is entirely unfamiliar to us. Yet in spite of this the Aborigines of Australia see their land with the utmost clarity, not so much as a natural phenomenon but as a supernatural entity existing within its own fullness. This world they call the *Lalan*, or Dreaming.

Flying in over the Kimberley region of Northwest Australia made me realize how different this continent is from others I have visited during my travels. The dry riverbeds, the scrubby hills and valleys, the deserted beaches along the coast, and the scoriated bluffs farther inland reminded me of the ravaged details of a man's face. As if slumbering on a balcony in the sun, its archaic visage remained upturned and expressionless. The Kimberley landscape appeared to be a region founded on dreams and visions. It can be understood only through the eyes of its original inhabitants, the men and women who lived by the law of the Wandjinas, those sacred spirit beings unique to this part of the world.

My first encounter with the Wandjina figures was among the

pages of the journal of George Grey, a British explorer who set himself the task of journeying on horseback through the Kimberley in 1838. He had been intent on discovering new grazing country that might encourage further colonization by adventurous overlanders interested in founding cattle stations of their own. Those were the days when Australia seemed like one vast emptiness, a frontier paradise, unpeopled except for a few benighted Aborigines who were considered to be barely human anyway. What lay within the purview of these explorers was a pristine landscape ripe for the taking. King and Country were the perfect insignia of possession. The real owners of the land were considered to be no more than interlopers.

That year, on an extremely hot morning in March, Grey and his party found themselves looking for a route through a range of rugged hills. Below them lay a fertile valley into which they were eager to descend. Rather than retrace their steps, Grey decided to scout ahead in the hope of discovering a way down. While returning to his party, he happened to notice the remains of native fires at the foot of some sandstone rocks. He resolved to investigate the area more closely and so made his way to the base of these cliffs. It was then, as he later related, that he "suddenly saw from one of them a most extraordinary large figure peering down at me. Upon examination, this proved to be a drawing at the entrance to a cave, which, entering, I found to contain, besides, many remarkable paintings."

What he saw was a group of Wandjinas painted in ochre and pipe clay on the rockface. Of course, he had no way of knowing what they were. He went on to record his observations in the prosaic language of the day. "I was certainly rather surprised at the moment that I first saw this gigantic head and upper part of a body [referring to the principal figure] bending over and staring grimly down at me." Furthermore, it was "impossible to convey in words an adequate idea of this uncouth and savage figure." Grey was left with no other recourse than to measure the images on the roof of the cave and note these down in his diary. He did, however, allow himself to compare the Wandjina's head, encircled as it was by "bright red rays," to "something like the rays which one sees proceeding from the sun when depicted on the signboard of a public house." It was evident that George Grey did not experience any profound feeling of religious awe in the presence of these spirit beings that day.

True to his vocation as explorer and observer, Grey spent the rest of the morning recording all that he saw. He drew pictures of the Wandjinas as best he could, detailing their large eyes, their nimbus and disembodied cloudlike body, together with what a later commentator regarded as indecipherable script etched into the nimbus itself. What Grey's sketches revealed, and what he alluded to in passing, was that these spirit figures did not possess mouths. Muteness was implicit in their gaze, a condition that the American poet Ezra Pound later sought to highlight in one of his Cantos when he likened the Wandjina to the embodiment of the "verbal perfection" known to be an attribute of the Paraclete. It was an idea that Pound may have inadvertently picked up from a reading of Virgil's *Aeneid*, where the inhabitants of the Underworld were said to forever hold their silence.

More than one hundred years passed before another Englishman set out on an expedition in pursuit of Grey's celebrated Wandjinas. Harvey Rouse, a jack-of-all-trades as well as part-time missionary among the Aborigines of the Kimberley, organized a donkey train into the region in an effort to rediscover the lost paintings. He was under the patronage of a well-known anthropologist of the day who provided him with the funds to make the journey. Because of his missionary activity, Rouse had taken the trouble to learn many of the languages spoken by the local tribes, so he was able to gain the cooperation of tribesmen in the region. He was also able to question them about the meaning of the Wandjina in the event that he stumbled upon them in his travels.

His Aboriginal guides led Rouse into a remote and inhospitable region inland from Walcott Inlet. Running low on rations, and some fifty miles from his headquarters, he nonetheless managed to push on to a saddle in a sandstone ridge, which he deduced from Grey's map was the likely location of the Wandjina cave. His guides knew of the cave but had no way of knowing which cave Grey had spoken of, since Grey's verbal description of the terrain in no way conformed to their perception of the region. To them it was not "remote and inhospitable" but a land profoundly imbued with spiritual values that could only be invoked by *kurara*, a term denoting the ability to "talk to the land." Fortunately for Rouse, his guides were able to "talk to the land" on his behalf and ascertain the location of the Wandjina cave he was looking for. Early in May 1947 he entered a natural hollow in the sandstone rocks and gazed for the first time at the sacred Wandjina of the Worora and Naringin peoples. He had rediscovered the mouthless spirit figures in their ancient sanctuary, a place long conjectured upon by scholars who had analyzed Grey's descriptions from the security of their studies.

My initial contact with the Wandjinas in Grey's pages had fired my enthusiasm to venture into their country. A few discreet inquiries soon confirmed that Mr. Rouse was probably still alive and living in Derby on the edge of the Kimberley. Finding him might well prove to be my first step if I were to gain access to the sanctuaries of these Wandjinas. Hoping to enter into a dialogue, a *kurara* so to speak, with the sacred land over which they presided, I had set myself the task of becoming a *kumarre*—that is, someone who belongs to the land—not a *kamaliwany*, or stranger.

Furthermore, I was fascinated with the prospect of coming into contact with a living paleolithic tradition. Ever since their discovery, the cave paintings and sculpture of Lascaux and Altamira have given rise to more questions than they have answers. Scholars have argued various hypotheses as to the likely reason for the painting of these mysterious tableaux by our forebears. But these have always been determined by minds in league with our time, not by those who performed their ritual acts of creation in the first place. The paleolithic vision has escaped us principally because we no longer know how to think in a preliterate way, nor do we take the trouble to discuss such issues with those people who might possess this vision today.

In Australia this tradition is still alive. Aboriginal men and women still perform secret rituals associated with their veneration of the Sky Heroes of the Dreaming. These cult heroes take the form of spirit beings whose shape and dimension resembles various species on earth. Marlu the Great Kangaroo or Maletji the Law Dog, Ungud the Rainbow Snake or the mouthless Wandjinas—all of them are celestial beings whose origins lie in the Dreaming. They are world creators and lawgivers, each a spirit being of a particularly luminous splendor whom all Aborigines revere through the enactment of secret rites, songs, and totemic dances. The Sky Heroes are not gods as such, but celestial entities capable of acting as companions and guides.

To understand their role one must first understand the essential nature of the Dreaming. Before time had been conceived, the Aborigines believed that the world was without form. To some it was *njidding*, or "cold"; to others the earth was merely "soft." It required a mighty act, a Seven Days of Creation in order that the world might become fit for life. This act was performed at the time of the Dreaming, that primordial moment when the earth was given its current form. To the Aborigines, the Sky Heroes made the earth. They emerged from below the surface and created the landforms, the mountains, the river systems, and all the species that walk upon it. When they had completed their act of creation they changed into the landmarks they had created. In so doing, they ensured that the earth became one vast memorial to themselves. No longer was it composed of rock, sand, soil, and minerals as such, but of their everlasting mythic presence.

The Dreaming represents a supernatural occurrence "before time," yet in contrast it is still happening today. Aborigines make no distinction between the world-creative moment of the Sky Heroes and their presence in the landscape right now. The Aborigines believe they are part of the Dreaming; or, if not, their ancestral home after death is the Dreaming. Life is a cyclic event not a continuum. A man is born as a result of a visionary event, a dream, and his spirit is destined to return to the reservoir of Spirit when he dies. His presence on earth is thus more a completion of the Dreaming event itself since his presence in life fulfills a part of the Dreaming cycle that he so reveres.

The Wandjinas of the Kimberley region were still living entities as far as I knew. They were not visual artifacts reflecting an age past, but the iconic presence of the Sky Heroes themselves. To enter their sphere meant that I would have the opportunity of engaging in a conversation with my own origins. After my voyage through mythic time on the back of Gelem and my encounter with the bird realm of Sengalang Burong, the prospect of coming face-to-face with the proto-visage of a divine being as it exists outside time filled me with anticipation. The sea and the forest had yielded up some of their secrets to me; now it was time for the earth to teach me a little more.

The outback town of Derby was a fitting place to begin my inquiries. Located on a peninsular jutting into King Sound, once the

largest pearling ground in the world, Derby seemed like a throw-
back to a more leisurely age. Its wide streets graced with baobabs
reflected a time when overlanders herded cattle along the main
thoroughfare to the finger wharf on the peninsula. Here they were
loaded aboard ships and transported to the abattoirs down south.
The Kimberley has always been regarded as prime cattle country,
and the great property-owning families that founded their agrarian
empires here in the last century are an intrinsic part of Australian
history and folklore. They came here to settle the land in the spirit
of Victorian enterprise. The fact that numerous Aboriginal tribes
had lived here for perhaps fifty thousand years prior to their arrival
was immaterial to them.

The shock of encounter between these two cultures was characterized by tribal massacres, human exploitation, and the progressive
encroachment by white people upon tribal lands. Government decrees were proclaimed through the barrel of a gun, and any
Aborigine caught spearing stock was liable to be shot on sight. The
supremacist attitudes of the colonizers had already been expressed
by George Grey on his 1838 expedition when he meditated, "I sat
in the fading light, looking at the beautiful scenery about me,
which now for the first time gladdened the eyes of Europeans; and
I wondered that so fair a land should only be the abode of savage
men whose anomalous position in so fertile a country cannot be
denied." Subsequent visitors concurred with Grey's observations,
and set about eliminating the Aborigines from the Kimberley region
altogether.

The Aboriginal hostel where I stayed provided me with my first
contact with Kimberley tribespeople, who often stayed here when
they came to town. Slenderly built, and possessing a diffident
grace, they appeared to be at ease whenever they walked across the
intervening lawn between the sleeping block and the canteen. I
was reminded of certain wild creatures that have long ago come to
terms with their environment, so shy and unforthcoming were they
when first approached. It was as if they were surrounded by an
invisible substance that protected them. In spite of the hardship
and oppression they had suffered in the past one hundred years,
these tribespeople still managed to retain strong links with their
culture and tradition. Such links with the past have enabled them
to survive to this day, it seemed.

Finding Harvey Rouse was at the top of my agenda. Unfortunately the telephone directory yielded nothing in the way of his address. When I approached the local librarian, however, she informed me that Mr. Rouse, though elderly, was indeed very much alive.

"He lives some way out of town on an industrial site," she informed me. "I believe he's the caretaker there."

"Does he comes to town much?"

"Oh, yes. He pops in here quite often. He's always researching something to do with Aboriginal culture. He's quite an eccentric, really. Last time I heard, he was translating the Bible into the Naringin language."

A Naringin Bible! The thought of Job's exploits being translated into a language older than those of the prophet himself warned me that I must approach Mr. Rouse with respect. To make the contents of the Bible available to no more than a thousand or so tribespeople was a singular act in itself. Such dedication reminded me of the work of medieval scribes who spent their lives copying obscure texts. Once a missionary, explorer, and now a translator, Mr. Rouse was clearly equipped to interpret the dream of Nebuchadnezzar for an illiterate minority. I only hoped that the significance of the Wandjina might prove to be no less elusive for me when I finally met up with him.

"You're in luck today," the librarian remarked, peering through the doorway into the wide, sunlit street beyond. "There's Mr. Rouse now. I see his vehicle pulling up outside."

Harvey Rouse was a small, wiry sort of man whom I judged to be in his late seventies, possibly older. Wearing a bush hat that had been pushed out of shape years ago, he walked in a hurried manner that belied his age. He came toward us along the path, his shirt buttoned almost to the neck, his knobby knees protruding from a pair of faded khaki shorts. He reminded me of a gremlin or a garden gnome. It was hard to believe that he had spent most of his life working among Aborigines in some of the most remote places in the world. His mannerisms were more like those of a staff sergeant or hospital orderly than those of a scholar.

The librarian introduced me to the explorer, and we shook hands. Knowing that Mr. Rouse was the first European since George Grey to step inside a Wandjina cave made him, in my eyes at least, someone special. As an old bushman who had spent many years of his life sitting around campfires learning the Naringin language from the last of the Aboriginal elders, he was in a category all his own. I was keen to know to what extent they had shared their secrets with him.

"Why don't you come to dinner this evening and we can talk," Mr. Rouse said, generously extending the invitation when I explained the reason for my visit to Derby. He agreed to pick me up in his aging Toyota outside the hostel at around six o'clock.

Later that evening Mr. Rouse drove me to his place on the outskirts of town. I soon found myself gazing at the high wire gate guarding the entry to an earth-moving machinery site deep in the scrub. There were no lights in the place. Mr. Rouse unlocked the chain on the gate, then drove his vehicle past the shadowy bulk of front-end loaders toward a group of buildings in the far corner. The atmosphere in the yard was like that of entering a Roman ruin at night. I felt somewhat uncomfortable, especially when I learned that Mr. Rouse had been forced to live out his twilight years in three old workman's huts that he had managed to scrounge from the Department of Main Roads.

"They travel everywhere with me," Mr. Rouse remarked with some pride. "The owner of the worksite offered me the land in return for caretaking duties when I retired. So I brought my huts over here from where I was living. You must think me a regular tortoise, carrying my house around like this!"

"You don't want to live in town?"

"I like the silence out here at night. Derby is too noisy for me. This place keeps me in touch with the bush."

Inside the first hut I was introduced to a world of cobwebs, large mosquitoes, a small table cluttered with food, a bed piled high with clothing, and a fridge. The bulb above our heads threw down a vague light, nothing more. A much-thumbed copy of the Bible lay by the window among assorted manuscripts and old newspapers. I immediately realized that "dinner" was likely to be a couple of cheese sandwiches washed down with a mug of tea. Old bushmen rarely linger over food; tinned beef and damper (bread made in a camp oven from flour mixed with water) form their staple diet when they're on the move.

"Tell me about the time when you found Grey's cave," I began as Mr. Rouse extracted a slab of cheese from a packet.

"During the war, it was," he replied. "I had been working on a mission in east Naringin country for a number of years. An anthropologist friend of mine in Sydney asked me if I might like to look for Grey's cave on his behalf. It was too far for him to come over here, and anyway nobody traveled in those days because of gasoline restrictions. Of course I jumped at the chance. I always wanted to rediscover those lost Wandjina paintings. But I needed a couple of good boys to help me find the cave. In the end I asked the administrator at the mission if he would give me my pick."

Mr. Rouse laughed at the memory.

"He agreed, but on the condition that I cut wood for him for three weeks. That's how I came by my Aboriginal guides. In the end they cost me a load of wood!"

"And a few blisters, I'll bet," I said. "Did they lead you straight to the cave?"

"Not at all. I had only a hand-traced map my friend had sent me. Trying to decipher this was no easy matter. We spent weeks wandering about country hoping to find what we were looking for. Real rubbish country it was, too. The donkeys were a godsend, though. Horses would never have been able to cross that terrain. Too rough."

"You found the cave in the end, though."

"Yeah. But I tell you it was a spooky place to come upon! In all my life I've never felt so strange entering a cave. The Wandjinas on the walls were like figures from outer space. Here I was, in the presence of a group of beings looking down at me, almost as if they were interrogating me with their gaze. They had huge eyes and no mouths. I felt as if I had stumbled into a sort of living hell, like you see on church walls in Europe sometimes."

"Can you recall what color the figures were?"

"White, mostly. With black eyes surrounded by orange, ocher-colored circles. Their noses were the same color. But what made them appear really odd was a thick orange nimbus, like a horse-shoe, with rays radiating from above their heads."

"Like the rays on the signboard of a public house," I said, recalling Grey's description.

"That's about right," Mr. Rouse agreed.

"Did they have bodies?"

"Sort of, but all that wasn't very clear. They looked vaguely like ghosts, I suppose. The paintings were in pretty poor shape, you must understand. The old fellas hadn't been up there to repaint them in years."

"The Aboriginal elders, you mean?"

"Yeah. In the old days, when the tradition was strong, they used to visit the cave each year before the wet season to perform rituals and repaint the Wandjina. According to Woolagoodja, one of my guides, they prayed to them when they wanted rain. That was their way of bringing on the wet season. He was a good man, old Woolly. He knew his stuff really well."

"Did he sing any songs while you were there?"

"Oh, yes. He repainted the Wandjina, too. With ocher and pipe clay. While he was doing this he sang a lot of songs. One of them went like this—"

Mr. Rouse paused in the act of making a sandwich. He stood under the pale light, a knife in one hand, and began to intone in flat, unmodulated voice: "Because you are looking so dull—you're not looking bright—I'll try and draw you. I'll try and put new paint on you people to make you new again. Please don't get wild and don't send rain! You must be very glad that I'm going to make you new again."

"When he finished repainting the Wandjina, did he say anything else?" I asked.

"I made you very good now," Mr. Rouse went on, his voice little more than a monotone. "I don't know how I did it. Very good indeed. You must be very glad because I've made your eye like new again. Your eye like new again. Your eye, you know, like my eye. I made it new for you people. My eye has life and your eye has life too. Because I made it new.

"Something like that, anyway," Mr. Rouse added, resuming his sandwich-making with gusto.

"You said the Wandjina were responsible for rain. Yet Woolagoodja implored these figures not to make it when he sang to them," I said.

Mr. Rouse grinned. He obviously relished my attempt to catch him out.

"That's the Aboriginal way," he explained. "The Wandjinas are associated with rain clouds, with thunder and lightning. If you ask the Wandjinas directly to provide rain, they're as likely not to listen to you. They're contrary, you see. But if you tell them you *don't* want any rain to fall, then there's a good possibility they'll send it anyway, just to spite you."

"As simple as that," I said.

"Not entirely. You see, this cave was devoted to the cult of Dalimen. A number of figures on the wall were female Wandjinas who represented young girls. According to old Woolly, these girls made love with Dalimen at the time of the Dreaming. Then they drifted along to another cave farther down the valley called Dondondji, which means "drying out place." This is where the female Wandjinas washed themselves after playing around with Dalimen. Woolly later showed me Dalimen's penis sitting up on a nearby hill as a piece of rock."

"Are you telling me these Wandjina sites are associated with more than rainmaking?"

"Aborigines are always thinking about sex," Mr. Rouse replied, a note of censure in his voice. The missionary in him seemed to fill the hut with an air of stricture as he spoke.

"You don't think their stories might simply be parables?" I said, hoping to appeal to Mr. Rouse's background as a man of God.

"Aboriginal gods are all bound up with nature," Mr. Rouse said, not wishing to give too much ground. "Their stories and myths are always associated with protecting food sources or making rain. That's about all. They don't have any religious significance as we know it."

"Don't you think that sex between Wandjinas might suggest a similar wish to encourage fecundity among other things? Nature, for instance. By talking about sexual activity they're really talking about renewal."

"That's nothing but mumbo-jumbo, if you'll pardon the expression!" Mr. Rouse countered. "All these spirit beings wandering about the earth are merely randy old animals in disguise. Take it from me: Aborigines like to dress up their own cravings and merely pretend it's a religion."

"Even Ungud, the Rainbow Snake?" I asked, thinking of the great fertility snake, maker of rivers and waterholes, which Aborigines throughout Australia revere.

"Sex! It's all sex, nothing more!" the small man railed, thrusting a cheese sandwich into my hand.

I was taken aback by Mr. Rouse's tirade. I had not imagined that a man who had spent so many years among the Aborigines could have such a narrow opinion about their beliefs. He had written a number of learned articles on these, I knew, which led me to wonder why he had been inclined to help them in the first place. I finally decided that a trace of fundamentalism in his thoughts made it impossible for him to look at Aboriginal spirituality with the wise eyes of a sage.

"Perhaps there's someone else in Derby you might recommend I talk to about the Wandjina," I said, hoping to change the subject.

"Well, there's my principal informant on the Naringin language," he suggested, seemingly impervious to the implied censure of my remark. "His name is Waljali. He's what they call a sites officer here in town. Between him and his friend, old Kamurro, I reckon they know about all there is to know on the Wandjina these days. Most of the old blokes have died, you see. And the young ones know nothing. All they're interested in is grog and women, nothing more. Kamurro happens to be a sorcerer, which makes him rather special. He knows a lot about the old ways."

"He's a medicine man?"

"They call them *barnmunji* around here. I wrote a paper on them once. Hold on, let me see if I can find it for you."

Mr. Rouse went to a cabinet by the wall next to his bed and rummaged in one of the drawers. He produced a sheaf of papers at last and handed them to me. The title of the article was "The Rai and the Inner Eye."

"You can have it," he said. "I've got no use for it anymore. It could prove interesting to you if you want to know more about Aboriginal ways. Don't know why, though," he added dismissively.

Flipping quickly through the pages, I came across a Naringin text with an English translation written underneath. A few words caught my interest at once: *Wandjina djiri: ru; dambun djuman mana, yadmerinanganari.* Underneath was transcribed: "Wandjina is the important one. We say concerning him that he designed the world."

Later, when Mr. Rouse had dropped me back at the hostel, I wasted no time in beginning his article on the *rai*. It was a remarkable document, unlike any I had come across before on the subject. Not only did it ascribe the creation of the world to the Wandjina,

but it also detailed the making of a *barnmunji* with the help of
spirit beings known as the *rai*. It seemed that these *rai* had the
power to transform a man into someone capable of seeing through
the veil of ordinary reality with the aid of a so-called inner eye—
that is, a quality of spiritual perception not available to the conventional run of men.

According to the document, the *rai* are spirit children who live
in the bush and wander about at night. Men can encounter them
only in their dreams. Furthermore, a *rai* is a sort of "spirit double"
of the man, and is therefore capable of telling him how his country
is faring when the man happens to be absent from it for some
reason. According to the text, the *rai* feeds on its own arm blood
and is therefore self-sustaining. The *rai's* main task is to give a
barnmunji the power of visionary perception so that he can see
with his inner eye, aided by the use of *gedji* or quartz crystals.
These are pressed into the *barnmunji's* body in a magical fashion.
But once the crystals are lodged in his body, he is equipped with
supernatural powers that enable him to attend to the sick, perform
new corroborees (sacred dances), and travel great distances through
the air.

My first impression after reading about the *rai* was to ask myself
whether Mr. Rouse had deliberately set out to mislead me. The
concept of the *rai* seemed so preposterous that I began to wonder
whether the old man had been affected by the sun. Spirit doubles,
inserting quartz crystals into the body, vampirelike creatures that
fed on their own arm blood, astral travel—these descriptions
seemed to draw their inspiration from the shadowy realm of the
occult rather than from any bona fide religious experience. Then
I recalled the first words of the text: "Wandjina is the important
one. He made the world." Such an emphatic statement made me
reconsider my initial doubts. I decided to suspend my judgment,
at least until after I had discussed these matters with the Aboriginal
elders Mr. Rouse had referred me to.

The Mowanjum Aboriginal community outside Derby was my
first stop. Mr. Rouse had advised me to go there and meet with
Waljali and Kamurro. He did point out, however, that these men
often paid visits to their tribal country, and so might not be at
home. Such was the nature of Aboriginal life today, where many
tribes found it impossible to live in the bush now that much of

their land belonged to pastoralists. The community had been founded for displaced Aborigines who wanted a secure place to bring up their children and be near to medical facilities. The word *mowanjum* meant "settled" or "on firm ground."

I bicycled out to the settlement early one morning. A collection of galvanized-iron shelters and abandoned motor vehicles met my gaze as I rode through the gate. People wandered aimlessly from one shelter to another as they attempted to put some order into an otherwise unvarying day. Hunting and foodgathering activities had given way to weekly government pension checks for most of these tribespeople as they struggled to come to terms with their state of exile. I felt a certain sadness watching children roll bicycle rims across a clearing, knowing that in the old days they would have been out in the bush with their kinsmen learning how to hunt.

One of these children soon led me to an encampment lying in the shade of some trees. A number of women were sitting on the ground, their dogs asleep nearby. When I approached and asked where I might find Waljali or Kamurro, they fell silent. They looked at me as if I were only half there. It was the look all oppressed people offer to those whom they believe to be responsible for their plight.

Eventually an older woman in the group pointed rather diffidently to my right. I noticed a solitary figure sitting cross-legged under a tree, his head bent over some object in his lap. At no time did the woman speak. I thanked the ladies and made my way over to the man. He stopped whatever he was doing to observe my approach.

"Are you Waljali, or Kamurro?" I asked.

I estimated the man to be in his late sixties. His features were slender, rather refined in appearance. A loosely clipped beard covered his jaw, and his graying hair was swept back from his forehead to reveal partial baldness. His eyes appraised me as if I were standing some distance away. Though I had approached him in the spirit of friendship, I knew this man was considering his response with some caution, uncertain as to my motives.

"Maybe I'm Kamurro," the man replied, revealing his identity at last. Then he resumed carving a baobab seed pod, a popular pastime among older Aborigines who like to make money from selling their artifacts to tourist shops. Already he had etched in the outlines of a kangaroo hunt across the surface of the nut.

"Is it true that you're a *barnmunji?*" I asked tentatively.

"Who told you about me?" Kamurro's voice was edgy.

"Mr. Rouse. He said you gave him a lot of information about the *rai.*"

"That was a long time ago, when things were good 'round here. Now all we do is sit about gettin' drunk."

"But nonetheless the *rai* still exist," I ventured.

" 'Course they do," Kamurro replied gruffly, rubbing his fingers over the baobab nut.

"And they give you power to see inside a person," I added.

"Mr. Rouse, he tellin' you too much," Kamurro responded cautiously. Yet I could see my interest in the doctrine of the *rai* had aroused him more than he cared to admit.

"Is it also true that you can fly through the air?" I asked.

Kamurro glanced up at me. I was immediately struck by the change in his manner. The apathy and aggression that had marred his earlier attitude toward me had all but disappeared. Instead a look of grudging complicity had begun to appear on his face.

"I tell you: That missionary fella has been tellin' you too much," he repeated.

Feeling that my presence had been accepted at last, I sat down on the ground opposite Kamurro. Meanwhile the women were watching us from a distance. I could tell they were curious about what was happening because they sent one of their dogs over to investigate. The dog walked up, sniffed my arm, then lay down nearby.

"The women are real busybodies. They want to know what we're talkin' about," Kamurro began with a small smile on his face. "But what they don't know is this dog understands nothin' about the *rai.* The spirits are too clever for 'im."

"Tell me about these spirits," I said.

"Well, we Aboriginal people aren't much without the help of the *rai,*" the old man went on. "They're the spirit people who made us. Without them we wouldn't be in this world."

"Not even as a result of a man and woman making love?" I suggested.

"That's white-man talk. Funny business with woman doesn't account for makin' a child. Your people only see things in one way. Always thinkin' 'bout sex," he added. His remark made me recall with some irony Mr. Rouse accusing Aborigines in much the same way.

Kamurro touched his temple and continued:

"The *rai*, they enter a man in his dream because they comin' from the Wandjina. That what important. They hop into a woman's body only after that happens, and make a baby. A man got to see the *rai* in his dream first. Everythin' goes on in our head, not down here." Kamurro patted his thigh to emphasize his point.

I gathered from Kamurro's explanation that in spite of his insistence on the *rai* being spirit entities that wandered about the bush at night, they were also much more. They appeared to be linked to the Wandjina in a spiritual way that could only be invoked in a dream. Physical paternity was so ingrained in my thought, however, that the idea of a person being dreamed into existence confounded me. Yet Kamurro was insistent that the "funny business" between man and woman was incidental to conception. A person was first conceived by the spirit of the *rai* before undergoing a period of physical growth in a woman's womb.

"If the *rai* are responsible for giving everyone life and making people who they are," I replied, "why is it that there are only very few *barnmunji* like yourself around?"

"Not everyone has the right to become a doctor-man. The *rai*, they give us special powers. These powers don't belong to everyone. The *rai* see you as being important. That's why they make me *barnmunji* and not some other fella," Kamurro explained.

"How do the *rai* enter you, and make you a *barnmunji*?"

"Only when the *gedji* crystals are placed inside you. Them spirit stones belongin' to the *rai*."

"Quartz crystals, you mean?"

"*Gedji*, they come from the *rai*," Kamurro insisted. "They don't come from the ground. To become a *barnmunji* you must have your insides taken out your body and replaced with *gedji*. Then the spirit of the *rai* goin' inside you. Once they're in your body you have power, what we call *kurunba*. You become a doctor-man, an expert. The *rai* make it possible for you to see all things. When you go out hunting, you can see through the bushes and know if a kangaroo is there. You can fly, too, that's right! Doctor-men can fly like birds. They can travel under the ground, too, like a lizard. Below the earth he rumbles along just like a goanna."

"How can you actually fly?" I asked, finding this revelation a little hard to accept.

"That's a secret," Kamurro replied, not wishing to reveal too much to me. "But I tell you, the *rai*, they teach us all we know. We can find out what's wrong with a fella when he's feeling sick, too. We look into his body and see the disease shinin' like a light. The healthy parts don't shine like the sick parts. Then we know what's wrong with a fella. The *rai*, they show us how to look inside his body. So for the *rai* to teach us how to fly isn't such a big thing."

"Are you ever called upon to cure people much these days?"

Kamurro glanced down at his baobab nut, as if embarrassed by my question.

"My people don't trust us doctor-men anymore," he said. "They go to white-men doctors in town and get pills. They like to sit in hospital beds and have nurses running around lookin' after them. My people like to have a white fella listen to their insides with something on his ears. A stethoscope, you blokes call it. They don't believe my inner eye can see what's wrong like they did in the old days. Much better than them white doctor-men with their shiny metal ears, anyway."

"Yet in spite of this your people still believe in the *rai*. Even though they go to white doctors, they haven't forgotten the old ways completely," I countered.

"They know they only born because of the *rai*, that's why. We teach them this when they're children. But that doesn't mean they want to listen to what I've got to say anymore."

Kamurro's dilemma was obvious. Not only did he find himself living on the fringe of white settlement, but it appeared that his skills as a *barnmunji* had been undermined by modern medical practice as a result. Sorcery and magic were no longer acceptable among his people now that they had become mendicants of the state. The old ways were considered to be inferior, little more than the remnants of their wild bush life, which for many Aborigines had become only a memory. To many of them, particularly the younger ones, Kamurro was an argumentative old man, out of touch with modern life.

"My people don't want to believe in my doctor ways because that would mean helpin' themselves. White medicine takes this away from us. It takes away our power," Kamurro added.

"You mean, white medicine and pension checks have stopped your people believing in the old ways," I said.

Kamurro barely nodded.

"*Rai*, they don't like people who don't believe in them. When they die, our people die," he added, a hint of bewilderment in his voice. It was clear that what might happen to his people once they ceased to believe in their culture had only just begun to dawn on him.

I was deeply touched by Kamurro's explanation of his people's beliefs. It seemed that I had been made privy to a kind of earthy logic that transcended any arguments that I might wish to put forth in reply. Here was a man who had seen his culture all but decimated by European settlement in the past one hundred years. The power to see with X-ray eyes, to fly through the air like a bird, or walk underground like a lizard—these things were in danger of disappearing from the world forever. I had the impression that Kamurro felt that his culture and beliefs had been irretrievably damaged by the aggressive and often thoughtless ways of white men. Furthermore, the old men like himself were powerless to do anything about it.

Nonetheless Kamurro had introduced me to a number of fascinating new concepts, not least being his people's belief in spiritual paternity. Mr. Rouse's insistence that sex was the motivating force behind most Aboriginal beliefs certainly came to grief on this concept. Although they acknowledged sexuality as a significant agent on one level, this did not preclude the acceptance of a spiritual agent at work also. The *rai*, those self-sustaining spirit entities, played a vital role not only in the making of a *barnmunji* but in the spiritualization of the fetus as well. Clearly, they were the "angels," so to speak, the invisible bearers who "entered" both the mind of the father and the womb of the mother. The quickening process involved much more than a physical transformation brought about by normal biological processes; it involved a mental transformation as a direct result of a human spirit's need to be born into the world.

I now realized that Grey's Wandjina figure, the one they call Dalimen, might have revealed only one aspect of his potency by his act of copulation with those female spirits, as Mr. Rouse had related to me earlier. What the old explorer probably had not known when he first discovered Grey's cave paintings was that there might be another side to the story—a secret known only to the tribal custodians of the cave itself. Perhaps, when Mr. Rouse made his journey in 1947, he had not earned the confidence of his

guides as much as he thought. Perhaps they had given him only
the outer layer of the myth while suppressing its true message.

I left Kamurro sitting on the ground where I had found him.
We agreed to meet again after I had located his friend Waljali and
talked to him. According to Kamurro, Waljali had moved into a
house in town to be close to his work as a sites officer recording
Aboriginal sacred places in conjunction with the government. Such
was the pressure these days to apportion the country into mining
leases that it had become necessary to assess the location of each
sacred site in advance. Some of the richest deposits of oil, minerals,
and diamonds in the country were reputed to lie buried under
Kimberley earth. The land of the Wandjina, once a speechless
place reflecting the world-creating activities of the Sky Heroes at
the time of the Dreaming, had been transformed into a national
resource. No wonder old Kamurro preferred to sit alone under a
tree carving baobab nuts, not wishing to go anywhere these days.
Probably he was fearful that his underground spirit journeys as a
barnmunji masquerading as a goanna might bring him in contact
with a drilling tip.

"You be careful," he said to me as I climbed onto my bicycle.

"What of?" I asked.

"The *rai*, they got to like you first. Otherwise you be in trouble.
They can trip you up pretty quick."

"Thanks for the advice, Kamurro. I'll keep my eyes open," I
called as I rode away from the old Aboriginal sorcerer.

Kamurro, meanwhile, picked up his baobab pod and began carving again as if nothing had happened. Clearly the hunting scene
he was carving on its surface reminded him of a time when men
really did move about with the aid of spirits.

TEN

At the hostel the next morning a young Aborigine came up to me as I was crossing the lawn for breakfast. I had not seen him before, so I assumed he must have arrived the previous evening from a remote Kimberley settlement. He wore a cowboy hat and was dressed in jeans and an open-necked check shirt divested of most of its buttons. I could see tribal initiation scars across his chest as he approached.

"You lookin' for Waljali?" he asked.

"How did you know?"

"Waljali tell me you lookin' for him. He says he be home if you want to see him today."

The knowledge that Waljali was looking for me came as a surprise. There was no way he would have known of my existence unless Mr. Rouse had already advised him. This was doubtful as I knew that Mr. Rouse believed Waljali to be still living at Mowanjum, not in town where the man had recently moved. In any event, my contact with Kamurro and Mr. Rouse had been so recent. Surely news couldn't travel that fast!

The Aborigine gave me Waljali's address, and I thanked him.

Borrowing the cook's bicycle again, I decided to ride across town in search of the man. I had begun to believe Waljali possessed knowledge of the Wandjina that he was interested in sharing. Otherwise why would he have requested a meeting with me so soon? I became aware that my presence in Derby was under some sort of surveillance. There were people out there who wanted to know what I was doing in town.

Waljali's house lay on a back street not far from the mudflats of Kings Sound. I noticed a four-wheel-drive vehicle parked out front. On the door of the vehicle was written "Aboriginal Sites Dept," so I knew I was on the right track.

A slender, rather ascetic figure met me as I entered the gate. Waljali's deepset eyes were filled with a distant, penetrating look as we shook hands. Some teeth were missing from his mouth; otherwise he reminded me of a monk. Everything about his manner reflected restraint. Only his chest betrayed the wild spirit of his origins—it, too, was scarred with the permanent weal marks of tribal initiation.

I introduced myself. Waljali barely spoke as he listened to my reasons for wanting to talk to him. He gave me the impression that he already knew why I had come. In the end my curiosity got the better of me, so I asked:

"Waljali, how did you know I wanted to see you?"

"Kamurro came here yesterday morning," Waljali said.

"How could he? I was with him at Mowanjum for most of the day."

"That's right," Waljali agreed. "He told me you were out there speakin' with him."

"How is that possible?" I asked, taken aback by Waljali's revelation. It did not seem possible that Kamurro could be in two places at once. I decided to voice my confusion to Waljali.

"He's a doctor-man," Waljali replied. "He knows how to be wherever he wants."

"I suppose he flew here."

Waljali shrugged, growing a trifle impatient with my penchant for exactitude in these matters.

"Kamurro flies through the air or travels underground—it doesn't make much difference," he said.

"What you're saying is that he was here with you at the same time as he was with me," I countered, my thoughts still in turmoil as I tried to come to terms with my first encounter with someone who had actually engaged in out-of-body travel.

"I told you, Kamurro is a doctor-man. These fellas know how to get about."

"How do they do it, then?"

"They use a *biju*, a rope that goes up into the air. Doctor-men climb this rope and fly wherever they want to go."

"Even while they are talking to someone?"

"This is something that happens in your head, not inside your body," Waljali replied. "When Kamurro came here to see me, it doesn't mean he came in his body. He came in my dream. I saw him in my dream, and he told me he was talkin' to a white fella. It must have been you," he added, a hint of a smile on his face. Those deep-set eyes of his looked like rock pools reflecting light.

"All right," I said. "So Kamurro told you about me. Did he tell you I wanted to find out more about the Wandjina?"

Waljali nodded.

"He told me you're a fella who wants to understand why the Wandjina are so important to Aborigines. It's somethin' we don't like to talk to white people about much."

"What are you afraid of?"

"We got plenty to be afraid of. White fellas have been takin' away our culture for generations. There's nothin' much left for us now that people have gone off with it. They're like crows: Real scavengers, they are," Waljali added.

"We've stolen your myths and stories, is that what you're saying?"

"I dunno. Maybe you have. All those stories my people told to Mr. Rouse, where are they now? We haven't got them anymore. He wrote them down and sent them off to Sydney. They got our stories down there somewhere now. Probably in boxes."

"Surely your people still recall what they told Mr. Rouse," I countered.

"Most of them old fellas he talked to are dead and gone. They take their stories with them to the grave. We got nothin' left," Waljali said.

Waljali's concern was obvious. The information that the elders of the tribe had given to Mr. Rouse in good faith all those years ago was no longer on the lips of the younger generation. Nor had the great myth cycles and rituals been passed on to the young men because of the cultural disruption and exile imposed upon Aborigines by European encroachment on their lands. The older men of the tribes refused to reveal what they knew for fear that it might not be accepted in the proper spirit. Rather than allow their knowledge to fall on deaf ears, the elders had decided to remain silent. Like the Wandjina, it appeared they had chosen to seal their lips forever.

"Why don't you ask Mr. Rouse to return your stories?" I suggested.

"We've tried that," Waljali said. "But he won't help us. He says our stories aren't true anymore. He tells us we must read the Bible and believe in Jesus Christ."

"He can't do that. The Wandjina stories are your Bible."

"All the spirits of our country have gone bush, he reckons. We not allowed to believe in them anymore. They put our stories in museums and libraries. Now we got nothin' to live by," Waljali said, without a trace of bitterness in his voice.

"What makes you think I might be any different from Mr. Rouse?" I said, trying to be my own devil's advocate.

"You *must* be different," Waljali almost pleaded. "We need help to get our culture back. You got to help us."

"All right. What do you want me to do?" I demanded.

"You're a writer-man. You got to tell the world about us. Tell people we Aborigines not livin' in our own country anymore— that it's been taken from us by big-money cattlemen and mining companies. They're all looked after pretty well by the government, that's for sure. Everybody's lookin' after these fellas, but not us Aborigines. That's what you've got to tell people. How our land has been taken from us. How we've lost our stories because we've lost our land."

Waljali's outburst brought home to me something that I had not thought about before: His people's beliefs were intimately associated with the land itself. It did not seem possible that a people could lose their sense of cultural identity in the wake of the loss of their tribal lands, yet this was exactly what Waljali was saying. As creation spirits, the Wandjinas had made the land for the Aborigines. They had ensured its sanctity by way of tribal stories handed down to each generation from the time of the Dreaming. These stories had belonged to the Aborigines through an act of inheritance. Now, it seemed, European property laws and the granting of mining rights had rendered the law of the Wandjina impotent.

Nonetheless, I could not quite understand why Kamurro and Waljali wanted to initiate me into their myth life. I was an outsider, after all, in principle little different to those who presented to them the public face of occupation and ownership. How were they to know whether I would not run off with their stories like Mr. Rouse? In trusting me they would have to believe I was prepared to present their case to the world as a people desperately trying to regain control over their culture, and their lives. These were inextricably intertwined. Aboriginal survival depended upon them holding onto what was theirs. For some reason Kamurro and Waljali wished to place their trust in me. Was it an act of faith on their part, or merely one of desperation?

"What do you reckon?" I heard Waljali remark.

"This is a big responsibility, Waljali. If Mr. Rouse isn't prepared to give your stories back to you, how am I supposed to help?"

"Some of us old fellas still know them. We could tell them to you, and then you can write them down for the next generation, and the generation after that."

"That's what Mr. Rouse was meant to have done for you."

"I know. But this time we stay close by you. We want you to write them down for us, and then hand them back right away."

"What's in it for me, Waljali?" I said, hoping to tempt him into offering what I wanted most.

Waljali looked at me, his deep-set eyes burrowing into mine.

"We take you to see the Wandjina," he said simply. "And teach you their law. This is what we give you."

It sounded like an excellent bargain. Knowing how difficult it would be to locate the Wandjina caves without Aboriginal help, I was prepared to barter almost anything in return for such an encounter.

Waljali told me a little about himself as we sat together on the steps out front. He had been brought up on the Kunmunya mission, not very far from Grey's cave. His father had been a Naringin, his mother a Worora. His early education had been at the mission school where he had been introduced to Christianity. While still a child he had contracted leprosy and was separated from his family and transferred to the Derby Leprosarium. Here he became an accomplished violin player and a car mechanic. Later he put his expertise to good use on his return to Kunmunya, where he spent many years working as a mechanic on pearling luggers in King Sound.

In his youth, Waljali was initiated into his totemic fraternity under the guidance of his kin brothers and uncles. About this time he was taken to visit the Wandjina caves scattered throughout the Kimberley. Not all of them belonged to his kin group, of course, which meant that his visits were made in the company of their respective custodians. These men revealed the sacred stories to him, and chanted the songs. The years of his early manhood had been dedicated to learning as much as possible from the tribal elders—the very knowledge he now realized was in danger of disappearing forever.

Since then Waljali had watched his country being overrun by European pastoralists, geologists, and more recently by mining contractors. The establishment of an iron ore mine on one of the islands offshore, not far from their bush community at Kunmunya, brought home to him the predatory nature of European exploitation. For years his people had tried to come to terms with the restrictive work practices of pastoralists, which forbade them from visiting their land whenever they wished to perform their sacred rites. Going on "walkabout," as it was called, had been forbidden to them because this traditional practice interfered with white men's concept of efficiency.

Now a new threat had manifested itself in the form of their land being dug up and shipped overseas to fuel foreign smelters. More recently, the establishment of one of the world's largest industrial diamond mines in the eastern Kimberley region further highlighted how potentially rich the region was. The world of the Sky Heroes and the Dreaming places of old, which Waljali's people used to visit as places of pilgrimage and meditation, these places were now under threat from economic exploitation that they found difficult to combat.

"Everywhere we look now we see the same thing goin' on," Waljali said. "They got uranium mines up in the Northern Territory. They want to build a gold mine at Coronation Peak where Ungud, the Rainbow Snake, lives. It never stops. They always diggin' up some place. White fellas always wantin' more.

They never satisfied with what they got. Money more important to them than spirit."

"By revealing the secrets of Wandjina to me, aren't you afraid you might lose everything?" I suggested.

"The Wandjina will protect us. That's all we got left. If we tell the world about them, then maybe everybody be afraid to touch us. If we keep them secret—" Waljali paused, aware perhaps of how much his next remark signaled the death knell of tribal secrecy as a central tenet of Aboriginal life, "then we lost. White people only care about what they know. We got to make sure they respect our culture. That means the Wandjina have got to come to our rescue."

It was evident that I had walked into a minefield more political than mythological. The hope of confining my interest in the Wandjina as religious and cultural exemplars had been dashed on the shoals of Aboriginal expectation, considering their personal agenda for survival. But was there anything new in this? Surely the Wandjina had always been supernatural beings to which the Aborigines could turn for help and guidance. Now the enemy was no longer the malignant spirits that inhabited rocky crevasses, waiting to pounce on unwary tribespeople. It was the geologists and seismic experts who wandered about the country in four-wheel-drive vehicles bearing their scientific equipment in shiny aluminum cases. Waljali's people needed protection from them more than they did their own spirits.

"I want to tell you somethin' important," Waljali broke my train of thought.

"Go on," I said.

"I'm a Yaada man," he breathed.

"What does that mean?"

"It means I'm a lawman. My *dji* [totem] is the kangaroo. Now I tell you the story of how Yaada, the kangaroo, gave the law to my people. Then maybe you understand why Wandjina so important to us."

Waljali began:

"One day, at the time of the Dreaming, a young boy took a little joey from a mother kangaroo's pouch for a pet. He liked to play with it. He was always kissin' it. So people decided to call the boy Muga, which means 'kiss.' To this day his people are called Muga.

"Anyway, this kangaroo grew up big and decided to run away from the Muga people. An old fella named Binniora, which means 'frog,' decided to hunt the kangaroo. He threw a spear he had made from a very strong tree that the Wandjina had created. He hit the kangaroo in the backside. The kangaroo, he kept on runnin' with the old fella chasin' him.

"After a while the kangaroo came to a big rock and sat down to rest. He looked back to see whether the old fella was still chasin' him, which he was. So he hit the road again, with blood comin' from him. Before he headed off, he put his picture on the rock. This picture is still there today. We call it Bangudda, which means 'kangaroo looking back.'

"Poor old kangaroo, he was getting weaker from loss of blood by this time," Waljali said. "Then a pack of dingoes attacked him and ripped away the skin from his ribs. Where he sat down to catch his breath again, we call that place Arrmbalma, which means 'the part of his body under his ribs.'

"The kangaroo looked at himself and groaned, 'My body aches.' When he looked down at the Wandjina spear in his side, he cried out, 'And my skin—look, it's shrivelin' up.'

"Then he keeled over and died. But what he didn't know was that he had become a Wandjina kangaroo, because of the sacred spear in his side. So he came back to life. After that, the people called the kangaroo Yaada, which means 'sick' or 'suffering.' It also means 'come back.'

"Anyway, the spear in his side became Yaada's sacred thing. It made him special, a Wandjina. It made him a lawman with the right to teach others. Yaada then hopped about the King Leopold Range all the way to the desert over at Fitzroy Crossin'. That's a long way from here, as you know. Over there the desert people, who didn't have much at all because the country was so dry, they were shown his sacred spear, and allowed to make one for themselves. Yaada gave them a sacred song, too, which they could sing at ceremonies, tellin' them all about the creation of their own country.

"That's the story of Yaada, the Wandjina kangaroo," Waljali added. "That's why I'm a Yaada man. My job is to preserve the law. Yaada gave the law to men."

The story of the sacred Wandjina kangaroo carried many implications for Waljali. Not only did it bind him to the concept of sickness and suffering as his bout with leprosy might suggest, it also possessed an inner message—a message he insisted was normally only revealed to a young man at the time of initiation.

"Yaada had an easy life when he was a baby," Waljali explained. "He was always being kissed by the boy Muga. So he had to escape. All men must leave their tribe for a time when they grow up. They must test themselves, otherwise they never get to become men. We call this a part of initiation.

"Then he was shot by Frog using a sacred spear made from Wandjina wood. The frog represents water, and his spear comes from the *Ungud* spirit. We say that Yaada received the waters of the *Ungud*, but without really knowin' about it. So wherever he runs now he's always tryin' to escape what is already in him—the sacred *Ungud* water.

"When he leaves his mark on the rock, the one we call Bangudda, this is for us to remember the story. Yaada's picture on the wall tells us a little bit about his sacred story. We never forget then."

"What about the dingo attack?" I asked.

"That's where Yaada really gets hurt. The dogs are tearin' him apart, causin' him to suffer a lot of pain. He cries out, tellin' the world how much he hurts. But he's really callin' out to the Wandjina, just like your Jesus Christ does when he dyin' up there on the Cross. He wants to be put out of his misery. That's when he get the name Yaada, which tells everyone how he suffered before he died."

"Yet still he managed to come back to life," I remarked.

"Because he's a Wandjina, that's why. He came back as a spirit kangaroo and then traveled about tellin' everyone how they must learn from what he'd been through. Everyone got to see the sacred water spear in his own side and know that it means somethin'," Waljali said.

"That he's a Wandjina?"

Waljali nodded.

"In the old days," he said, "we always think of the Wandjinas as different from ourselves. They were around at the time of the Dreamin'. But we say that the Dreamin' is always with us. We don't think of it as somethin' that happened way back in the past. Today we Aboriginal people got to start seein' the Wandjinas as part of us, not just as spirit beings painted on rocks like in the old days."

It was a remarkable confession. Not only had Waljali introduced me to the hidden aspects of the Yaada myth for the first time, he had also interpreted its meaning. I could see now why he wanted my help. The man was struggling to reinterpret the culture of his people in a way that might make it relevant for future generations. He did not want to see the Wandjina reduced to a museum exhibit or become the centerpiece of some future tour program to the region. He wanted people to understand that the world-creating activities of the Sky Heroes were more than just events of the past, but that they were also happening today. He was determined not to let the Wandjinas die out, knowing that if they did so it would likely prove to be the end of his people.

"I want you to write this story down," Waljali said. "It's important for everyone to know about Yaada."

"Do you really believe the Wandjinas have a story to tell for everyone?" I tested him.

"Wandjina made this land. People got to understand. Wandjina and Ungud, they powerful spirits. Everythin' belongs to them."

"Are Wandjina and Ungud one and the same?"

"They half and half," Waljali admitted. "They both come from water. Ungud, he sacred like Wandjina. Ungud, he the water snake—what you call the Rainbow Serpent."

"Tell me, Waljali, why is the Wandjina always painted without a mouth?"

Waljali thought for a moment. I could see that he was grappling with something in his mind. Explaining the character of a spirit was not an event he engaged in every day.

"I tell you a secret," he said at last. "His lips are closed because we believe Wandjina doesn't want to say anythin' anymore. Some of the old fellas believe Ungud closed his mouth to stop the rain. They say if Wandjina opened his mouth, it would never stop rainin'."

This was a significant piece of information. Waljali's entire being, it seemed, was based upon the sufferings of a sacred kangaroo who had become a Wandjina. It made him different, a man set apart from others. Furthermore, it made me realize that the time he had spent in the leprosarium as a youth had likely made him more conscious of his relationship with Yaada. Between them they had both learned what it was like to suffer for the sake of others. No wonder Waljali felt the law of the Wandjina to be so important. The spear of Yaada had become a symbol of all that his people needed to retain if they were to survive.

But his revelations had not ended there. He had also helped me to understand the subtle difference between the Wandjina and the sacred snake, Ungud. They were siblings since both were responsible for rain. As well, they had participated in the act of world creation at the time of the Dreaming. If there was any difference in their nature, then it probably stemmed from their respective specialties. Whereas Ungud was a maker of rivers and waterholes, the Wandjinas made rock formations, hills, and plains, as well as rain.

"Is there a spirit being guiding Wandjina and Ungud? A spirit above them both?" I asked.

"Yeah. We say that Ngadjaia, he's the first spirit. But he never came down to earth," replied Waljali. "Maybe you should talk to my friend Bungana. He knows more about that fella than I do."

"Who is Bungana?"

"He's a Worora man. He knows a lot about these things. I take you to him tomorrow."

My discussions with Waljali on the subject of his beliefs had evoked in me a feeling of excitement. I don't know why, but I had begun to feel as if I were being drawn closer to the very source of things. Waljali had mentioned to me that the Wandjina were made by the wind, a singular act in itself. It seemed that the realm of the Sky Heroes was dominated by the idea of nature as the orchestrator of all creation. Could it be that the Wandjinas were merely the embodiment of all nature's gestures, or did they live a celestial life independent of people? It was a question I still could not quite fathom. I welcomed the opportunity to speak with Waljali's friend, Bungana. Perhaps he would be able to provide the answer.

The following day Waljali picked me up outside the hostel and drove me to another Aboriginal community on the outskirts of town, not far from where he lived. We drove along a street filled with houses that had been made available to the local Aborigines at a modest rent by the local council. Most of the houses were in a state of disrepair, however, their windows broken and doors hanging from their hinges, reflecting the disinterest Aborigines often manifest toward possessions, particularly their houses. The squalor of the place was brought about by a people who had not yet come to terms with their transition from a nomadic life-style to that of urban dwellers. It was also a condition derived from their feeling of not belonging in their own land.

Bungana turned out to be an important elder of the Worora people. We found him sitting outside his house under a baobab tree, a canvas shoulder bag beside him on the ground. He wore a panama hat and a soiled kerchief around his neck. His drooping features reminded me of a cocker spaniel. But for all that, Bungana was pleased to have visitors call upon him. He greeted Waljali with a few words in Naringin, then he addressed me:

"You come a long way to be with us, all right."

"How did you know I was coming?" I asked.

"People talk. They say you want to hear 'bout Wandjina. Is that true?"

I nodded. "Knowing more about the Wandjina would make my trip worthwhile," I said.

"We all journey long way to be in this place. Don't matter too much where we comin' from," Bungana replied. "You white fellas like to travel all the time in one direction. You don't like to turn 'round and come back any place. That's because you don't want to listen to spirit," he added as he adjusted his panama hat.

"Retracing your steps isn't all that easy."

"You got to sometimes. You got to think about things. Black-fellas always thinkin' about where we come from. We always like to go back to places we know, so we can talk about what made us in the first place."

It was evident from Bungana's remarks that Aborigines did not see themselves as separate from the physical world around them, but rather they saw themselves as identifying closely with it. Returning again and again to their own country, the country of their forefathers, was an act of renewal for them, a sign that they belonged. After all, they owned little but their Dreaming territory, and the totem they had been given at birth. Possessing a totem—whether an animal, a bird, or even a plant—gave them access to a particular kind of sensibility that they would not have possessed otherwise. Was a kangaroo the man, or was it a badge of identity? It was a question I put to my two friends.

"Kangaroo and me are one," Waljali explained. "He and me are one flesh. Sure he doesn't look like me, but we one *ingáhnj*—what you call spirit. I got the *ingáhnj* of the kangaroo inside me, that's why I can't eat him. To eat him would be to eat myself. That's forbidden."

"We blackfellas not cannibals, no sir!" Bungana echoed.

"Your totem comes to you when you first dreamt by your father," Waljali went on. "This means you're born with the *ingáhnj* of an animal or bird inside you. Everything I do is laid down by my totem. He's the boss."

"So every Aborigine is identified in some way with nature," I said.

"That's right," Bungana said. "We've got all of nature inside us. That way we never feel alone when we're out in the bush. Nature is our friend, maybe even our brother."

"I tell you secret," Bungana continued, rearranging his kerchief so that the knot did not interfere with his Adam's apple. "You got to know how Ngadjaia shows himself. We say Ngadjaia never comes down to earth, but this is wrong. He come down all right. He put his spirit into nature. We see it this way," he added, preparing to explain it to me in more detail.

"Ngadjaia is the one who made us and made the old-time people. He's the one who sends the rain. When you see a frog's egg in the water, you know it's the eye of the water, Ngadjaia's eye. The waters are always movin' about. But under the water Wandjina is always there, holdin' it together. We born out of the Wandjina water. He's the one who made us; our fathers and mothers only found us there. But you never see Ngadjaia: He invisible. He only shows himself as Ungud or Wandjina. Look, I show you somethin'."

Bungana reached into his shoulder bag and produced an object wrapped in a piece of cloth. As he unraveled the bundle a section of shell or bone—it was hard to tell which—emerged from the cloth. No more than four to six inches in length, the object reminded me of a sculptured image. Arms, legs, a clearly defined body, and what appeared to be an open-holed face greeted my gaze. Remnants of dried flesh were attached to its surface. The figure was a perfect imitation of a man.

Bungana placed the object on the palm of his hand.

"You look, this is Wandjina," he pronounced. "This is how Ngadjaia revealed himself to my people."

"What you see is the bone from a sweet-water turtle's throat," Waljali remarked.

"How can it possibly be a Wandjina?" I said.

"Ngadjaia made the turtle," Bungana went on. "He made this piece of bone in the shape of Wandjina and put it inside the turtle. Ngadjaia made its eyes, legs, arms, and body. When we catch a turtle and put it in the fire to cook, we always remember Wandjina. Because Wandjina, he's in the throat of the sweet-water turtle when we open it up. We see the shape of Wandjina before our eyes. This is how he looks when he comin' a paintin' on the rock."

"I tell you a secret," Waljali remarked. He glanced about us to make sure no one might be in our vicinity—a woman or uninitiated youth perhaps. "What you're seeing here is *ungud*, something sacred. We believe this Wandjina is a gift of Ngadjaia, the invisible spirit."

I realized that what lay before me in the form of a sweet-water turtle's throat bone embodied an important part of mythic doctrine for the Kimberley tribespeople. More than anything, this bony icon represented nature as a carrier of ideas. Was it possible that Ngadjaia, the invisible Creator, had made the turtle's throat bone the bearer of his image on earth? Waljali and Bungana seemed to think so. Moreover, I was also beginning to recognize the mysterious link that existed between man and nature. They came together in the Wandjina, a Sky Hero who had chosen to reside in the throat of a sweet-water turtle. It was as if, for the first time in my life, I were gazing at the origin of my own prehistory. According to my friends the human form may have been derived from the throat bone of this animal that had preceded man on earth by many millions of years. In other words, we had been carried about as a kernel of an idea in the throat of a turtle until our time came to enter this world.

During our discussion I noticed that Waljali and Bungana's demeanor had begun to change. They reminded me of men attempting to reaffirm their traditional authority as *imiini*, or "great men." Talking about their beliefs had helped to raise their spirits considerably. They had made me a mirror in which they could see, reflected back at them, what they normally tried to conceal. At the same time it was clear that they felt rather vulnerable in my presence. They had told me secrets about the Wandjina's hidden form known only to fully initiated tribesmen like themselves. They had opened their hearts to me as they had to no other.

Waljali picked up a stick and began to draw on the ground. I watched him inscribe the outline of a map that looked vaguely like that of Australia.

"Maybe it's time I tell you something," he said.

Waljali proceeded to mark on his map a grid made up of small circles, all linked by a network of paths that extended into the ocean itself.

"This is where we live," he explained when he had finished his map. "My people see Australia this way."

"Where are the mountains and rivers?" I asked, hoping to find some recognizable feature among the lines and circles.

"They're not important. What we believe is important are the stories. Everythin' the Sky Heroes created is with us today as a story. You see these little circles"—he pointed to the grid across the map—"well, each one of them represents a story. The lines linking them tells you the direction of where the story goes."

"So that Aborigines all over Australia are able to know what is happening elsewhere," I reasoned.

"They a part of the story, too. Each tribe knows a little bit of a story comin' from his territory. When you put all these little bits together you have the complete story of Australia. Nobody knows all of it, that's for sure. But together we all know it. That's why we all brothers," Waljali added.

"We call this *wunnan*," Bungana said. "That's the word for sharing stories. You call it 'trading.' We trade stories across the country. We see Australia as a big man, a body lying in the ocean, all crisscrossed with stories."

I turned to Waljali.

"What does he mean?" I asked.

"We think of Australia as *bandaiyan*, a living body," he replied. "It's not just rocks and earth that you see with your eyes. It's something that lives and breathes the same way we do."

"The country has arms and legs?"

"Sure it does. The front we call *wadi*, which means the belly section. That's because the continent is lying flat on its back—like a man floating in the water. Deep down under the water are his

buttocks, what we call *wambalma*. The leg joints run into the
pelvis and right across to the other side of the country."

"Inside the body of this man lives Ungud, the Rainbow Snake,"
Bungana said. "He makes sure nature grows on the outside of his
body, like the hair on your head. We live on all these things
growin' on his body. Kangaroo, goanna, crocodile, fish."

"Around here," Waljali added, touching his rib section, "we call
ungnu djullu. The ribs go right across the country above the navel,
the *wangigit*. You call the navel Ayers Rock, where all the tourists
go to climb over it. That's a white man's name, not ours. But we
know it as the navel of this man, *wangigit*."

"The part below the navel is *wambut* or the man's private part,"
Bungana said, indicating his pubic area. "There's a woman's part,
too, called *ambut*. And the head, blackfellas know this as
ulangun."

"All across the Top End of Australia is *ulangun*," Waljali elaborated. "Cape York, Arnhem Land, the Kimberley where we are
now, Bathurst Island—all of them are part of the man's head."

"That's how we see Australia," Bungana said. "*Bandaiyan*. He's
a big body."

I was deeply touched by the cosmic anatomy lesson my friends
had given me. Regarding the earth as an endless story or a giant
man suggested to me that Aborigines lived within their own myth.
The poetic nature of their perception made it difficult to distinguish
between a reality based upon normal observation and one derived
from the Dreaming itself. Which one was more real? An ancient
land mass formed by geomorphic frisson, or one created from the
bedrock of myth? A shapeless template masquerading as the geological descendant of the legendary Gondwanaland, or a massive arte-
rial system of stories that formed the life blood of its people? I had
no way of knowing, but I suspected the latter explanation helped
people live more complete lives than any knowledge of the former.

"What you're saying is that everyone in the world is part of the
same body," I said.

"That's right," Waljali replied. "All of us, black and white.
Australia is a big body filled with stories. They like the veins in
your arm. We—you and I—are just like the blood flowing in them.
We carry the stories wherever we go. Without the stories the world
is no more, we say. It's finished."

Meanwhile Bungana wrapped up his bony Wandjina and tucked it away in his shoulder bag.

"You better write down how important Wandjina is to the world. Tell people. That way, everyone be all right," he said.

I recalled the remark made by Woolagoodja, now long dead, which I had read in Mr. Rouse's text on the *rai* back in my hostel room: "Wandjina is the important one. He made the world."

"Maybe you better come with me tomorrow," Waljali suggested.

"Where to?" I asked.

"I take you into the Kimberley. Then you can see Wandjina for yourself."

"What about Bungana? Is he coming too?"

"I'm too old," Bungana said. "You go with Waljali. He show you things only blackfellas ever seen. He teach you things."

So I was to visit the Wandjina caves at last. It was as if the *rai* had lowered an aerial rope to me, inviting me to ascend into their realm. Although I possessed no scars on my chest demonstrating my initiation into manhood, nonetheless I felt that I had passed through some sort of test while talking with these two elderly Kimberley tribesmen. Would the Wandjina instill in me their sense of *ingáhnj*, their living spirit? Only time would tell.

"You better take Kamurro along, too," Bungana suggested. "He know a lot about Wandjina places. Some of it is his country."

"He comin'," Waljali replied.

"Have you asked him already?" I said.

Bungana nodded sagely.

"A little bird already over at Mowanjum tellin' him to pack his swag, I reckon," he announced.

"A *rai*, you mean," I ventured.

Waljali looked at Bungana and then grinned at me.

"Maybe we find this fella's Dreamin' country out there some place," he said to his friend.

"Sounds to me like he got a bit of goanna in him. Maybe that's his totem," Bungana replied, adjusting his kerchief once more. "He got to learn to walk underground some time if he want to find Wandjina, though," he added after a short pause.

ELEVEN

"It's a long drive," Kamurro observed from where he sat in the back of the Toyota, jammed in among our bedrolls and camping gear, as we drove north into the unclouded Kimberley sunlight.

"How long?" I asked, glancing at Waljali as he veered to miss a dead cow lying bloated by the roadside, its guts already picked over by dingoes. It had been knocked down by a road train.

"Two days maybe," Waljali replied. "The Gibb River road, it's full of holes. We got to take our time."

He was talking about one of the most remote tracks in all Australia. Through fossilized reefs and mountain ranges the Gibb River road wound, providing the only link many lonely cattle stations have with the outside world. High hills, sparsely layered with scrub, testified to a time when the region was at the mercy of vigorous geological upheaval. Here, too, family dynasties rose and fell amid luxuriant pastures brought on by drenching monsoon rains, followed by extended dry spells that often brought ruin. Harsh and unyielding, the Kimberley landscape inspired its own sense of grandeur, for it was a country born out of an archaic encounter between land, man, and Wandjinas.

It didn't take long to realize I was not making any ordinary journey into the hinterland. Traveling with a *barnmunji* on the one hand and an *imiini* on the other was enough to ensure that events and places would take on their own special flavor. The stillness and abstract beauty of the land stretching beyond the roadside combined to make me feel that I was entering a visionary landscape as mysterious as any one might find among the gilded panoramas of a Persian miniature.

The truth was I had become aware of a significant shift in my attitude since Waljali had confronted me with the prospect of helping his people. That Mr. Rouse, his early mentor, had chosen to withhold their past in order to strengthen his influence over them only made me more conscious of my responsibility. Waljali was asking me to enter into the spirit of the Wandjina in the hope that I might understand more fully the serpentine world of Ungud and his spirit counterparts, the *rai*. This was the reason he had invited Kamurro to join us on our trip north. He knew that the old *barnmunji* understood the *rai* better than any man alive. With his help I might be initiated into what was most secret about the Dreaming, and so begin to understand the special relationship Aborigines have with the land.

I also sensed that Waljali and Kamurro were keen to make this pilgrimage back to their tribal territory. They were both quite old now, and the likelihood of their ever journeying to the great Wandjina centers again was becoming increasingly remote. While in their youth they might have regularly gone to these centers for ceremonies and singsongs, their days of living a full ritual life were almost over. Retouching the figures and uttering the prayers as Woolagoodja had done in the old days were fast becoming events of the past for them. Ever since the various tribes had retreated to Derby, the Naringin and Worora found themselves fenced in by memories, unable to summon up the energy to break free from the sycophancy engendered by government handouts.

My presence, however, had given these men new enthusiasm for the old ways. In me they could see someone who understood their deep need to express the mysterious power of the Sky Heroes, and the hold their myth life had over them. I was their lightning rod so to speak, able to draw to me all their undischarged fears of becoming an extinct race. What they wanted was to believe in their own survival, to know there was still room enough in the world for them to exist. Even to contemplate the demise of the Wandjinas was a painful experience for them, for they knew their caves would become anonymous pavilions if this were to happen. They did not wish to see them reduced to little more than crypts for the bones of their ancestors. Nor did they wish to see them crumbling into dust, uncared for, and without benefit of Dreaming rituals. It was a prospect they had discussed among themselves a good deal. My appearance had merely forced them to come to their own defense.

"Where do you plan to stop tonight?" I asked.

"Windjana Gorge," Waljali replied. "It's a place made by the Maletji dogs when they come through here givin' people the law."

"I thought Ungud, the Rainbow Snake, made the land," I remarked.

"I told you: Every spirit made the land. Wandjina, Ungud, the Maletji dogs, Yaadi, the great kangaroo. We believe everythin' in nature has given us somethin'."

It was a curious feeling, knowing we were journeying across a landscape molded by spirit beings. I had never considered what it would be like to confront a rock formation that was the representation of a pair of divine testicles or the dung of a spirit dog. As we drove north Waljali and Kamurro pointed out features that were similar to these. Under their guidance I no longer felt we had been traveling across country in the wake of someone else's dust, but that we had been participating in a dream journey into the very substance of myth. Divine stories had become the bones of the earth. Each rock outcrop, red-tinged in the afternoon sunlight, drew forth a desire to know more about what had inspired the Sky Heroes to appear here in the first place.

When we reached the gorge shortly before dusk, it was to find ourselves alone but for baobab trees clinging to the rock face near the entrance, and the sight of freshwater crocodiles sunning themselves by rock pools. Antediluvial and asleep, these creatures offered a perfect counterpoint to this otherwise tranquil setting. Still, their menace seemed to have left its imprint on the air in the gorge. One could almost feel the savage bite of their jaws in every small breath of wind.

We camped in a clearing by the entrance. Later, around a fire, we lay back on our bedrolls after a simple meal washed downed with tea, and Waljali and Kamurro produced their tobacco tins. Conversation drifted from one topic to another until Waljali finally decided to tell me the story of Pigeon, an Aborigine living around the turn of the century, who had chosen to oppose the white man with his gun.

"He was a real wild fella, that one," Waljali remarked with a grin. "He was always gettin' into trouble for cattle-stealin'. That was his trade. When the police caught him one day and put him in jail, he played along with them for a while and worked as a tracker. He took to huntin' his own people, or lookin' for fellas who'd got bushed. But it didn't mean he'd stopped hatin' whitefellas for what they were doin' to our people. He just kept his hurt inside."

"What else could he do if he wanted to keep on livin'?" Kamurro reasoned.

"By and by he killed a policeman at Lillimooloola outpost, not far from here."

Waljali pointed down the road.

"Did they arrest him?" I asked.

"He took off through this gorge," Waljali said. "They sent out a party of stockmen and police on horseback to try and catch him. But Pigeon, he waited 'til they had ridden into the gorge. Then he and a few mates that were along for the ride ambushed 'em. The fight went on for maybe three hours. Poor old Pigeon got hit that day, but he managed to get away. For the next three years he killed whitefellas' cattle and frightened the hell out of 'em. He didn't like what they were doin' to the Kimberley, runnin' cattle an' all. It was his country, not theirs. They were ridin' roughshod all over our sacred Dreaming places. They were shootin' his people. They were forcin' the game to go 'nother place."

"The troopers cornered Pigeon not far from here," Kamurro said.

"A few years later, that was," Waljali went on. "In Tunnel Creek, where a Maletji dog gave birth to pups. They shot him stone dead. He was the last Aborigine to take on the whitefellas at their own game. We always think of Pigeon as our hero," Waljali added.

"That's because he used to breathe through his feet," Kamurro said. "When the police shot him in the chest he never used to die. Our people used to say his nose was in his toes!"

"The *rai* looked after him, I reckon," Waljali said.

The idea of a man breathing through his feet did not seem so unusual in the context of what these men had already told me. Still, Pigeon's exploits did represent a willingness to resist invasion on the part of the original inhabitants, even if the results ultimately proved to be fruitless. It seemed that people like Pigeon were always considered to be outcasts, rogues, not patriots prepared to die in defense of their own kind.

"Before I born," Kamurro said, his weathered face as worn as a stockman's chaps, "my spirit child was livin' in a freshwater turtle. I showed myself one day to my father when he come down to the pool to drink. He see me in his dream then, and went back to my mother and told her, 'You havin' a boy pretty soon.' I climbed inside my mother with them words. By and by I was born at Umbandji. That my country. I was born belly-up like my totem, the turtle. When I get a bit older my mother, she rub charcoal on my face. This so I would become strong and black, a big fella. Later she built a fire and steamed me all over."

"Why did she do that?" I asked.

"That part of teachin' me the law," Kamurro explained. "As a little fella, while she steamin' me she says, 'Don't you steal anything from other people. And don't you go snatchin' another man's wife.'

"Then she steamed my eyes and says, 'Don't look at other people's business or cause trouble. That not right.' After that, she warmed my body all over and says, 'You behave yourself. Don't you go beggin' from people. Hold yourself up tall.' Then she steamed my nose and says, 'Don't you be a nosy parker. Mind your business.'

"Last thing she do," Kamurro added, pausing to light his cigarette. "She hold me in her arms toward the morning sun and says, 'You must always be givin', because that givin' reason is the law. Be delightful like the sunset, always pleasant and generous. If you give selfishly, then you pretty well finished, a rubbish blackfella.' That what my mother said to me, anyway," Kamurro concluded, his cigarette smoldering.

I was deeply impressed by what Kamurro had told me. Here were commandments far older than the Mosaic law, it seemed. Their uncluttered truth derived its authority from the beauty of dawn and the dying light of sunset. I had traveled uncounted miles, across oceans and through forests, to discover the link between morality, ethics, and nature. Who would have imagined that at the point of confluence between the cleansing power of smoke and a child offered up to the sun I might find the genesis of law? To think that goodness lay in measuring oneself against a sunset's reddening haze. Yet Kamurro's mother had explained what I had always instinctively believed: that the observation of nature alone provides us with our most enduring image of rectitude.

Was this what Pigeon had fought so desperately to preserve? Gazing up at the night sky as I lay under my blanket, I kept asking myself whether Pigeon's last stand, though of course futile considering the superior firepower of his opponents, represented his people's last opportunity to remain culturally independent. At the very least, his ability to breathe through his feet had ensured him of a measure of protection. His example, both as cattle rustler and outlaw, meant that Pigeon had been elevated to the pantheon of Sky Heroes, there to live on with Ungud and the Wandjinas. If, like Kamurro, he had been dreamed into existence among the reefs of Windjana Gorge, where we camped, I suspected that his exploits more properly reflected the laws of nature. In the end breathing through his feet had been a soul-raising gesture, a gesture of courage designed to taunt those who were after him.

The feeling that we, too, might be breathing through our feet was further enhanced the next day when we continued north along the Gibb River Road. High bluffs made up of igneous rock walls shone black through pale green shrubbery. Dead cattle and the occasional kangaroo knocked down by trucks gathered flies by the roadside. Fording shallow creeks and watercourses bearing names such as Mistake Creek, Marchfly Glen, Dogchain Creek, Bullfrog Hole, and Saddler's Springs suggested a reality tied firmly to nature and the idea of survival. The early pioneers had made it their business to identify a place by resorting to small events in their lives—in contrast to Waljali's people, who sought to identify such places, each according to its mythic importance. Was it any wonder that Aborigines sometimes felt they were walking on air?

Meanwhile, I was content to listen to Waljali and Kamurro as they explained their beliefs to me. As ancient as they appeared on the surface, I somehow felt that I had heard them all before—as if they were part of my own memory and consciousness. Both men introduced me to a way of viewing the world entirely conditioned by mythic encounters between Sky Heroes and men. It was a world in which I felt I was beginning to belong. Jolting along the road toward Grey's cave in distant Worora country was like crossing over from one order of reality into another. The realm of the Dreaming, when time didn't matter, seemed to envelop us.

"When we make contact with Ungud," Kamurro explained, his voice little more than a whisper from the backseat, "we call this *wananinj*, which means we able to see spiritual things and travel to our country. That happens when we place bullroarers in the sand and tie a piece of string covered with feathers to them. We hold onto the string and fly to our country."

"Does your body fly there, too?" I asked.

Kamurro scoffed at my suggestion.

"Not your body but your *biljur*, your spirit. It goes there," he said. "You whitefellas always worried about whether your body goin' some place. I tell you, death is nothin'. When we leave this place, we goin' back to *Lalan*, to the Dreamin'. Why we worry about it if our body isn't travelin' along to our country? In our minds we're movin' about, that's enough. Our *biljur* leaves our bodies and heads off when it wants. It's free."

"We blackfellas travel in our minds," Waljali said. "I remember doin' this when I was livin' in a different place one time, a long way from my family. I got pretty homesick, and wanted to see them. I said to myself, 'I'm off to see them right now.'

"I gave a big yawn. I soon begin to dream. In my dream I make connection with my mother and family over there, where they were livin'. I go into their dreams as a baler shell, which is their totem. That's what I become. As soon as I yawn they all sit down to greet me.

"My mother says to my people, 'Hey. Waljali, he's comin' to visit us.' By and by they all see me comin'. I come up to them and they say, 'Here's Waljali.' Then we all sit down and talk. When I wake up later, I know me and my family have been tellin' each other a lot of things. We've been talkin' to one another."

"We all dream, Waljali," I argued.

"Sure we do," Waljali replied. "But when me and my family get together later, we always talk about what we said to one another in our baler dream. That's the difference. We've both traveled to see one another in the same dream."

It was clear that, as we negotiated the rough red road ahead, our dream of traveling toward distant kinsmen had become more real. Somewhere out there I knew the Wandjinas were waiting for us, their wide eyes and mouthless faces observing our approach. They who had arrived in the region wearing *gadidja* sandals, those sandals of invisibility, were now watching us as if we were *djalng-guru*, or craft-carriers of old. When we did finally turn off the Gibb River Road and make our way along a bush track, it was with the knowledge that Grey's cave lay somewhere nearby, among the crumbling rock outcrop and stony gullies, a solitary mausoleum to a Sky Hero.

"This is the home of Dalimen Wandjina," Waljali informed me as he changed down a gear in order to climb a slab of stone lying across the track. "He was a pretty randy fella in *Lalan* time."

"I'm told he liked the girls," I said.

"Sure he liked them. He come up to some girls who liked him so much one day, they opened their legs to him. They had a good time together, playin' 'round with one another. But the girls were only young, see? What you call virgins. They were too small for him. The girls were keen on him anyway, and called out, 'Come on, Dalimen, you can do it. Make us bigger.' Pretty soon he had a bit of fun with the eldest girl."

"What happened then?"

"She asked Dalimen to swim with them together—at a place called Djeri-ngarin, which means 'laughing place.' Then they went to Low-ngarin, where Dalimen grew hungry. 'Let's eat,' he said. The girls whispered among themselves, so he said, 'All right. Let's get hold of one another and play 'round again.' So they called the place Low-ngarin, which means 'the place of love.' What happened here is that Dalimen got his cock jammed in one of the girls and it hurt him for a time."

"I suppose he lost interest in them after that," I said.

Waljali chuckled.

"Not Dalimen," he said. "He played 'round with one of the girls at a place called Banganan, which means the 'juices of a woman.' The other girls made a bed out of paperbark for him, and they all went at it. He kept pushing into them so hard that eventually his cock broke in half. He was all knocked up. He reckoned it was time he left these girls, otherwise they might make him into nothin'. He figured it was best if he made himself into a paintin' instead, a Wandjina, at Banganan."

"How did he do that?"

"He just went into the rock and left his mark on the wall. That's how he did it," Waljali explained.

"You mean the Wandjina paintings are not made by men?"

"They're made by Wandjina. Dalimen made it when he go into the rock. That's why they sacred to Aboriginal people. They're not paintings. They're the Wandjina."

Here was my first encounter with the belief that a spirit entity was capable of creating an image of itself for men to see. The painting of Dalimen, therefore, suggested that it was not an art object as such; it was the way the deity chose to manifest itself so that people might be reminded of its existence. Men like Waljali and Kamurro were, in the true sense, custodians of the divine image. Their work at retouching the painting was a subsidiary activity since the real imprint of the Wandjina was both on the wall and in their minds. They were merely there to act as go-betweens. The Wandjina relied on them to maintain their visual presence on the rock, no more. After all, it was impossible for the spirit entity's imaginative presence to suffer depredation at the hands of the weather: It was eternal.

Meanwhile, as we drove toward the region of divine sexual encounter, Waljali told me that the moral to the Dalimen tale lay in the risk caused by unrestrained sexual activity, particularly with immature girls. A progenitor of all uninhibited passion, Dalimen had imbued the surrounding hills with his divine potency. Thus we were no longer driving through uncharted territory that merely recorded obscure British place names; we were journeying through a land fortified by qualities attributed to spirits who flew through the air with the aid of winged shoes, none other than the *gadidja* sandals belonging to the Wandjinas. This feeling was further reinforced by my companions' silence. They, too, had fallen under the spell of Dalimen as we watched the track ahead disappear before our eyes.

Waljali stopped the vehicle at last and indicated that we should walk the rest of the way to the cave. The ground had become so uneven that there was little chance of driving the vehicle any farther without causing it damage. Collecting a water bottle, I fol-

lowed Waljali and Kamurro as they clambered over rocks. Soon
we came upon the opening to a cave that I recognized from the
sketch George Grey had published in his journal. Long spinifex
grass and a few low trees partially obscured the opening. Otherwise
the entrance was much as it was when Grey had made his discovery
last century.

"This is Dalimen's home," Waljali whispered.

I stepped inside. Above me I noticed the figure of a Wandjina,
its cloud-white face surrounded by a horseshoe-shaped nimbus
daubed in orange ochre. Charcoal-black eyes stared down at me,
absorbing me in their vacant gaze. In that instant Grey's surprise
and my own became one and the same as I tried to come to terms
with this powerful spiritual figure. Where else but in a Byzantine
church had I ever seen such an austere rendition of a deity? Like
a pantocrator in the dome of a chapel in Greece, the figure of the
Wandjina did indeed "stare grimly down at me" as Grey had so aptly
described. It was enough just to stand there, my neck cramping under
the strain, knowing that this image represented the culmination of
my journey. Dalimen Wandjina, that figure of purest potency, maker
of rain and bestower of fertility, hovered above my head, his massive
head empty of words. I had entered a precinct dedicated to the memory of a time when spirits wandered freely upon the earth, their
silence as succinct as any catechism uttered by priests.

"They're the girls he made love to," Waljali said, pointing out
four smaller Wandjinas in another part of the cave.

"The Dalimen story don't end with him becomin' a paintin'
here," Kamurro remarked.

"Is there more to the tale?" I asked.

"Sure there is," he replied, sitting on a rock and producing his
tobacco tin. "We tell it like this. One day the Duminite people
came, pushing each other all the way to Bungalaru. That mean
'rise up' and 'spurt out' as it does when a fella is playin' 'round
with girls. These people pushed each other to Rurunguruma over
there in the scrub." Kamurro pointed toward the bush outside the
cave. "Rurunguruma means the rustling sound grass makes when
you walk through it. Or when you playin' 'round with girls in it,
maybe! Anyway, them fellas laid the girls down in the grass and
had some more fun with them. They went at it like dogs, randy
buggers they were! They jammed their cocks in them women so
hard they hurt themselves.

"Anyway, along came a fella named Wanambul. He was a devil man who was sort of blind, and he prodded around with a stick to help him get along. He came to this place called Yuwala, and immediately he started to smell somethin'. Of course it was women-smell, so he named the place Yuwala. 'Randy old buggers,' he called them. 'Always playin' 'round with women. I'll teach you somethin'.' So he called out to Ngadjaia, the top spirit above, and asked him to throw down fire. When Ngadjaia heard about them fellas playin' 'round with young girls he was real angry, see? 'I'll throw somethin' down, all right,' he said to Wanambul. He got hold of a firestick, lightning maybe, and threw it into the grass. Pretty soon a fire blew up all over the place."

"What happened to the people?" I asked.

"They were afraid," Kamurro continued. "The blaze came so close, it scorched them all. Pretty soon their faces were many-colored. They tried to run away but the fire chased them, burning their bodies so they cried out in pain. Even their backs split open in the heat. Their legs and arms got burnt many colors, too. Them people had nowhere to go. They stopped at a place called Mariyangu where they said, 'This is where we stay. No more runnin' away. The fire might burn us, make us many-colored, but we not goin' any further. This our country,' they said.

"Today, when we go to Mariyangu," Kamurro added, "we think about them people. We think about Dalimen and his girls. They Wandjinas now, so they here to remind us what they do in *Lalan* time."

"You don't regard their behavior as a bad example, perhaps?" I said. "Not what you might expect from Wandjinas?"

Kamurro looked at me, his weathered face filled with a look of forbearance, as if he had half expected me to register disquiet over Dalimen's unseemly actions.

"At the time of the Dreamin'," he said, twisting tobacco strands from the end of his newly made cigarette, "men didn't know what was right or wrong. They tryin' things out for our sake. We learn from their mistakes. That's why they become Wandjinas. Dalimen important to us because he teach us about the law. Our job is to keep the law, so we come here to this cave to remember Dalimen's story when we with him."

"We sing his songs and remember," Waljali echoed. "That's why we always comin' up here in the old days to perform ceremonies."

"I tell you somethin'," Kamurro said. "Dalimen not just a name. It means 'from his spirit.' He come from the arm muscle of Ngadjaia, so he's not just an ordinary fella. Where his people stopped at Mariyangu, that's where Ngadjaia threw down fire and made it their totem country. So you see, this story not just a story about playin' 'round with women. It's a story about holdin' onto the law, about holding onto our land."

In his quiet way old Kamurro had given me a lesson in how to interpret mythology. What on the surface had seemed little more than a bizarre narrative about sexual incontinence turned out to be something far more important. Dalimen's actions were conditioned by a desire on the part of Kamurro's ancestors to fix the boundaries of their tribal country. Ngadjaia's intercession had served to emphasize the divine nature of such activity, thus affirming the link between all human and celestial enterprise. The rustling grass, so full of sexual splendor, was but a backdrop to a more fertile liaison between men and Sky Heroes. The bushfire that had pursued them, burning into their bodies the memory of pain and anguish, had also invested them with the knowledge that in flight the unity of their character had become fragmented. Their many-colored bodies were a further testimony to this fact.

Dalimen's apotheosis in the cave roof as a Wandjina reflected the power of mythic expression to convey complex ideas in a relatively simple form. Dalimen was superhuman. Whatever he did denoted a mystery in itself. His actions were but a veil concealing his true intent. His passional nature echoed his desire to draw together various elements. Fire, pain, sexual intimacy and desire, the yearning of innocence to be embraced by contingency, multiplicity, and death—all these were essential if one was to survive. Dalimen was a consummate *djalng-guru*, a true craft-carrier and bearer of revelation. No wonder Waljali and Kamurro were so keen to regard his image on the rock as the incarnation of their own belief in immortality. The penumbra encircling Dalimen's head appeared to glow as the first rudimentary halo.

"Come on now," Waljali remarked softly. "We take you to meet another fella."

I looked around. In this wilderness who but a Wandjina spirit could survive alone?

"Which fella?" I asked.

"You'll see pretty soon."

Back at the Gibb River Road we turned right and headed toward Derby. Only then did Waljali tell me that he wanted to pay a visit to a gentleman by the name of Krunmurra, a Wandjina custodian who lived at Gibb River cattle station.

"Maybe he take you out to visit Wanalirri cave," he said.

"Can't you take me there?"

Waljali shook his head.

"It's his place. He knows the stories. You go with him. Kamurro and me, we stay at Gibb River. We got friends there," he added evasively.

"Are you sure I'll be all right?"

"Wanalirri is an important place. Big Wandjina center. Lots of power there," Waljali replied. "Better you be with Krunmurra than with me or Kamurro. We tell you stories about Dalimen; he tell you about Wanalirri."

"Yeah," Kamurro said. "Wanalirri, he belong to Krunmurra, not us."

A decision had been made. I was to be handed over to another man much as if I had been a message-stick destined for a far country. It was clear that Waljali and Kamurro felt uncomfortable about visiting another man's Wandjina place. Wanalirri was not in their country. To go there unannounced would be to invite retribution on the part of the traditional owner. Each Wandjina belonged to a certain Dreaming territory. No man could visit a site without first approaching its custodian.

Gibb River Station turned out to be an old family property that had only recently been sold back to the original Aboriginal inhabitants. A landmark sale completed with the aid of a government grant, it meant that the Naringin people were once again in control of their tribal country. It also meant that the sacred centers scattered throughout the region would be protected from further encroachment by pastoralists. Wanalirri cave, the home of Wodjin Wandjina, and nearby Tunbai Plain, were located four hours to the east of the homestead. By the time we arrived at the station it was too late to begin the journey to the cave, so we camped with Krunmurra and his friends.

My meeting with Krunmurra took place outside his galvanized-iron lean-to some distance from the main house. Though the Aborigines now owned the property, the homestead was still occupied by a white manager. Krunmurra and his kinsmen were content to live as they had always lived—outside on the bare earth, close to their horses and under the stars at night.

Krunmurra was a thin-bodied man, probably in his late forties, though he looked much older. He walked with a limp, the result of a bad fall from a horse while out mustering cattle. His face reminded me of someone who had met with a few hard knocks in his time. Krunmurra later told me that he had once been kicked in the head by a horse. It was no wonder that his entire presence suggested a walking wound.

As we sat by the fire that evening Waljali explained the reason for our visit. Krunmurra did not say much. He seemed content to listen to his more vocal compatriots who regaled him with gossip from Derby. Krunmurra gave me the impression that he had made his peace with the dilemma of being a black man in a white man's country. Now that he had formally become a landowner, the prospect of assuming the mantle of an *imiini* like Waljali and Kamurro was not so remote after all.

"He says it's all right," Waljali remarked. "Tomorrow you take the Toyota and travel with Krunmurra. He show you where to go."

Looking across the fire, I noticed that Krunmurra had pulled his Stetson well down over his eyes, as if he considered our planned excursion of the next day to be a duty rather than a pleasure.

"He all right," Kamurro said, observing Krunmurra's behavior. "Head pretty sore, maybe."

Early the next morning we drove away from the homestead in an easterly direction. Krunmurra told me to head back to the Gibb River Road and proceed north again. It was noticeable that Waljali and Kamurro were not on hand to bid good-bye before we left. The beer they had consumed the night before must have left them with hangovers. Or perhaps their encounter with Dalimen had aroused old memories more in keeping with a dream rendezvous with the *rai*. It was hard to tell which.

Driving along a track east of the Gibb River Road soon led us into rough country. Four-wheel-drive became essential as we negotiated dry creekbeds filled with stones or climbed eroded gullies. Deep ruts, high spinifex grass that speared the radiator, and anthills that rose out of the scrub like sentinels further emphasized

the loneliness of the region. Nor did Krunmurra's continued silence make the journey any easier. His only communication was
made with the occasional hand gesture whenever it was time to
change direction. Nonetheless his prowess as a navigator was uncanny. At no time did I get the feeling that we had become lost.

Around midmorning we stopped to boil a billy. Krunmurra made
a small fire while I filled the billy with water. As soon as I had
poured the tea and offered Krunmurra a biscuit he seemed to relax.
For the first time he looked at me as though I were more than
just his driver.

"Much farther to go?" I asked.

"Little bit," Krunmurra answered vaguely.

An eagle floating in the air above widened the circle of its flight
as we sipped our tea.

"This little bit dangerous for you. What we call *jumirirri*,"
he added.

"Journeying to Wanalirri, you mean?"

Krunmurra nodded.

"You got to speak with the country," he said. "When it know
you, it lets you come in. We say you no longer a *kamaliwany*, a
stranger. Then you be a guest."

"I don't really want to return to Gibb River just yet."

"Maybe I talk to the land for you. That way you be all right."

Then Krunmurra murmured: "Wanalirri cave sacred to Tumbi,
the owl."

"Tell me about it," I said, sensing that the old drover appeared
ready to trust me at last.

"We say that one day at *Lalan* time two kids found an owl on
the ground," Krunmurra began to relate the story of Wanalirri.
"They thought it was a honeysucker, but it was really Tumbi, the
sacred owl. Anyway, these boys did bad things to Tumbi. They
pulled out all the feathers from his head and tail. They put grass
up his nose and blinded him. After that they threw him in the air
and told him to fly away. But he couldn't. He fell back to the
ground. Then Tumbi got angry with the way the boys were treatin'
him and he flew away. When the boys found out he'd gone, they
forgot all about him.

"Like I told you, Tumbi was a sacred bird. He was the son of
Wandjina. He flew up into the sky and told the head Wandjina

what the boys had done. Pretty soon the head Wandjina asked Wodjin to call up all the Wandjinas to hear what Tumbi had to stay. They came from all over the Kimberley—from Calder and Regent rivers, from King Leopold Range, every place—and they had a meeting. They decided to teach the people a lesson.

"But the birds and animals 'round the place wouldn't tell the Wandjinas where the people were hidin'. They felt sorry for them. So Wodjin, he produced a bicycle lizard from his cock. This lizard hurried about the country and soon found the people hidin' on Tunbai Plain, over there—"

Krunmurra pointed in a northerly direction.

"Before they attacked the people," he continued, "the Wandjinas decided to initiate themselves. They cut their cocks with stone knives and blood began to flow. Wodjin said, 'I want to be light, like air, so I can catch up with anyone who tries to escape.' The trouble was Wodjin got sick, and his body blew up big with water."

"Like a raincloud," I suggested.

"He filled up with rain, all right. When he stroked his beard, rain fell from his body and flooded all over Tunbai Plain. He made a big flood."

"Did the people drown?"

"Some did. But most of them were killed by the Wandjinas. They were forced back into a muddy waterhole made by brolga birds dancing on the wet ground. Sometimes Wandjinas were hit by the people's spears, but it was water not blood that come out of them."

"Were the two boys killed in the battle?"

"They got away," Krunmurra replied. "Seein' the rain and lightnin' and their people drownin' in the flood frightened them too much. The Wandjinas, they chased after them anyway. One Wandjina pretended to be a kangaroo and asked them to hop into his pouch. As soon as the boys did this, the Wandjina tricked them and changed into a baobab tree. He wouldn't let them go from inside his trunk. The people tried to cut a hole in the tree and let the boys out. When they did this, the Wandjina flowed out lookin' like water. No one could catch him! He just flowed away. The boys stayed inside the baobab where they died."

"Where did the Wandjinas go after the battle at Tunbai?"

"Tumbi felt much better about things now all the people were dead," Krunmurra resumed. "He called up a whirlwind and swept the plain clean of the dead bodies. Then the Wandjinas, they sat down in a cave not far away to decide on what to do. But Wodjin, he cut his foot real bad while he was climbin' up to the cave. So he called the cave Wanalirri, which means 'cut.' He reckoned it was time to become a picture on the wall after that, and stay in the cave. He's there now. That's his Dreamin' place."

My tea had cooled considerably by the time I remembered to take another sip. Krunmurra's recitation of events at Tunbai and Wanalirri at the time of the Dreaming was far more interesting. Tumbi's gaze had absorbed me at a glance. Wodjin's lizardlike penis had inseminated the earth. Blood had been transformed into life-giving waters, initiation augmented, sacrilege condemned. The brolga birds had danced up a storm and the Wandjinas had assumed the forms of kangaroo, baobab, and water, deceiving transgressors at every turn. Wisdom had been mocked and a flood unleashed upon the world. Apocalyptic images of death by drowning in a mire of desecrated earth had inadvertently fallen from Krunmurra's lips. He had tamed the ancient ground with his words, made a myth out of its geogenic moments. Wandjinas and men had engaged in a battle royal on the Tunbai Plain that would define forever their relationship with one another.

"We better git along," Krunmurra said, climbing unsteadily to his feet. He kicked earth over the smoldering coals.

The final part of our journey involved a trek on foot into the Wanalirri cave area. I helped Krunmurra negotiate the rocky terrain as we made our way along a ridge. Such was his lack of concern for either distance or time that he did not indicate how far we might yet have to travel. We plodded along, arm in arm, an unexpected intimacy developing between us. The remoteness, heat, and silence of the region had forced us to draw strength from one another.

At last Krunmurra called a halt at a point on the ridge from where we could look down into the valley. Red stones and pale green undergrowth met our gaze. Below, the dry watercouse appeared as if it had not seen rain in years. A stillness pervaded the air. Krunmurra raised his hand then, and pointed to the far slope.

"Wanalirri cave over there," he said.

Halfway down the slope opposite I noticed what appeared to be an extended overhang. It was partially concealed behind low scrub and shade.

"That's the home of Wodjin and Tumbi. This my Dreamin' place," Krunmurra revealed.

"Your spirit home?"

"Yeah. My father dreamed me when he was droving cattle 'round here. I came to him one night when there was plenty of thunder and lightnin'. I told him I wanted to be born. He heard me in his dream and told my mother when he got back to Gibb River. By and by I came along. My father gave me the totem name of Wanalirri in memory of this place and the big storm, like the one Wodjin made when he get angry with the people."

"Why are you telling me this?"

"Only way you understand my people. We part of the land. We the same. That's why we able to talk to our country, make *kurara*. It's a sacred thing, *kurara*. The Wandjina, they teach us how to talk to the land, hear what it has to say. We don't want to hurt the land because it like us, a body. Every part of the land is part of us. If I don't respect my country, then pretty soon it turn against me. Kangaroos, they go first. Then all the other birds and animals, they follow. That why we always listen to the Wandjinas, to Wodjin, to Tumbi the owl. They all spirits. They come from Ngadjaia, the number one spirit up top. He invisible, sure. But the Wandjinas, they still with us, carin' for us all the time. They give us the law. We learn the law, generation to generation. My father, he teach me. Then I teach my kids not to hurt the land, not to treat Tumbi in a bad way, just like he taught me. It's all the same. You whitefellas got to understand how to care for this country. Not dig it up, or hurt it when you want to make a bit of money. This place sacred, see? Pretty soon it's goin' to get angry and maybe roll over and toss us all into the sea if we not careful. Then we have another flood, maybe—"

"Like the one at Tunbai," I interrupted.

"Yeah. That be another time when we all die," Krunmurra agreed. "Maybe we don't come back a third time. Maybe that be the end for us. Anyway," he added. "You better git down there and have a look at Wandjina."

"Aren't you coming?"

Krunmurra tapped his lame leg.

"Too hard for me now," he said. "I'm buggered. You go. You be all right. I watch you."

I glanced at Krunmurra. His battered face seemed to be somewhat diminished by his trek along the ridge. Or was it the recent confession of his secret name, that of Wanalirri, which had made him feel unable to continue our trek? In any event I felt a tenderness toward him. We were no longer merely traveling companions who had been thrown together by accident. Nor were we two people helping one another across a broken landscape. We had become more like father and son, content to console one another through the act of sharing knowledge 'generation to generation' as Krunmurra explained it.

"Go on now, git along," he urged me as he sat down on a rock and produced his tobacco tin.

I started down the hillside. The bright sunlight removed all trace of my shadow. Silence and a sense of ageless calm accompanied me as I clambered over rocks. Contorted trees in the dry creekbed below merely accentuated the feeling I had begun to experience— that of stumbling into a landscape populated by invisible spirit beings, energies, and powers. I was Wodjin, staggering up to the cave entrance, my foot bearing a primordial wound. I was Tumbi, blind, featherless, and naked, pronouncing the end of the world under a deluge of waters. This was the moment I had been waiting for. I had become a living vestige of my own origins. The world as it once was had begun to surge through my veins, the baptismal blood of Sky Heroes, the wordless wonder of Wandjinas as they fashioned order out of chaos. I was about to climb up to the cave where I was born and confront the august countenance of my maker, he who had dreamed me into existence. Only one question remained: Would Wodjin announce to me my totem, as a father does to his son?

I climbed up to the ledge underneath the overhang. Before me on the rock lay a fresco of Wandjina paintings many yards in length. I counted nearly twenty of them, along with numerous Ungud snake heads and various totemic animals. One Wandjina image stood out from the rest. This was Wodjin. From his left shoulder grew a native plum tree representing the tree of life. His sceptered stance on the rock face was in keeping with his regal presence. Once I had located the image of Tumbi, the sacred owl, lower down on the rock, I knew I had discovered all the principal combatants from the Tunbai battle. Here indeed the drowning of the First Inhabitants of the world had been truly immortalized.

More significantly, I had stumbled upon a cenotaph dedicated to the memory of all those tribesmen who had engaged in spiritual warfare in the past. The Wanalirri cave was like a Tomb of the Unknown Soldier in which lay the undying spirit of every tribesman who had ever trod this country in pursuit of a sustaining ideal. Flood and fire had not daunted him. Defeat at the hands of Sky Heroes had not annihilated him. Though white occupation had nearly destroyed the law, he had still managed to survive. For his myth was the myth of betrayal and his determination not to lie down and die. In every tribesman a Pigeon was secretly hiding, breathing through his feet. Now his only avenue of escape lay in an act of *wananinj*, of flight to the realm of the spirit, Ngadjaia's abode, beyond the white, rain-bearing Wandjina clouds, toward that haven of peace he has always sought.

While I stood there, gazing at the cloudy face of Wodjin above my head, I heard a strange, peeling noise drifting across the valley. At first I thought it was the sound of wind ricocheting among the stony outcrops. Slowly, however, I began to recognize a distant voice calling to me—that of Krunmurra chanting some sort of song, a prayer probably, from his lookout on the far side of the valley. When I studied the rocks on the opposite ridge, I could not see him anywhere. It was as if he had put on his *gadidja* sandals and disappeared! The gentle echo of his chant was all that remained of him as he gave thanks to the Wandjinas for allowing me, a white man, to enter their sacred precinct. I stood quite still and listened intently to his every word:

Wandjina, let us look up to him.
His feet are great as he leaves
The sacred water, his beauty
All that we desire to look upon.

There we fought him, on this
Battlefield we engaged in combat.
He put down a baobab tree, here
The Wandjina put down a tree

That burst under the weight
Of water, flowing as his blood.

The evening star as it sets, this
And all stars you made us adore.
Wodjin, Ngadjaia's son, painted
Himself at Wanalirri, his good
Arms strong from knowing the law.

Galaru, the flashing one, a flash
Of lightning—and Jagu-gugu
That roll of thunder, they make
The ground boggy, allow the
Pandanus leaf to droop low.

So kneel down, let the rain
Wet everything. The rain,
The rain! Everywhere it drizzles.
We cut the grass it pushes up,
Clear the ground with fire
So green shoots might grow.

Galaru kneels down, feels
The pandanus leaves, his
Baler shell deep in the bog.
He watches the rain dripping
Dripping upon sacred earth.

Hearing this prayer made me shiver. Like Galaru's lightning
bolt, Wodjin's pronouncement had affected me deeply. I had become his victim, a prisoner in the baobab tree like the two brothers
who had taunted Tumbi. Yet in spite of this he had stimulated
me into seeing things differently. Sky, sun, trees, animals, and
stars—the whole of nature lay before me. All of it was modeled on
the formless essence of Ngadjaia and his emissaries. I had become a
part of the Dreaming, my ancestors those Sky Heroes who had
made rivers, mountains, and deserts. The earth was in my bones,
each fibula and rib a blend of its elements. For the first time I no
longer felt like a *kamaliwany*, a stranger in this land. Someone
had thrown down an aerial rope for me to climb, and now I was
able to travel great distances, traverse mountains with the help of

my *gadidja* sandals. Wodjin and Dalimen had made me feel free, freer than I had ever felt before. For they had taught me how to dream an interior landscape for myself. In me their law, the law of the Wandjinas had been realized. No more need I fear for my safety in this wide brown land. The *rai* had made sure of that. Krunmurra's voice, the voice I had heard drifting across the valley a few moments before, had become the voice of the mouthless Wandjinas, calling me back to where I always knew I belonged.

"Hey, you!" Krunmurra called out. "You better git over here before it gets dark. Otherwise you might end up a Wandjina paintin' like Wodjin."

It was a risk I was prepared to take. After all, Dalimen's girls had finally managed to seduce me just as they had every tribesman who had ever been privileged to walk this sacred earth since the time of the Dreaming. I now understood what *wananinj* really meant, for I, too, had learned how to make contact with spirit entities by becoming a part of their mysterious landscape. This landscape of the imagination was made up of all humanity's dreams, desires, and visions—and a belief that somewhere outside time and space there existed an utterly resolved universe that we all secretly wished to inhabit. This universe, I now realized, was none other than the topography of Ngadjaia's realm brought down to earth. Wodjin was his incarnation, his memory, his desire to manifest himself to all men. My good fortune was to have seen him before the Wandjinas had chosen to quit this world for good.

"All right, I'm coming," I called back, knowing that by leaving Wanalirri cave and crossing over the gully again I was bridging a gulf between myself and my past that had existed for far too long.

AFTERWORD

As I flew over inland Australia on my way back to Sydney, it was not difficult to lose my thoughts for a moment in the expanse of red-tinged earth below. Down there everything seemed indifferent to any desire to impart order to space, or to imagine secret pockets of luxuriance. In a desert environment it is only natural to want to discover a wellspring of sorts, something to relieve the monotony of sand, empty watercourses, and dry lakebeds. Only the blue haze over the MacDonnell Ranges near Alice Springs, or the red reaches of the Simpson Desert provided the occasional contrast as I flew south.

I kept thinking of Waljali's story map of the continent. From this elevation it was much easier to recognize the innumerable circles of thought, of myth, of memory linked by narrative tracks joining each to each. The land continued to slumber under a patchwork of tales, its revelation as seamless as any well-made quilt. Knowing now what I did about the evolution of myth on landscape, it was hard not to regard the earth below as anything less than the articulation of some cosmic design. I could see *bandaiyan*, Kamurro's "big man," lying there wallowing in a timeless narrative of his own.

Wodjin had certainly won an important victory at Tunbai. The battle to make men realize how fragile their environment was had been hard-fought. There too impiety had been vanquished. Mistreating Tumbi, the wise owl, had brought its just reward. Entombment in a baobab, that gangly water tree, had meant that all Aborigines were beholden to the Wandjinas' law. I for one had begun to accept the universality of this law and its wider ramifications. However high we flew, the view would remain the same. Feathers or no feathers, the Sky Heroes still possess the power to exercise their right over the domain of earth. It is their kingdom of worship.

Visiting the Wandjina caves in the Kimberley had been a rare privilege. The mouthless gaze of Dalimen and Wodjin would remain with me always, this much I knew. Their existence would not be so difficult to recall either, since on my return to Derby old Bungana had generously given me his turtle-bone Wandjina as a memento. In a sense he had bestowed on me a tiny icon of his Sky Hero, at least in the form it chose as its manifestation on earth. I in turn had dutifully typed out their myths and handed them over to Waljali and Kamurro in fulfillment of my part of the bargain. Between a myth and a memory-bone we had become blood brothers, it seemed. The task for Waljali and his friends was to make these stories relevant for the next generation.

The most vivid memory of our encounter was the sense of camaraderie that had grown up between us after our visit to the Wandjina caves. These three men and I were like *imiini* together, men of the law who wanted to see the continuity of a tradition maintained. We each represented the two blades of a boomerang, weaving an arc of return through the invisible air of belief. My Aboriginal friends stood for the old ways, those primordial values, a loyalty to the Sky Heroes of the Dreaming and their world-creating endeavors. I, on the other hand, stood for the need to preserve these values in the interest of worldwide harmony. When representatives of a people who still retain a paleolithic vision meet someone from the outside world, it is important that they all sit down and share their knowledge. This we had done, exchanging ideas that were as old as time—indeed, as old as humankind's attempts to make sense of the world by telling a tale.

The truth was that I had been introduced to a very ancient,

though living, perspective, one that was shared equally by my friends in the Torres Strait and in the forests of Borneo. Jack Wailu and Aki were men of knowledge, too, and true messengers, sharing the same vision of an undifferentiated world as Krunmurra. I'm sure Mr. Noa on Mer would have found much in common with Patrick Wrynkye, the *tuah rumah* from the Genswai longhouse on the Layar River. For they lived in an "age of souls" that was discontinuous and irreducible to a set of dates on a calendar. This age transcends the problem of "living with the times," that inescapable pastime that many today find so alluring.

I had come to the conclusion that these men shared the same vision of their respective spirit entities living in the same world as themselves. Malu, Sengalang Burong, or Ungud did not live outside this world, but in it as spiritual realities. These spirit entities existed as objects of veneration as well as subjects of creation. Not only did they create themselves by creating the world, but they became entities of pure transparency able to contemplate themselves through the eyes of all they had created. They became the mirror reflecting themselves in all the forms of creation. Men such as Lui Bon and Sumbeng were merely manipulators of that reflection. They had learned the art of angling the light so that it permitted others to experience illumination, each according to their capacities.

This art is the art of telling a story. The feats of Gelem, Serong Gunting, and Dalimen live on in the act of narration. When a man opens his mouth and links together experience, he is enacting something special. He is engendering continuity out of random events, a thread of coherence out of chaos. The story is the single most powerful form of defense that we have against the threat of falling into the abyss of meaninglessness. For it allows us to resurrect presences, invoke that which has grown distant, intensify all that we feel. Without the story we are left with the mute face of the Wandjina, whose very silence we associate with resolution. The story does not resolve anything; it only provides us with the tools by which we try to make sense of reality.

I had begun my quest to learn more about the way traditional peoples cope with a changing world in the hope of receiving some answers to questions affecting the way we address these changes ourselves. Modern science and our ability to compress time have brought us to the brink of annihilation. Though we may no longer be looking down the tunnel of a rocket silo, we are engaged in a relentless process of resource exploitation that threatens to denude the planet. The modern economy, it seems, is wedded to conspicuous consumption with no likelihood of divorce. At the same time the economical impulse has enchained countless millions of people to a treadmill more spiritually debilitating than is perhaps fully realized. The rise of mental disability and new psychic disorders are symptoms of a terminal disease facing the entire world.

Some 250 million people exist outside this economic nexus, however. They live in jungles, deserts, and remote wilderness areas throughout the world. Until recently these regions were considered to be too difficult (i.e., uneconomic) to develop. While their lands were not viewed as prospective resource zones, their way of life continued to remain intact. They could hunt and fish, farm village gardens, and graze livestock in accordance with age-old customs devised in cooperation with the spirits of nature. These spirits were their helpmates. They were free to venerate their celestial friends with the aid of ritual and ceremony, knowing that to do so meant the preservation of the natural order. The law of Malu, *Adat*, and the law of the Sky Heroes are spiritual and regulatory systems typical the world over. Like the Wandjina, they "hold" things together.

But when these regions where a subsistence way of life continued to thrive became the target for resource development, an entirely new situation arose. Not only did these people find their land, their forests, and their grazing rights taken away from them, they also experienced the erosion of their cultural assets. These were increasingly undermined by modern technology confronting their environment in the form of mining equipment, tractors, fences, roads, airstrips, electricity and telephones, modern medicine and education, not to mention the introduction of alien foodstuffs brought in to compensate for their loss of traditional food caused by the physical disruption of their land and life-style. In time, these independent peoples, blessed with a visionary gift and a profound sense of identity, found themselves reduced to mendicant status, at the mercy of government agents and experts.

I had grown increasingly concerned about the hiatus emerging between these two perspectives. The exploiter and the exploited were locked into a relationship whereby each began to need one another, but for reasons not in keeping with the continuing survival of one of the parties, namely the traditional peoples of the earth. Their environment and their life-style was most under threat. The miners, loggers, and pastoralists could always move elsewhere to set up shop, at least in the short term. But in the long term even this would prove impossible, given that natural resources are finite and are not easily renewable unless cared for.

Making contact with men of knowledge, those traditional seers, had been my first step in understanding the problem. The *zogo le*, *tuai burong*, and *barnmunji* that I met were my introduction to a different way of viewing the natural world. Previously I had seen it as little more than an open-cut mine, a roll of newspaper, or a tank of gasoline. My new friends had taught me to view it in a different way. Nature was not something that could be converted into an economic reality, but a chalice bearing invisible essences denoting spiritual and physical well-being. These, my friends maintained, were priceless. Ketupong's cry on a forest track was as important to their survival as a tonne of hardwood is to us. The problem I asked myself was this: Could a means be found whereby these realities might learn how to accommodate one another?

In order to find an answer to such questions I had deliberately set out to place myself within nature's field of force. Following in Gelem's footsteps, listening to Bejampong's call, and acknowledging the power of the *rai* had brought me into contact with a fragile yet mysterious world. It was a world governed by the power of myth. The myth is nature's other voice. It speaks to us through the language of visionary acts—acts that germinate in the stillness of the forest, in the silence of the plain, in the emptiness of the desert. They are not perpetrated by men, nor are they the result of an imaginative thought process. They rely on the infinitely slow unfolding of sublime experience for their realization. This experience is the preserve of the spirit of nature. Nature lives its own metaphor and reveals its intent by way of a totality of perceptions better known to us as intuition. We are able to *feel* nature's intentions when we are in tune with the evolution of its forms.

From my first meeting with Mr. Issau on Thursday Island to my last with Krunmurra outside his cave, I had come to realize that these men thought as nature does. This is not to say that they had the mind of a crocodile or a kangaroo, but that they regarded themselves as nature's heralds on behalf of these creatures. They echoed the message that nature wished to announce to the world. This message is simple: Every species; every genus and phylum; every breed, race, and tribe are all inextricably linked. They are part of *bandaiyan*, nature's "big body" of which we, too, are an integral part. Larry's wife confirmed this fact to him when she imitated her totem before she died. Nature used her totem to pronounce the Last Rites. Her limbs waving had become the flippers of a turtle announcing the contiguity of all life.

Clearly, traditional peoples are equipped with a seventh sense that we may do well to acquire before it is too late. It is none other than the sense of wonder. Instead of dissecting reality as we do through our innumerable scientific disciplines, these people have chosen to invest it with mystery, a "wholly otherness," something beyond the sphere of the usual. Wherever a mind finds itself exposed in a spirit of absolved submission to impressions of the universe, it is able to experience intuitions and feelings of something that is, as it were, a sheer "overplus," in addition to normal reality. This overplus becomes a glimpse of the Eternal, the invisible form of Kree Raja Petara, Augud, and Ngadjaia, the "number one spirit up top." The seventh sense, the sense of wonder and awe, allows us to enter Wodjin's cave and know he has been there before us.

Whenever I discussed spiritual matters with my friends, I was struck by the sense of awe and reverence that permeated their thoughts. At these times they were no longer tribesmen afflicted with the normal worries and cares of this life; they had become men of distinction, wise men, seers almost, as they expounded the mysteries of nature. They reveled in the opportunity to escape conventional reality and tramp the lofty summits with their spirits and Sky Heroes. There they felt freer, more able to be themselves—or more exactly, to be somebody other than themselves. They had allowed a state of *mysterium tremendum* to wash over them like a gentle tide, filling their minds with the tranquil mood of deepest worship. While we spoke together, I realized that this state was an attitude of the soul, thrillingly vibrant, that passed from them only when our discussion terminated and we again entered the profane world of everyday experience.

In this I perceived something significant: that we were implicitly acknowledging the existence of two worlds, the material and the metaphysical. My friends, nevertheless, accepted these worlds as intertwined—so much so that a man could participate in both if he so wished. Sumbeng's voyage up the Mandai River accompanying the dead, Kamurro's ability to fly through the air on an aerial rope, or Jack's Solomon Islander friend who transformed himself into a booby bird are but a few examples of how men crossed over into the realm of the spirits. What these men had taught me was that by detaching oneself from ordinary reality it was possible to experience one of those marvelously full and powerful moments that rise up in defiance of death.

Of course Mr. Benny-Father, Bungana, and Patrick are old men now. They do not have long to live. The *ayu* in their *gayu* will soon depart just as nature ordains, leaving their *semangat* free to float airily toward the summits beyond the Kupuas Hula Mountains. As men of knowledge they possess something as rare as sapphires, and, unfortunately, when they depart, this knowledge will go with them. When Sumbeng sings his last death dirge the Mandai River will dry up forever. While Jack Wailu can still wield an ax, his cane windbreak will keep out the prevailing winds of disbelief. But once they have gone we will be left with a world dominated by signs not symbols, quantities not qualities, realities not visions. The fluted call of Nendak or Embuas will have been silenced. The omen birds will no longer augur the lives of men. This is the penalty we must pay for wanting to invade the realms of Sengalang Burong, Malu, and Wodjin in order to pursue our own material ends. Their myths and sacred stories will have been shipped off to feed the insatiable appetite of industry's furnaces elsewhere in the world. No wonder Waljali wanted me to write down his stories before it was too late. Retrieving something from the flames might help to keep Dalimen's potency rising up at Banganan cave a little longer.

The truth is that many today feel ashamed at the way things are arranged, ashamed of all those heavy trucks that pass through our being, those industries, factories, stores, theaters, public monuments that constitute much more than the backdrop to our individual lives. We are ashamed of the sordid movement of men, and not just around us either. Yet equally we are aware that nature, so much more powerful than ourselves, makes ten times less noise—and that nature within man (in the form of reason, that is) doesn't make any noise at all. Our increasing dominion over nature has intensified our self-awareness at the expense of our ability to forget ourselves, which is the only genuine form of nourishment available to us anyway. What we have forgotten is that in order to become a god, we must remain unaware of ourselves.

This was the first lesson I had learned from my friends. They had taught me to revere that moment when one leaves oneself while pursuing a vision of absoluteness. Listening to them relate their myths, I knew they were taking leave of themselves. They were entering into a more rarified sphere where things meant much more than they seemed. Furthermore, adopting Sumbeng's technique of looking inside a word for a different order of reality, I had discovered that in absoluteness, a word pertaining to untrammeled freedom and detachment, the sun roamed the sky in its Latin guise of *sol*. The sun of reason rose over their stories, bathing them in a lucid light, a light capable of illuminating the summit, the axis of the heavens, where men lie down to sleep without dreams. It was this summit that men like Timothy China glimpsed each time he sang the praises of Nam Kerem, his turtle god, while palm leaves rustled overhead.

It is time we carried off the fire in clamshells once more and used it to rekindle myriad hearths. Waiat, that savage god of defloration, is, like Dalimen, a god who cannot contain himself. He abounds in potency, in seminal fire. He encourages us to engender new forms within ourselves. He ejaculates the word. All stories, all myths are conceived out of his supreme act of love. This act of love comes about when men and nature are drawn together as one. They embrace one another, they sing one another's praises. Birds, fish, animals, and flowers become human exemplars. They constitute our *unthinking* beauty, the beauty we harbor when we smell a rose or pat a horse. We are nourished by these encounters as all pretension and modesty fall away, and we become, for an instant, rose and horse. This is the fire Waiat's acolytes carried so triumphantly along the beach in clamshells. It is the fire Iniamuris swallowed in the act of consuming Geigi, the great trevally fish.

*   *   *

Here I was then, flying high over Australia, conscious that my world had been transformed. Though I was heading back to more familiar territory, I was also aware that my encounters over the past months had changed my perspective. I carried within me the pleas of men on beaches, in jungles, and alone among caves in the wilderness who wanted to hold on to their heritage. They did not wish to see nature denuded of its lofty spirit, its celsitude. They wanted the call of the omen birds, the blue *zeg* light of Malu, and the mouthless Wandjina to remain in the world as visionary edifices, supreme and unconquered. They had asked me to reawaken people's desire to enter into their own myth, become a dugong man, and roam the world like Gelem. They wanted me to harbor the possibility for transformation as I set out on my voyage of revelation, just like Gelem did when he arrived at Mer and became a hill above the beach, or Malu when he revealed himself to Dog's wife, Kabur, as a divine octopus.

My friends had taught me to recognize that myths constitute a living reality of their own. They are not the basis for a comprehensible story, with a beginning, middle, and end as we demand of ours. Myths do not have to make sense in order to convey their inherent truth. On the reefs about Erub and Mer, in the forests of Central Borneo, and among the rocky outcrops of the Kimberley I had been brought in contact with an ancient way of investing reality with an interior dimension—a dimension not ordered by the rational faculties of men, past or present. I had been made aware of the sheer anarchy of the mythic structure as a way of transcending the deliberations of individuals and their desire to make sense of their predicament. What my friends had taught me was to accept a degree of unpredictability in the way the gods worked as a method of evoking a real sense of wonder within myself. In other words, awe was as important as narrative in the realization of a good story.

When I returned to Sydney the inevitable pile of mail awaited me on my desk. After months in the wilderness it seemed curious to be gazing at foreign stamps, each a symbol of a world alien to my own. Among them, I noticed a letter from Thursday Island. On the reverse of the envelope Larry Passi's name was clearly printed.

I opened the letter and read:

Bala Jim,

I know this will surprise you. Writing is not what I do best. I like a story, but putting words down on paper isn't easy. Anyway I wanted to tell you something important. It's about Jack Wailu. No, he's not dead and gone, in fact he's with us in a big way!

We had a dance festival here recently. All the boys came over from Boigu, Mabuiag, Moa, and the other islands. They danced real well. Plenty of dugong dances. The *daris* decorating their heads this year were pretty good too. Mr. Issau was there too. He told a lot of stories, and everybody felt that something important was happening to us.

Anyway, Jack came over with his dancers from Mer. Guess what. They brought Wasikor with them! The first time since anyone can remember.

The night his boys danced everyone wanted to come and look. Because it was a new dance! Yes, *bala*, a new dance. He danced a story about Nimau coming back to Mer. She is alive after all! And for the first time since I can remember, they played Wasikor. I can tell you everyone was real pleased.

Jack told me to tell you this. He said, "Tell *Bala* he was right. We got a new dance, and we feel good about it." That is what I'm telling you on his behalf.

I hope you are well. I'm feeling much better. The crocodile in me has been chewing over a lot of things lately. This is true. We got a good culture up here. We got to hold on to it.

Oh yes, old Lui Bon says "hello" too. He's dreaming of coral a lot of late.

Your good friend,
Bala (Brother) Larry

It appeared that Nimau had finally returned to her mate. The drums of Mer were together again. Echoing the waves crashing against the reef, they beat out a rhythm of renewal on the beach at Las. Jack Wailu was sitting cross-legged on the sand outside his windbreak, the shark-shaped torso of Wasikor lying across his lap. Or was it Nimau? Tagai's canoe was there too, already half submerged by the tide and the night. The stars of the Southern Cross had beached themselves on the shore of one man's vision and his desire to restore Meriam culture to its rightful place. The omen bird that had brought us together had done so in the nick of time, it seemed. Between us we had managed to devise a way of bringing about Nimau's return to the Torres Strait, and so revive Wasikor from his long sleep.

I unfolded the cloth covering the Wandjina turtle-bone Bungana had given me in Derby. The microcosmic god-man lay on my desk, its slender image reminding me of nature's message. All earth is an icon, and we must adore it as a gift of grace. Clearly this was why Bungana had given it to me: He had wanted me to remember the importance of the Wandjina for the survival of the world. I was reminded of a remark made by Giovanni Battista Vico, an Italian philosopher of the eighteenth century, when he wrote in his *Scienza Nuova:* "Poetic vision, which was the primitive wisdom of paganism, must have begun with a metaphysic, not reasoned and abstract like that of modern educated men, but felt and imagined, such as must have been that of primitive man. This was their own poetry, which with them was inborn, an innate faculty, for nature had furnished them with such feelings and imaginings, a faculty born of the ignorance of causes, and therefore begetting a universal sense of wonder. . . . Such poetry had a divine origin, [and] in this way the first men fashioned things out of ideas."

Thanks to my friends I felt that I, too, had become the possessor of this unique faculty of imagination. Now, like Larry and Lui Bon, I would be able to watch coral whenever I wanted the crocodile in me to digest what might have in the past been unpalatable. The key to this new way of thinking rested with the gesture made by Kamurro's mother when she had raised her infant son above her head. "Be delightful like the sunset" had been her entreaty to the Wandjina on his behalf, knowing that in the end all human values rest in nature's desire to be at one with itself.

ABOUT THE AUTHOR

James G. Cowan is a distinguished author and poet. He has spent much of his life exploring the world of traditional peoples such as the Berbers of Morocco, the Tuareg of the Central Sahara, and the Australian Aborigines. He spent a decade living and traveling in Europe and North America, and then returned to Australia, where he embarked on a series of books that explored the agricultural peoples of early Australia. These books were followed by others dealing with Aboriginal metaphysics and cosmology. James Cowan has also written fiction, contributed articles to magazines, given lectures, and made documentaries for Australian television.

OTHER BELL TOWER BOOKS

The pure sound of the bell summons us
into the present moment.
The timeless ring of truth
is expressed in many different voices,
each one magnifying and illuminating the sacred.
The clarity of its song resonates within us
and calls us away from those things which often distract us—
that which was, that which might be—
to That Which Is.

Being Home
A Book of Meditations
by Gunilla Norris
An exquisite modern book of hours, a celebration of mindfulness in
everyday activities.
Hardcover 0-517-58159-0 1991

Nourishing Wisdom
A New Understanding of Eating
by Marc David
A practical way out of dietary confusion, a book that advocates aware-
ness in eating and reveals how our attitude to food reflects our attitude
to life.
Hardcover 0-517-57636-8 1991

Sanctuaries: The Northeast
*A Guide to Lodgings in Monasteries, Abbeys, and Retreats of the
United States*
by Jack and Marcia Kelly
The first in a series of regional guides for those in search of renewal
and a little peace.
Softcover 0-517-57727-5 1991

Grace Unfolding
Psychotherapy in the Spirit of the Tao-te ching
by Greg Johanson and Ron Kurtz
The interaction of client and therapist illuminated through the gentle power and wisdom of Lao Tzu's ancient Chinese classic.
Hardcover 0-517-58449-2 1991

Self-Reliance
The Wisdom of Ralph Waldo Emerson as Inspiration for Daily Living
Selected and with an introduction by Richard Whelan
A distillation of Emerson's essential spiritual writings for contemporary readers.
Softcover 0-517-58512-X 1991

Compassion in Action
Setting Out on the Path of Service
by Ram Dass and Mirabai Bush
Heartfelt encouragement and advice for those ready to commit time and energy to relieving suffering in the world.
Softcover 0-517-57635-X 1992

Letters from a Wild State
Rediscovering Our True Relationship to Nature
by James G. Cowan
A luminous interpretation of Aboriginal spiritual experience applied to the leading issue of our time: the care of the earth.
Hardcover 0-517-58770-X 1992

Silence, Simplicity, and Solitude
A Guide for Spiritual Retreat
by David A. Cooper
This classic guide to meditation and other traditional spiritual practice is required reading for anyone contemplating a retreat.
Hardcover 0-517-58620-7 1992

The Heart of Stillness
The Elements of Spiritual Practice
by David A. Cooper
A comprehensive guidebook to the basic principles of inner work—a companion volume to *Silence, Simplicity & Solitude*.
Hardcover 0-517-58621-5 1992

One Hundred Graces
Selected by Marcia and Jack Kelly
With calligraphy by Christopher Gausby
A collection of mealtime graces from many traditions, beautifully inscribed in calligraphy reminiscent of the manuscripts of medieval Europe.
Hardcover 0-517-58567-7 1992

Sanctuaries: The West Coast and Southwest
A Guide to Lodgings in Monasteries, Abbeys, and Retreats of the United States
by Marcia and Jack Kelly
The second volume of what *The New York Times* called "the Michelin Guide of the retreat set."
Softcover 0-517-88007-5 1993

Becoming Bread
Meditations on Loving and Transformation
by Gunilla Norris
A book linking the food of the spirit—love—with the food of the body—bread. More meditations by the author of *Being Home*.
Hardcover 0-517-59168-5 1993

Pilgrimage to Dzhvari
A Woman's Journey of Spiritual Awakening
by Valeria Alfeyeva
A powerful and eloquent account of a contemporary Russian woman's discovery of her Christian heritage. A modern *Way of the Pilgrim*.
Hardcover 0-517-59194-4 1993

Bell Tower books are for sale at your local bookstore,
or you may call 1-800-733-3000 (with a credit card).